REFORM OF
BRITISH CENTRAL GOVERNMENT

THE REFORM SERIES

Reform of British Central Government

J. H. ROBERTSON

1971

CHATTO & WINDUS
CHARLES KNIGHT
LONDON

Chatto & Windus Ltd.
Charles Knight & Co. Ltd.
London

*

Clarke, Irwin & Co. Ltd.
Toronto

C

SBN 7011 1743 5

Printed in Great Britain by
R. & R. Clark Ltd.
Edinburgh

Contents

Preface

Any student of British Government is likely to have mixed feelings about his subject, to feel at times that parliamentary Government in Britain is beyond reform, and at other times to be strongly aware of its fine traditions and achievements. It seems best to declare at the outset that a love/hate relationship of this kind is one of the conflicts running through this book. I hope the reader will regard it as a valuable, perhaps a necessary, ingredient. A combination of iconoclastic impatience with an urge to re-establish the shining traditions of the past is probably quite a good recipe for reform.

Another conflict may seem to be apparent too–a conflict between the general and the particular, the rhetorical and the practical. Many people suppose that self-government, participation, democracy, and such high-flown political concepts, occupy a different universe of discourse from the detailed exposition of committee structures and financial procedures and management systems. Those who feel at home discussing the first often have little respect for those who expound the second, and vice versa. But that cannot be a happy situation. The attempt has to be made to fuse political concept with administrative detail. The reform of government requires our changing political perceptions to take specific shape in real-life institutions and procedures; while, if our political perceptions are not to degenerate into mere slogans, they in turn must reflect the changing nature of administrative reality.

Finally, a third conflict may seem to run through the book–this time a conflict between historical description and logical analysis. Again I ask the reader to see the resolution of this conflict as fruitful. For successful reform depends on harnessing the evolutionary momentum of the past to the fulfilment of present and future needs.

Historical exposition has to stop at some particular point in time, and the right point to stop is clearly June 1970. Ten years of unsuccessful reform under Conservative and Labour Governments ended then–unsuccessful because, even in the case of the supposedly reforming Labour Governments of 1964 and 1966, the attempted reforms fell into no coherent strategy. In June 1970 a period of what promised to be much more radical reform began, under a new Conservative Government embarking upon it from a strong base of study and analysis carried out in opposition. June 1970 is thus the obvious point from which to take stock. That, then, is what I aim to do–to bring the outline story up to 1970, and to take that date as the vantage point from which to look forward into the future.

However, now that the Conservatives under Mr Heath have been in office for nearly a year, it is sensible to consider what progress they have been making during that time. To what extent have they, in fact, been following the diagnosis and treatment expounded in later chapters? The answer is that, in broad outline, Mr Heath's Government seem to be following the prescription offered here, even if there are many differences in points of detail and progress is rather slower than one might have hoped.

One of the most important elements in the 'new style of government' has been to strengthen the government's hold on the commanding heights of national policy-making. The White Paper of October 1970 on 'The Reorganisation of Central Government' (Cmnd. 4506) described the aims as follows:

(i) To improve the quality of policy formulation and decision-taking in government by presenting Ministers, collectively in Cabinet and individually within their departments, with well-defined options, costed where possible, and relating the choice between options to the contribution they can make to meeting national needs. This is not confined to new policies and new decisions, but implies also the continuing examination, on a systematic and critical basis, of the existing activities of government.

(ii) To improve the framework within which public policy is formulated by matching the field of responsibility of government departments to coherent fields of policy and administration.

(iii) To ensure that the government machine responds and adapts itself to new policies and programmes as these emerge, within the broad framework of the main departmental fields of responsibility.

The measures taken to achieve these aims include:

(a) the unification in a smaller number of larger Departments of functions previously carried out in a larger number of smaller ones;

(b) the improvement of the organisation and procedures for enabling the Cabinet to take collective policy decisions, by the creation of a Central Policy Review Staff (Lord Rothschild's think-tank) in

vii

the Cabinet office; and also by instituting regular, systematic reviews of the objectives of government activity under the procedure now known as Programmes Analysis and Review.

The second element in Mr Heath's approach to the reform of government is to be 'a sustained effort to ensure that, among those functions which remain a necessary part of central government, executive blocks of work will be delegated to accountable units of management' (Cmnd. 4506). This will lessen the load on Ministers and on departmental top management. It will also open up the activities of government to scrutiny by Parliament and the public.

This brings us to the third element in the present government's strategy of reform – the reform of Parliament. A new system of Select Committees of the House of Commons has been set up, which goes at least some way towards the Expenditure and Administration Committee envisaged in Chapter 9 below. In the words of the Green Paper published in October 1970 (Cmnd. 4507) this is intended to provide 'an effective machinery of scrutiny without in any way impairing the responsibility of Ministers to Parliament or detracting from the importance of proceedings on the Floor of the House'. It will represent 'a significant strengthening of the parliamentary system'.

These changes, it is true, fall short of what is suggested in later chapters. There are still too many Whitehall ministries and departments. There is still no Prime Minister's Office, and the Rothschild think-tank may prove an ineffective substitute for a properly established research, planning and management services capability in a Prime Minister's Office. The position of the Civil Service Department remains unsatisfactory. The component parts of the new Department of the Environment (transport, building, housing and local government) lie very uneasily together. It was a pity to have placed partial responsibility for the country's industrial infrastructure in the Department of Trade and Industry instead of creating a department with comprehensive responsibility for its various constituent elements. For all these reasons a further re-allocation of functions between departments seems inevitable before long, probably on the lines summarised on page 157 below. Rationalisation of the parliamentary Select Committee system has further to go; a glaring inadequacy remains in respect of parliamentary scrutiny of taxation; and little has yet been done to reinforce and modernise the supporting staffs of Parliament. Finally, it will take two or three years to get results from rationalisation down the line in Whitehall, as accountable management begins to take effect.

But, in spite of all this, a long stride forward has been taken. The central institutions of parliamentary government are already much

PREFACE

strengthened, and the way is open for further progress. Progress will be hastened by the Heath Government's comprehensive approach to such questions as tax reform and tax simplification, as announced in the 1971 Budget, and in particular by the Government's evident intention to have at least some major issues of policy openly discussed–witness the Green Papers on Value Added Tax and Corporation Tax Reform.

When we turn to the complex issues (discussed in Chapter 4 below) of industrial efficiency, industrial relations, companies legislation, monopoly and competition, consumer protection and prices and incomes, progress has been patchier and less certain in its direction. The Prices and Incomes Board, the Industrial Reorganisation Corporation, and some of the little Neddies have been dismantled, together with the Consumer Council, in accordance with the new policy of disengagement and competition; and the trade unions are being brought within the framework of democratic control under the law. But little has yet been done with regard to companies legislation generally; or with regard to monopolies, mergers and competition; or consumer protection. Government intervention to control prices and incomes has seemed arbitrary and spasmodic. Conservative policy towards the nationalised industries has seemed confused.

It looks as if a Conservative Administration – even a reforming one – may have to learn the hard way that free enterprise alone no longer provides a sufficient basis for a healthy industrial society; and that, for example, it cannot simply be left to the labour market to determine our relative incomes for us. It may take traumatic episodes like the nationalisation of Rolls Royce to demonstrate that disengagement pure and simple, as a government policy towards industry, ignores the realities of the modern world. These realities demand not only an end to detailed intervention by government in the affairs of industry, but also the creation of an effective framework of democratic scrutiny and control over industrial and commercial behaviour through Parliament and the Courts.

When we come to the question of geographical devolution, the philosophy underlying the present government's approach is less clear still. The Redcliffe-Maud proposals for local government in England have been rejected (Cmnd. 4584). The Crowther Commission's report on the Constitution is still awaited. So far there is little positive sign of a comprehensive approach to the proper allocation of government functions at national, regional and local levels, as described in Chapter 6 below.

But, taken all in all, there is good reason to hope that the reforms on which the present government has embarked are leading in the right direction. It is not unreasonable to hope that, by the time of the next

ix

general election, the institutions of parliamentary democracy in Britain will have been much strengthened, and that at the same time commercial and individual enterprise will have been much invigorated. Nor will it be altogether surprising if, by then, a supposedly right-wing Conservative Government–which has turned its back on the Butskellite consensus of the 1950s and 1960s–will have proved a far more effective instrument, not only of private capitalism but also of democratic socialism, than any of its predecessors. Such a development (as suggested in Chapter 11) could largely invalidate the existing structure of party politics and party political debate. And that could prove to be one of the most important aspects of the late-20th-century reform of British central government.

Acknowledgements

I have made use of quotations from a number of published works. References to these works, their authors and their publishers appear in the Notes at the end of each chapter. I gratefully acknowledge the dublishers' permission to use these quotations, and also the permission of the Editor of the *Spectator* to use material which appeared in the issue of 9th August 1968.

Many friends and colleagues have talked and argued with me over the years about various aspects of government reform. Their contributions to my thinking and therefore to this book cannot be measured or easily identified, but I recognise it and am grateful for it. In particular, Charles Read and David Peretz read the manuscript and made helpful comments.

Judith Kenney took charge of the typing and has helped in other ways. Her quickness and efficiency have lightened the burdens of authorship. She has my sincere thanks.

My greatest debt of gratitude is to my wife, Anne, not only for her support and forbearance, but also for her shared interest in the subject matter of the book. She has helped me much in writing it, and has suggested many improvements to earlier versions of the text.

JAMES ROBERTSON
April 1971

I

The Whole Organisation of the State

When I considered these things and the men who were
directing public affairs, and made a closer study, as I grew
older, of law and custom, the harder it seemed to me to
govern a state rightly . . . The result was that I, who had at
first been full of eagerness for a public career, when I saw
all this happening and everything going to pieces, fell at
last into bewilderment. I did not cease to think in what
way this situation might be amended, and in particular
the whole organisation of the state.

PLATO: Seventh Letter, 331 D:
Cornford's Translation

GREAT BRITAIN LTD

It is fanciful to suppose, as some business barons do, that governing
a democratic country is the same as running a company. However, there
is no harm in being fanciful, especially at the beginning of a serious book
like this. So let us see if there are any lessons to be learned from the
story of the little, old firm of HMG Enterprises which has grown over
the years into the large industrial corporation known as Great Britain
Ltd.

We have to go back to the second half of the nineteenth century,
when a chairman and chief executive called Gladstone consolidated the
business in its modern form. Managing it was fairly straightforward
then. There were only a comparatively few, well defined products,
basically very similar to those manufactured under the 'Crown' trade-
mark in earlier times. Gladstone did not even find it necessary to put in
much new, purpose-built plant. He simply took over the machinery
installed by his predecessors and made a number of modifications to it.

For many years, while the product range remained small, all went
well. The old machinery, driven by steam and hot air, worked pretty
smoothly. The local people were proud of the firm, and used to con-
gratulate themselves that HMG Enterprises was the best-run business
in the world. It was not until the number of products began to grow,
and the frequency of product changes began to increase, and the firm

I

itself began to expand, and the existing machinery became older, that trouble really began. Then stoppages in the production line, and breakdowns in marketing plans, began to happen more and more often.

Successive boards of directors were constantly having bright ideas about what new products to put on the market, and how to make them, and how to cure the breakdowns. But as they had no long-term marketing strategy and as they did not recognise the need to re-plan and re-design the production line for the new products, improvisation was the order of the day. The machinery underwent almost continual modification. Sometimes new attachments were made to existing machines; sometimes two or more machines would be cannibalised; from time to time an entirely new machine would be brought into the production line. The result of all this piecemeal modification was that different parts of a machine tended to clash with one another. Sometimes whole machines were installed in this way; as soon as one machine began operating, another automatically switched on and fouled it up. Normally this resulted by mistake, but there was one chairman and chief executive, who adopted this approach as part of a deliberate management philosophy. He took the view that this was, in fact, the best way to assemble machines, so that–as he put it–they would strike sparks from one another and engender an atmosphere of creative tension. For a while, everybody thought this was very scientific, part of a white-hot technological revolution. 'Aha!' they said, 'this man really knows about running a factory.'

In the course of time the plant acquired a number of curious features. For example, there was the experiment with a double governor on the main power drive. The old governor had tended to run very slow; in spite of many attempts to correct it, including a complete stripping down in 1962, the fault persisted. So the board of directors who took office in 1964 had the ingenious idea of fitting a second governor, which they would set to run fast. According to local gossip some of the less sophisticated members of the board hoped that this device would enable them to run the plant fast *and* slow at the same time. What actually happened was a production crisis of the first order–and, of course, plenty of sparks and tension in the factory. In due course, the second governor was quietly disengaged and then abolished.

Even without distractions of this magnitude, operating the plant had become quite a problem. An immense amount of effort from the workers and dedicated service from the foremen was needed to keep the old, increasingly complicated machinery going. Boilers wheezed, fly-wheels flew, belts creaked and strained, cogs clashed; every now and then a safety valve would blow its top. Mechanics and operators worked in a frenzy, rushing around with oil-cans, testing pressures, repairing emergency faults, shouting instructions to each other, holding hurried conferences in various parts of the factory. No one had a moment to think about tomorrow's problems; everyone was fully pre-occupied with today's.

What was to be done?

The first thought of every board of directors was that closer co-ordination and inspection of various parts of the production process should improve its efficiency. So experienced workers would be taken off the production line to co-ordinate and inspect those who remained. Some time later, when a new board of directors had taken office, they too would have the same idea and would arrange for more men to be taken from the production line to co-ordinate and inspect the original co-ordinators and inspectors. This process continued and, over the years, a longer and longer hierarchy of co-ordinators and inspectors developed. One of the disadvantages of this was that the directors became further and further removed from the men who were doing the actual job of production, marketing, or whatever, and began to feel less and less responsible for what happened.

As things deteriorated, successive boards of directors found it more and more difficult to decide how they ought to run the firm. So they began to bring in more and more outside advisers to tell them what to do, and to give them moral support. At the same time they commissioned consultants, and also groups of distinguished customers, to look at various aspects of the firm's work and make suggestions about how they might be improved.

Unfortunately all these advisers, customers and consultants really only added to the difficulties of managing the factory efficiently. For a start, they did not always agree with one another. Often the air of the factory was loud with the noise of conflicting recommendations and advice above the din of the machinery. This caused great excitement for the mechanics and operators and tended to distract them from their work. Furthermore, all the advisers, customers and consultants had to be looked after. Mechanics and operators had to be taken off the machines to show them round and see that they had everything they

3

needed. Finally, the visitors were not always asked to look at the right things.

A good example of this was the assignment carried out by the consultancy firm Fulton Hunt Associates on the personnel problems of the firm. The consultants' terms of reference precluded them from looking at the firm's machinery and plant and also from examining the company's management and control procedures. Instead, they mounted a painstaking enquiry into twenty-three different blocks of work on twelve parts of the factory floor, analysing the main elements in each man's job and assessing the qualifications and experience of the individual workmen concerned. They found that although the firm was now attempting to manufacture twentieth-century products many of the men retained a nineteenth-century outlook towards their work. This was natural enough considering the working environment. All the same, Fulton Hunt gave the poor foremen a very black mark.

The remedies they proposed for the problems of the firm were as follows: every job in the factory should be evaluated; the distinction between different types of workmen (foremen, mechanics, fitters and so forth) should be eliminated; a massive training programme should be put in hand; improved promotion procedures should be introduced; and so on. Fulton Hunt said they were confident that if these proposals were carried through they would provide a basis for the progressive conduct of Great Britain Ltd.

This was, of course, an exaggerated claim. Everyone knew, for example, that the central factory's power plant was hopelessly out of date. No amount of improved personnel management on the shop-floor would achieve anything unless something was done about the old pink boiler and the old blue boiler in the boiler-house (or 'gas-works' as it was sometimes known). There was, in fact, a boiler-house supervisor, or 'Leader of the House' as he was called, who recognised this and became very angry about the performance of the boilers. His solution, which became known as 'the cross man's reform', was that the boilers should be stoked in the mornings as well as in the afternoons. This solution did not, however, go sufficiently near to the root of the problem to improve matters.

By the late 1960s poor old Great Britain Ltd., which (as HMG Enterprises in the old days) had been regarded as one of the most progressive and best-managed firms in the business, had become almost a byword for bad management. The real trouble was that successive

THE WHOLE ORGANISATION OF THE STATE

boards of directors failed to understand the basic problem facing the company. While they asked Fulton Hunt to examine the firm's personnel problems, they were asking a distinguished group of customers known as the Maud Group to look at the organisation of the firm's outlying establishments (managed by what were known as 'local authorities'), and yet another group of distinguished customers (the Crowther Group) to look at the firm's 'constitution'. It was a long time before the directors came to see that all those enquiries were concerned with related aspects of the same problem: how should the firm be re-organised and re-equipped as a whole, to cope with all the new markets and product lines of the last hundred years, and to take advantage of the new production processes that had been developed during that time? To put it another way, it was a long time before they came to see that the very nature of the business had changed. Which is why, when a new board of directors took office in 1970 with much talk of "a new style of management", most people were healthily sceptical.

Well, enough is enough, as Mr Macmillan is supposed to have said to Mr Selwyn Lloyd, and we have had enough of the story of HMG Enterprises to suggest the theme of this book. It is that, in words used by Sir Robert Morant, one of the great administrative reformers of the century, the efforts of those who have recently tried to modernise our system of government are 'as though a man had been seeking to build a substantial house by working spasmodically on odd portions of the structure on quite isolated plans, fashioning minute details of some upper parts, when he has not set up, nor indeed even planned out, the substructure which is their sole possible foundation and stay: his very best efforts being thus necessarily rendered abortive by the fact that, while he is hammering at this portion of it or that, he possesses no clearly thought-out plan of the structure as a whole.' Morant was talking about the educational reformers active at the turn of the century, but his words are equally applicable to the government reformers of the 1960s. The need now is to think out clearly a plan for the structure of British government as a whole.

The Conservative Governments which were in office from 1951 to 1964 failed to recognise this. The Labour Government of 1964 to 1970 recognised that reforms were necessary, but misconceived the nature of the problem. This was partly because they saw it through the eyes of economists and partly because they saw it in terms of a crusade against the 'Establishment', rather than as a question of how we could make more effective our decision-making apparatus as a society. While Mr Heath and his advisers were in opposition they tackled the problem in a more serious, coherent, analytical way than any politicians in this country have ever done before. David Howell's pamphlet on *A New Style of Government*, which was published by the Conservative Political Centre shortly before the 1970 General Election, sketched an admirably comprehensive approach to reforming the executive, parliamentary and judicial functions of government.

But do the Conservatives recognise that this approach implies a new relationship between the public sector and the private sector that could almost be construed as a breakthrough to a modern, effective and humane form of socialism? Or do they regard it as a way of putting the clock back to an obsolete form of capitalism? Although they have been in power for some months now and have put some of their reforms in train, the answer is not yet entirely clear.

THE NEED FOR REFORM

Between 1960 and 1963 I had the great privilege and good fortune to assist Sir Norman Brook (the late Lord Normanbrook) in his work as Secretary of the Cabinet and Head of the Home Civil Service. From this unique vantage point it was apparent that the present Cabinet system and associated central government machinery was rapidly becoming an ineffective instrument of decision and action, in spite of all that the best, pre-eminently professional, civil servants could do to make it work. During those years it also became clear to me that effective reform of the Civil Service could not take place except in the context of wider changes in government as a whole. Then, during the following two years in the Ministry of Defence, I had first-hand experience of the great waste of human endeavour now endemic at working levels in the Whitehall bureaucracy, fragmented in its structure, uncertain of its objectives, confused in its methods of work, and unaccountable for its performance. That the ministers formally responsible for the Ministry of Defence during that period, Mr Peter Thorneycroft (now Lord Thorneycroft) under the Conservatives and Mr Denis Healey under the Labour Government, were more than averagely able, only confirmed that the system itself needed overhauling.

As I have said, Conservative administrations between 1951 and 1964 had had no coherent philosophy of government reform. Meanwhile, in

THE WHOLE ORGANISATION OF THE STATE

1964 and 1965 it was becoming apparent that the new Labour Government's approach was misconceived. The creation of so many new ministries and departments; the appointment of an even larger number of ministers than under the previous Conservative Government; the explosion in Civil Service numbers; the deliberate introduction of conflict, described by Mr Harold Wilson as 'creative tension', between departments; and the amateurish and even spiteful approach to the problems of the Civil Service adopted by some of the new Government's advisers from the universities–all this was bound to aggravate the existing faults in the system.

At the same time developments were gathering momentum elsewhere that would be closely relevant to eventual reform. Significant progress was being made, especially in the United States, in computing, decision theory, organisation theory and the behavioural and management sciences. It was becoming clear that cybernetics and the 'information revolution' would contribute more in the long run to the reform of government than the ideas of the orthodox academic economists who were then taking over Whitehall.

Thus by 1965 it was beyond doubt, I felt, that our system of central government called for fundamental measures of reform; that the prospects for effective reform during the following five years were small; and that the really important developments for the future were taking place outside the sphere of government altogether. Since then, three years with CEIR (now Scientific Control Systems) Ltd., Dr Maurice Kendall's management and computer consultancy, provided some insight into the potential and the limitations–and into the long-term possibilities–of computing and management science. Two years subsequently with the Inter-Bank Research Organisation provided an opportunity to wrestle with some of the problems looming up in the 1970s and 1980s. Participation in studies of various aspects of government, notably as Adviser to the House of Commons Select Committee on Procedure in their 1969 enquiry into parliamentary control of public expenditure, strengthened my conviction that radical and comprehensive government reform was urgent and that by 1970 comparatively little had been done about it.

In the history of science there always comes a time when an old theory cannot be further elaborated. Increasing cumbersomeness simply makes it less and less effective as an instrument of scientific thought. All the ramifications and qualifications, the epicycles piled on epicycles,

B   7

which were needed in the fifteenth and sixteenth centuries to reconcile the Ptolemaic system of astronomy with newly observed phenomena, were bound to give place sooner or later to a simpler and more powerful explanation. A new vision of the Universe was needed, a new perspective to bring the new problems into focus. Men had to recognise that the world went round the sun. The Copernican revolution had to come. Similarly in the history of institutions there comes a time when further piecemeal change is not enough; patching up symptoms only makes matters worse; the underlying problems have to be identified and solved. It is my firm belief that under Mr. Heath's Conservative Administration one of these turning points in the history of British government is now approaching.

The main institutions of British central government, including the two Houses of Parliament, the Cabinet and the Civil Service, took something like their present shape in the second half of the nineteenth century. More precisely, one might say that the 1860s were the crucial years. They saw acceptance of the reformed Civil Service on Northcote–Trevelyan lines; they saw the Gladstonian principles of parliamentary control of government expenditure embodied in a new Exchequer and Audit Department and Public Accounts Committee of the House of Commons; Bagehot published *The English Constitution* and Mill published *Representative Government*. The 1860s also saw the final emergence of the Liberal Party. In short, the transfer of power from the aristocracy to the middle classes, originated by the industrial revolution and given momentum by the Great Reform Bill of 1832, was at last consolidated in the institutions of Whitehall and Westminster, in the political philosophy and the party-political structure of the day. The piecemeal changes of the preceding hundred years achieved their synthesis in the political ideas and institutions of Gladstonian Liberalism.

The innumerable changes which have taken place in the pattern of government since 1870 reflect our growing acceptance that government must play a more and more important part in our affairs. For example, the efficiency of our industry and our education have become vital to our well-being, perhaps our survival, as a nation; government's concern with them has become close and direct. The comparatively small and scattered social services of the nineteenth century have developed and coalesced into the welfare state; government is now concerned with most aspects of the welfare of the individual citizen. As the government has found it necessary to take on increasing responsibilities in fields such as medicine and the universities, doctors and professors have become increasingly accountable to society for their performance and not just to their own individual professional consciences. Similarly, laisser faire economic theory is no longer accepted; government has assumed responsibility for the country's economic and financial affairs, and for securing economic growth; business has become too important to be left to the businessmen. And so on.

These trends themselves reflect deeper changes. The scale and complexity of men's activity has grown enormously, primarily owing to advances in science and technology. Motorways and other modern civil engineering projects, aviation and defence projects, the developing of new towns and conurbations, the provision of health and social security services–matters of this kind raise social problems of a scale which virtually precludes local or private control. No man is an island any longer; and the interdependence of different commercial and industrial activities has reached the point where no firm, however large, can be an island either. At the same time, the development of communications, and especially of the press and broadcasting, has focussed attention on government and has encouraged people to look increasingly to it for guidance and action. The nineteenth and early twentieth-century extensions of the franchise, the expansion of education, and the gradual spread of scientific attitudes, have encouraged people to seek an increasing measure of control over the way in which the country's business is managed. In this sense, the continual growth in the functions of the State reflects a continually growing measure of self-government. It is difficult to see how this general trend could ever be reversed.

Although these great changes have taken place in the intervening years and much of Gladstone's political philosophy has now been superseded, our general notion of what the British system of government is and how its various parts are supposed to work together remains largely unchanged. No new philosophy of government has replaced the thinking of Bagehot and Mill. Indeed, one of the most remarkable things about British government in the twentieth century is that it has worked so well; we may justifiably be proud of the resilience and adaptability of our Victorian heritage. But it is now time for us in our turn to evolve a new synthesis of our own.

SELF-GOVERNMENT

We badly need a simpler and more effective system of government

9

than we have today, cleaned of the myriad barnacles and encrustations of a century of piecemeal growth. Its structure must be rooted in a new conception of government–a new basic premise that will bring the whole range of problems into clear focus. In fact, this basic premise is to hand–so obvious, like the world going round the sun or Hans Andersen's emperor's lack of clothes, that most of us cannot see it. *It is up to us to govern ourselves.* Government is no longer the means by which the rulers rule the ruled; it is our means to order our own affairs. Many of the shortcomings of British government today derive from the simple fact that we have been trying to run a self-governing society with the institutions of a governed society. We have been trying to operate the parliamentary democracy of today with forms of government suited to the parliamentary monarchy of a century or more ago. We have been trying to fly a jumbo-jet with horses for the engines.

Important consequences follow, once we accept that it is up to us to govern ourselves. Some of these are briefly sketched in the next few pages. They will emerge in greater substance from the more detailed description and analysis in later chapters.

One is that government is no longer fundamentally about something called power–as many political and social scientists still delude themselves. Fundamentally it is about taking collective decisions and collective action. Reforming the system of government is no longer primarily a question of shifting something called power from one section of the community to another, as it was in this country in the nineteenth century and still is in some other countries today. It is about improving society's mechanisms for taking collective decisions and collective action. Questions about power are secondary problems. We need to know about the mechanics of power and about the way people behave in power situations, so that we may be able to construct an effective system of social decision-making and action. We need to know how politicians and officials tick and how their organisations behave and evolve, so that we can design their treadmill–their rat-race–in such a way that they will adequately perform the function we, as a society, require of them. At present the political rat-race and the Westminster and Whitehall treadmill are not very well designed for this purpose.

Those who live in the so-called corridors of power do, in point of fact, have very little power, certainly very little power of positive action. What power they do have is mainly the power of obstruction, inertia and delay. In 1945 the Labour Party naively welcomed its election victory with a cheer of 'We are the masters now!', and one suspects that even in 1964 those who entered Whitehall with the victorious Labour Government expected to find something called 'power' in the corridors of Downing Street and Great George Street – the *efficient* counterpart, as Bagehot[1] might have put it, to the *dignified* aspects of ministerial life, such as official cars, red despatch boxes and attentive secretaries. But alas! they were deceived. Just as Pompey and his soldiers found no god in the Holy of Holies when they stormed the Temple of Jerusalem, so an incoming government finds the Cabinet Room empty of any tangible source of power. All they find are decisions to be made – difficult ones at that. Decisions are what government is about.

The fact that government is no longer basically about power and that there is no Aladdin's lamp at the service of those who sit in the so-called seats of power, explains another important feature of the situation. The impetus for action cannot normally come from inside the government itself. It is not only that the system does not work that way; those who work within it are actually its prisoners. The drive has to come from pressures of outside opinion, public and parliamentary opinion, impelling ministers to impel officials to take effective thought and action. Without this drive the machine is inert and powerless. *A fortiori*, the existing system of government cannot reform itself from within. Successful reform will only come from re-invigorating and re-focussing the political and parliamentary energies that drive the machine of government, and at the same time making the machine of government more responsive to them. Many of the abortive reforms of recent years have failed because they did not take account of this.

The next point is related. As we become self-governing it becomes nonsense to suppose that democracy and efficient government are in conflict with one another. They cannot be. In a self-governing society it must be part of the definition of government efficiency that governmental processes are democratic, and part of the definition of effective democracy that governmental processes are efficient. The notion that democracy and efficient government are incompatible stemmed from the time when a genuine difference of interest between the rulers and the ruled was possible, and the one might conflict with the other. Like so much conventional wisdom, it continues to be propounded long after the conditions that gave rise to it have disappeared. It has become what Samuel Brittan has described, in a related context, as a 'bogus dilemma'.[2]

We can put this point another way by saying that the system of government has become an integral part of the larger system of society. The State can no longer be regarded sensibly as something super-imposed on society from outside. (In fact, how many of us do still believe that the State has a separate existence of its own?) Thus, although the starting point for this book is the need to reform the Executive–the part of the system commonly known as Whitehall, the people traditionally known as the King's or the Queen's servants, the servants of the Crown–we shall find that the Executive cannot be reformed in isolation. We have to look at the Executive's relationship with the Legislature and the Judiciary, and also at the central government's relationship with regional and local authorities. We shall find that reform of the Executive is bound up closely with reform of the Legislature and the Judiciary, and that reform of central government is bound up closely with reform of regional and local government.

We shall also find that reform of the Executive raises questions about the relationship between the public service and the private sector. For example, reforming the government's organisation and practices in the financial and monetary field will necessarily involve clarifying and re-defining the existing relationships between the Treasury, the Bank of England and the City. More generally, we shall find that the devolution of responsibility which is now so necessary in government *may* involve removing certain functions from government altogether, into the private sector–though to suppose that it *must* do so in any particular case would be primitive and doctrinaire.

In short, we shall find that in a society where the State has withered away–or ought to have withered away, at least as a separate operational entity–we can no longer deal with the executive arm of central government as if it were outside society as a whole. Ministries, departments and other government bodies are among the various kinds of institutions we use to handle our affairs. A self-governing society needs to re-define the roles and inter-relationships, the responsibilities and the forms of accountability, of these institutions. Reform of government must be based on a 'systems analysis' of government's role in modern society. Although the term 'systems analysis' in this context does not refer to the detailed analysis of routine transactions and documentation normally carried out by the computer systems analyst, it refers to a process which is conceptually very similar–the analysis of what decisions various organisations have to take and what information has to flow through them and between them.

THE WHOLE ORGANISATION OF THE STATE

This brings us to the concepts of cybernetics. These are implicit in many recent developments in government, and in what we shall be saying about them in the following chapters. Indeed, it is no historical accident that the field of scientific enquiry known as cybernetics has developed in parallel with the evolution of self-government in society, just as it is no accident that 'cybernetics' means *the science of government or steering* in its derivation from the Greek. It is, of course, the term used to describe studies in the field of communication and control, information-handling and decision-making. In the last ten or fifteen years great advances have been made in this field, not least in understanding the logic of self-regulating and self-organising systems.

An important feature of the cybernetic approach is the idea of a hierarchical system, in which the various elements interlock with one another. The way such a system works—and re-organises itself when necessary—is determined largely by the operating functions of its various elements and the relationships between them. Higher-level decisions set the framework, or lay down the ground-rules, within which lower-level functions are carried out. Higher-level decisions are reached with the 'participation' of the lower-level elements responsible for carrying them out. The whole system is served by information flows linking its various parts, ensuring that whenever a decision has to be made or action has to be taken the relevant information is available, and ensuring that when action has been taken there is adequate 'feed-back' of information about its effects.

This approach to a generalised systems theory was originally developed mainly by communications engineers, mathematicians and biologists—people like Shannon, Norbert Weiner, Stafford Beer and Von Bertalanffy.[3] But in the behavioural and social sciences too the concepts of self-organisation and participation are playing an increasingly important role. In personnel management and industrial relations, as well as in politics, participation has already become an idea to conjure with. Precisely what it means in practical terms, and precisely how it is related to the similar concept of self-government, are questions that need detailed examination in particular circumstances. But in general it is coming to be accepted that the individual employee or worker must be given some opportunity to have a say about the business he is working for, if it is to run efficiently. Similarly, the individual citizen must be given a say in the affairs of his society if he is not to become alienated from it. Not only is there no conflict between democracy and efficient

13

government, but government simply will not work any more without a considerable measure of democratic participation. Beyond a certain point the disaffection of important sectors of society, such as young people or organised working people, and their rejection of the formal institutions of government as effective instruments of self-government, will lead to breakdown.

Finally, what is the basic problem facing all human societies today? Surely, it is how to cope with the continuing process of social and economic and technical change, as the so-called Information Revolution gathers momentum and as the world moves towards Daniel Bell's[4] post-industrial society and Marshall McLuhan's[5] global village. As men, we have it in our power to shape this process of change. It is not enough, as it might be for academics, merely to observe it, quantify it, and predict it. The point is not to explain the world but to change it, as a certain philosopher said over a century ago; as another said several centuries earlier, it is reserved only for God and angels to be lookers on in this theatre of man's life. As members of a self-governing society we need to equip ourselves and our statesmen with the apparatus of government–the mechanisms of decision–to enable us to plan and control the future course of events.

It follows that the mechanisms of institutional change in government have become a matter of prime importance to us. How, in practice, can we ensure a continuing match or fit between the institutions themselves and the issues with which they have to deal? It is not just a question of governing ourselves decently in today's situation; it is a question of organising ourselves adequately to meet tomorrow's. Thus there is no question of once-for-all reforms. It is a question of equipping ourselves with a self-organising capability in Westminster and Whitehall. That, essentially, is what government reform is about today.

A COPERNICAN REVOLUTION

Where have we come from? Where are we now? Where do we want to go? As we look forward and imagine what sort of a world society we may be inhabiting in the twenty-first century, what sort of problems we shall face and how we ought to be organising ourselves to face them, it is illuminating to look back over the way government has developed in this country during the last seventy or a hundred years, and to consider how the changes that have taken place should now be consolidated.

This is the aim of the following eight chapters– Chapter 2 to Chapter 9. They deal with particular aspects of government. Their first purpose is to describe how our institutions have actually changed during the transition towards effective self-government, and to show how, from the detailed accumulation of piecemeal change (which may necessarily be rather confusing to describe), there does in fact emerge a pattern that reflects the simple concepts of self-government and cybernetics outlined earlier in this chapter. Their second purpose is to suggest, again in sufficient detail to be illustrative, how the confusion created by the accumulation of past changes should now be resolved, and how the concepts of self-government and cybernetics should now be applied, so as to give us a simpler, more coherent and more effective system of government for the future. But, just as the account given of past events is not intended as a comprehensive history, so the proposals for the future are intended more as a basis for intelligent discussion of how Mr. Heath's existing reforms should be pursued further, than as a comprehensive blue-print. In these matters there are no uniquely correct solutions, and for practical purposes a blue-print can emerge only from the processes of public and parliamentary scrutiny and debate. That, indeed, is the burden of my song.

In Chapter 10 we shall be looking at the methodology of government, and at what will be involved in developing the state of the art in accordance with more firmly established principles and concepts than we possess today. Finally, in the last chapter we shall consider the way forward, in the wider context of possible future developments in the political and international spheres.

My interest in the reform of government was stimulated originally by the inefficiency of the existing system from the point of view of the government employee who wanted to get things done. Subsequently, I came to see that the same inefficiency was also intolerable from the point of view of people who wanted fair, intelligible treatment at the hands of government and who wanted to participate intelligently in governing themselves. It is for such people, as well as for people like my former colleagues in Whitehall, that this book is intended.

It is my hope that it will do something to accelerate the Copernican revolution in British government, which is now under way. In talking of such a revolution, we are not, of course, talking of the destructive kind of revolution that replaces one species of incompetence or barbarism with another, nor of the hot-air kind of revolution recently popularised

15

by the drop-outs and media-men. We are talking of an historic revolution that, running much deeper than either of those, transforms the political ideas and institutions of a society and raises its members to new levels of social purpose and action. This is a creative, constructive revolution that will sooner or later be accomplished, quietly and peacefully, not primarily by civil servants or politicians or experts of one kind and another, and certainly not by adolescent 'revolutionaries', but by the growing army of all kinds of people in every corner of Britain whose self-respect will no longer allow them to endure a system of government that is out of tune with the times, and a way of managing their affairs that they do not understand.

NOTES ON CHAPTER I

General

The approach outlined in this Chapter lay behind the evidence which I submitted to the Fulton Committee on the Civil Service; see the Fulton Committee's Report (HMSO, 1968), Volume 5 (2) pp. 1021 to 1084. It is also to be found in Broadsheet 513 published by Political and Economic Planning (PEP) in July 1969 under the title *Renewal of British Government*. Although not myself a Conservative, I agreed with much of *A New Style of Government* written by David Howell, MP, and published by the Conservative Political Centre in May 1970. Although not myself a Socialist, I admired Dr Jeremy Bray's attempt in *Decision in Government* (Gollancz, 1970) to develop a 'model' of the State as a relationship between the members of society rather than an entity imposed on them from above.

I cannot remember when I was first struck by the concept of a Copernican revolution in government. Arthur Koestler's *The Act of Creation* (Hutchinson, 1963) and T. S. Kuhn's *The Structure of Scientific Revolutions* (Chicago U.P., 1962) interestingly describe the process of re-structuring the categories of scientific thought that takes place when a scientific revolution occurs. This creative re-structuring process in science closely parallels the process of re-structuring that has to take place in the categories of government action and political debate for reform of government to be achieved.

Note 1. Walter Bagehot: *The English Constitution* (with an Introduction by R. H. S. Crossman, MP): Fontana Library, 1968: page 61.

Note 2. Samuel Brittan: *Left or Right, The Bogus Dilemma*: Secker and Warburg, 1968.

Note 3. Norbert Weiner: *Cybernetics*: Technology Press and John Wiley, 1948. This was the start of what has now grown into a truly enormous literature on cybernetics and systems theory. Stafford Beer's publications include *Cybernetics in Management*: English Universities Press, 1959.

Note 4. See, for example, Herman Kahn and Anthony J. Wiener: *The Year 2000*: Macmillan, 1967: page 24.

Note 5. Marshall McLuhan: *Understanding Media*: Routledge and Kegan Paul, 1964.

2

The Changing Shape of Government

> It is as though, in his pictures, an artist were to bring
> together hands, feet, head and other limbs from quite
> different models, each part being admirably drawn in
> itself but without any common relation to a single body.
> COPERNICUS: *On the Revolution of the Heavenly Spheres*

What impact has been made by the changes in the role of government in society on the size and shape of the government and the way it does its work? What problems have these changes raised?

The most obvious consequence has been the government's growth in size. Take the size of the Cabinet for a start. Disraeli had a Cabinet of twelve; in 1880 Gladstone was obliged to raise the number to fourteen; by 1914 the peace-time Cabinet had grown to nineteen members; in the 1960s both Sir Alec Douglas-Home and Mr Wilson had Cabinets of twenty-three. Between 1910 and 1966 the total number of non-Cabinet ministers rose from 29 to over 70. During the same period the number of ministerial departments rose from 16 to 25. Going back as far as 1854, the date of the famous Northcote–Trevelyan Report on the Civil Service, the number of non-industrial civil servants was only about 16,000. By 1970 the Ministry of Technology alone was employing well over twice that number, and the total had grown to well over 750,000. In 1870 central government expenditure was running at about £18 million. By 1970 the corresponding figure was £12,000 million, and total *public* expenditure was running at £18,000 million–in the region of two-fifths or possibly half of the national income, according to the definitions used.

For, of course, it is not only the central government that has grown in numbers and size. Local government has expanded hugely. Many other different kinds of public undertakings have been created too, including nationalised industries, hospital boards and other public corporations and bodies. As these various kinds of public agency have grown up, they have expanded into one another's territory and the traditional demarcation lines between them have become blurred.

Moreover, while the public sector has been expanding in this way, the scale of industrial and commercial activities has been increasing similarly, with the result that the distinction between the public and private sectors has become much less clear-cut than it used to be. Our mixed economy has come to be composed of a spectrum of institutions ranging from central government departments like the Cabinet Office at one end to small family firms at the other. There are not two clearly distinguishable types of undertaking, public and private, but numerous different types with a wide variety of constitutional, legal, financial and managerial characteristics. Comparable problems of efficiency, account-ability and control are common to them all. In order to understand these problems we badly need to develop a comprehensive conceptual frame-work for all these undertakings, in place of the anecdotal case studies which have traditionally passed for the study of public administration in this country. But that is by the way.

As the scale of central government activity has grown, so has its complexity; as its various component parts have expanded towards one another, they have become more and more closely interdependent. In the nineteenth century the government's tasks were confined largely to external affairs, defence, law and order, regulating trade, and raising the revenue—the traditional activities of government by the Crown. They fell into separate, well-defined compartments and very little co-ordination between them was needed. Since then, as the central government's responsibilities have expanded to cover every aspect of national life, its functions have become more and more closely inter-woven with one another, and it has no longer been possible to try to handle them in separate compartments. To meet the continually increasing need for co-ordination there has grown up, out of the Committee of Imperial Defence and its secretariat, set up in 1904, the whole machinery of Cabinet Committees, supported by the Cabinet Office, which exists today.

Not only have the once separate functions of government drawn much more closely together over the years, but the relative importance of different functions has begun to change more rapidly in step with the growing rate of economic, technological and social change. This has led to an accelerating process of structural change as the allocation of re-sponsibilities has shifted between existing ministries and as new ministries have been set up to handle new responsibilities. As we shall see, a kind of rhythm of fragmentation and re-integration looms out of this misty process of structural change–the proliferation of new ministries as new tasks have arisen for which no existing ministry has seemed suitable, and the amalgamation of two or more ministries as, with the passage of time, their tasks have become more and more closely related. This is a continuing process, which provides the mechanism for changing the categories into which government work is divided at any particular time. As the pace of economic and social change accelerates, the process of structural change in government is inevitably accelerating too. We have to learn to understand it, as a permanent feature of the scene, and to plan and control it more deliberately than we have done hitherto.

Growth in the scale of government has radically changed the nature of Civil Service work. The traditional job of Whitehall civil servants was to serve the ministers who formed the government of the day–to help them with their business in Parliament, to draft letters and speeches for them, to conduct interviews for them and issue instructions on their behalf to those who would have to carry them out. This was fundamentally a secretariat service, as titles like Permanent Secretary, Assistant Secretary and so forth suggest. Lord Strang, speaking of the Foreign Office at the turn of the century, describes it as little more than a clerical office for the Foreign Secretary. The Foreign Office

> had only a very small part to play, by comparison with our own times, in the formulation of policy, for it was not recognised as having any advisory duties. It was in fact little more than the Secretary of State's clerical organisation. There was, of course, much copying, cyphering and filing to be done. But of drafting (which appertains essentially to the advisory role) there was very little by modern standards ... Lord Salisbury never consulted his Permanent Under-Secretary, Sir Philip Currie, on any matter of importance, did much of his work at home, and on occasion kept his transactions with other governments completely secret from the Foreign Office. Sir Thomas Sanderson who succeeded Currie as Permanent Under-Secretary did not regard it as incumbent on him, or indeed proper for him, to volunteer advice on policy to his Minister.[1]

Perhaps the staff of the Foreign Office had an unusually restricted role. But it was generally accepted that the staff of the Whitehall Offices were, as their titles suggest, little more than ministers' secretaries.

THE CHANGING SHAPE OF GOVERNMENT

Since then the secretariat function has been augmented by a growing managerial function. Most ministries now have large direct or indirect responsibilities for managing hospitals, transport, the armed forces, industries, or social services; and even traditional activities like preparing the budget or controlling Civil Service personnel now have to be treated as major managerial functions and not simply as appendages to the personal work of ministers. The Permanent Secretary in most ministries is now a director-general as well as a top secretary.

The managerial functions of government have been most clearly recognised in the public corporations and nationalised industries, where the task of officials—in, say, the National Coal Board or British Rail—is to manage their industry to the best of their professional ability within a framework of targets and constraints laid down by the minister. As we shall see, the introduction of 'accountable management' and 'management by objectives' will involve extending the same principle to many other areas of government work in addition to the nationalised industries. But so far, in the absence of a modern style of management in government, growing complexity and the need for closer and closer co-ordination have led to changes in working methods that have been detrimental to effective and responsible management.

UNDESIRABLE FEATURES

In the traditional type of Civil Service secretariat work, responsibilities were clear-cut and the chain of command ran straight. The main flow of information ran vertically up and down clearly defined channels of communication. Decisions of any importance would have to be taken by the minister. Communication with another ministry was normally conducted at arm's length with official formality, on behalf of the minister himself. As recently as the early 1950s I can remember being instructed by one of the old-stagers how to write formal letters from the Colonial Office to other departments, beginning 'Sir, I am directed by Mr. Secretary Lyttelton . . .' and ending 'I am, Sir, your most obedient servant'. It was with a daring sense of modernity that in correspondence with members of the public one discarded this style in favour of the chattier and more personal 'Dear Sir . . . Yours faithfully'.

Today, of course, the old formal procedures are quite out-of-date. Ministers cannot in any real sense be responsible for many of the decisions taken by their ministries, simply because there are so many. Informal communication between ministries takes place constantly at every level. A vast network of inter-departmental committees has grown up, as a substructure to the Cabinet, and similar committee structures exist within ministries too. My own work as an Assistant Secretary in the Ministry of Defence in 1964 and 1965 was mainly concerned with inter-departmental working parties of a 'steering' committee. Before decisions could be taken, the recommendations of this committee, framed after argument about the conclusions of the working parties, had first to be considered by a number of other committees: first by two committees of principal military officers (one for administrative questions, the other for personnel questions) and one committee of Second Permanent Secretaries (for questions of finance and civilian management); secondly by a combined committee composed of these three; and thirdly by the Defence Council. On matters of particular importance the Service Boards might also be brought in. The Ministry of Defence then contained twenty separate hierarchies with heads at Board level or above and was perhaps particularly committee-ridden for that reason. But by 1970 this mode of work had become general in all Whitehall departments. It involves a dangerous dilution of any real sense of personal responsibility and accountability on the part of ministers and officials alike.

Lord Hankey, it is true, went on record as saying, 'It is sheer nonsense to say that the committee system means delay and passing on responsibility. A good chairman will never tolerate that. He will watch the situation every day, ever on the lookout for a hitch, finding a solution for every difficulty, never allowing matters to stand still. The truth is that the committee system is only pernicious when it is badly run.'[2] But that was wishful thinking by the biggest committee man of them all. The committee system inevitably becomes pernicious as soon as it becomes the normal way of doing business. It means that negotiation takes the place of administration, compromise the place of decision, exchange of opinions the place of analysis, and talk the place of action. There must be very few people in the central Whitehall departments today who do not recognise the truth of this.

All the unplanned developments in central government over the years have had a number of other undesirable results. There are too many different authorities with fingers in the same pie. There is too much centralisation, partly because there are so many authorities to be co-ordinated and partly because of an obsolete system of financial and parliamentary control. There is too much secrecy. There is too little forward planning. These shortcomings are inter-related. They all derive from an attempt to handle the tasks and the scale of late twentieth-century government with a system of institutions and procedures based on the assumptions of the nineteenth century.

As an example of too many different authorities take the number of ministers and ministries. Does anyone really suppose that the government's functions can be divided between more than twenty ministries in such a way that the minister in charge of each has a reasonably well-defined and self-contained sphere of individual responsibility? Can the Cabinet, even with the support of its committee substructure and its secretariat, effectively co-ordinate work which is split up into more than twenty different compartments? Could a Cabinet twenty-three strong ever comprise an effective decision-making body? Could fifty or so senior ministers, let alone another forty, ever really share collective responsibility for government policy? The answer to all these questions is clearly 'No'. By the 1960s the twin doctrines of individual and collective ministerial responsibility had become little more than a fiction.

The size of the Cabinet was, of course, recognised as a problem a long time ago, and through the years various solutions have been propounded The Haldane Committee in 1918 thought that the Cabinet should be small in number—preferably ten or at the most twelve.[3] In 1947 L. S. Amery[4] argued in favour of a small policy-making Cabinet; he was convinced that a Cabinet consisting of a score of ministers was quite incapable of either thinking out a definite policy or of securing its execution. Many others have considered the question of how the Cabinet should be composed. None has hit on a generally accepted answer, but all without exception have agreed that the Cabinet should be smaller than it is today.

Most recent Prime Ministers seem to have accepted this view, in theory. But in practice, they usually seem to have discovered, as Abraham Lincoln did when filling his government posts, that there are 'too many pigs for the tits'. They have found the personal and political pressures to increase the number of offices more compelling than the claim of efficient government that the number should be reduced. Surely it is time that Parliament assumed responsibility for scrutinising their actions in this respect, in order to redress the balance.

The prevailing tendency to enlarge the number of ministries and to blur responsibilities between them has been accentuated by the traditional methods of organisational change. In the first place, when new

C   23

ministries or departments are set up to do new tasks there is always quite a long time-lag before the corresponding old ones are wound up. Secondly, as the demarcations between existing departments become obsolescent, the first step towards their integration is often the creation of a new one to co-ordinate them. Thus the Ministry of Defence was set up in 1946 alongside the Service Ministries and, even seven years after their merger in a unified Ministry of Defence in 1964, there are still four departments where previously there were three. Similarly, the Department of Economic Affairs (now defunct) was set up alongside, not instead of, the other economic ministries. For these reasons there has been an apparently inevitable tendency for the number of ministers and senior officials to grow, and for the confusion of functions and responsibilities between them to become worse and worse confounded.

This confusion of responsibilities reflects confusion about objectives. To put it bluntly, ministers in recent governments have not known precisely what they have been trying to do. They decide that it is no longer sensible to manage the country's defence effort on the basis that sea-warfare, land-warfare and air-warfare are separate activities, so they set up a Ministry of Defence to manage it on the basis that they are not; but they leave the existing Departments to continue to try to manage it as if they are. They no longer wish to manage the economy in the traditional way, so they set up a Department of Economic Affairs to try to manage it in a new way; but they leave the Treasury to carry on more or less as before, in tandem. They decide that the Board of Trade has not been active enough in promoting efficiency in industry; so they set up a Ministry of Technology, not instead of it but alongside it. And so on.

This fragmentation of government work and the confusion of responsibilities between different authorities inevitably leads to excessive centralisation. Responsibility can only be decentralised to the level at which decisions fall within the province of a single authority; responsibilities cannot be decentralised at all if they are not clearly defined. This centralising tendency has been greatly reinforced by the Gladstonian system of financial control imposed on government departments by the Treasury on behalf of Parliament. We shall consider this further in Chapter 7. The important point is that Parliament has been concerned to control the amounts of money spent on different kinds of resources (or 'inputs' as they are often called) like staff or travelling expenses or supplies, rather than to control the amounts of money spent for different purposes (or 'outputs'). This, as we shall see, has led to detailed centralised control over the way government officials do their work.

SECRECY

Too much secrecy has followed from excessive centralisation as night follows day. They are opposite sides of the same coin. It is popularly supposed that the Official Secrets Act is to blame for this. In my experience that is not so. Official Secrets Act or no, civil servants are the prisoners of the system within which politicians require them to work. Unless that system is changed, the problem of excessive secrecy will remain.

What passes between a minister and his Civil Service advisers must be confidential. This kind of secrecy is a necessary adjunct to our system of parliamentary and cabinet government. It would become virtually impossible for ministers to carry collective responsibility in Parliament for the government's decisions, if the whole process by which they reached these decisions, including all the arguments, counter-arguments, doubts, hopes, and fears expressed by individual ministers, was public knowledge. Parliament is the forum for public political debate; the Cabinet is not. Similarly, in discharging their individual responsibility for the work of a ministry, ministers must be allowed to enjoy the confidential advice of their officials, and to accept it or reject it without the fact being made known. The words in which Sir John Anderson (Lord Waverley) described the relationship to be maintained between a minister and his civil servants are still valid today.

In my experience, the relationship between a Minister and his senior departmental advisers is of a very close and intimate character. The civil servant is the recipient of many confidences, and I have never known such confidence abused. If the Minister feels he can tell his departmental adviser frankly what his difficulties are–difficulties with his political opponents and with his party colleagues–the adviser will be in a position to apply far more intelligently and helpfully the departmental advice which it is his main function to contribute. It is upon the effectiveness of the partnership established between the Minister, irrespective of party, and his chief permanent advisers, that the practical results attained largely depend. This applies not only in administration

25

but also in the transactions of parliamentary business. No head of a department can perform his duties adequately unless he is thoroughly familiar with parliamentary forms and procedure.[5]

No doubt we have to preserve this convention of political confidentiality. But what is wrong is that it now extends to wide areas of activity to which it is irrelevant. There is still an area of central government activity in which political and parliamentary considerations are paramount. But the greater part of government work today, where professional, technical and routine administrative considerations are of primary importance, falls outside this area. Ministers' decisions are part of the political process, and the precise manner in which they reach them should be shielded from the public eye. But the facts upon which ministers have to base their decisions, and the professional or technical evaluation of these facts, are not part of the political process and should be public knowledge. At present, routine decisions of government officials far from the centre of affairs, and routine information which they compile, must be kept confidential in order to shield their minister from the possibility of political attack. This is wrong for two reasons. First, it means that Parliament and the public have no means of telling whether the professionals are doing a good job, and thus no means of bringing pressure to bear on them to improve their performance if necessary. Second, it means that Parliament and the public have no means of knowing whether ministers are taking whatever political decisions may be necessary, and thus no means of judging ministers' decisions against the facts and holding ministers accountable for their performance.

When one thinks of it, it is really very odd that since the time of Crichel Down in 1954 no minister has had to resign because shortcomings in his performance as a departmental minister have been publicly disclosed. And it must be a long time since any senior government official was retired early because his performance fell short of the standard exacted by public scrutiny. This is not because the performance of successive governments has been outstandingly good in recent decades. It is because ministers and civil servants alike are now shielded from any effective form of accountability. Because of the obscurity in which the business of government is conducted, ministers can always shuffle off the blame, by implication if not explicitly, on to their officials – and vice versa.

THE CHANGING SHAPE OF GOVERNMENT

The Prime Minister's position in this respect is of particular importance. The extent to which a Prime Minister can politically dominate his Cabinet and his parliamentary colleagues today as compared with a hundred years ago may be open to argument. But there is no doubt that as the leader of the government—the conductor of the orchestra, you might say—he is required to exercise much more positive direction than Gladstone or Disraeli was. In the nineteenth century, ministers could be allowed a good deal of independence to pursue self-contained departmental policies, and the Prime Minister was only the first among equals. Today he has become much more like an executive chairman and managing director. He now has a real job of his own to do organising and co-ordinating the activities of his government. He now needs a proper department of his own to help him in this task; and his performance in discharging it needs to be brought out into the open under more effective scrutiny than it is today.

The obscurity in which government business is conducted is also a factor contributing to serious failures in forward planning. Lack of forward planning has always been recognised as a problem in central government. Sir Henry Taylor referred to it in 1836 as a 'great evil and want' and thought it indicated 'something fatally amiss in the very idea of statesmanship on which our system of administration is based.'[6] Since then, of course, the need to plan for the future has become much more important, as the time scale of human activities and enterprises has lengthened. The design and construction of a power station, a motorway, an aircraft or a new town take years to complete. In even more complex matters, such as the reconstruction of the country's education system, armed forces, or civil service, for example, an even longer period will be required. There are many spheres in which we now have to plan, to think constructively, and to take decisions, ten, twenty or even thirty years ahead.

At first sight the underlying political conditions appear unfavourable to long term planning. The government of the day has a five-year term at most, and the mainspring of our political process is the conflict between one group of politicians who are determined to return to office on completion of their current term and another group who are determined to throw them out. This means that political leaders will be inclined to postpone difficult decisions until their urgency, in terms of electoral advantage and disadvantage, outweighs their difficulty. We must accept this as a fact of life and draw the logical conclusion. Major

27

premise: politicians will not take decisions until they have become electorally urgent. Minor premise: we want politicians to take the decisions necessary for long term planning. Conclusion: we must find some way of making these decisions electorally urgent. That is to say, we must make it possible for the public to know what decisions are required today if we are to avoid running into difficulties in ten, twenty or thirty years time; and we must make it possible to see whether these decisions are going by default.

In practice, this means that Parliament and the public must press for the publication of much more information about possible eventualities and the various plans and projects which could be adopted to meet them, together with the dates by which decisions must be taken. Making the decision will be the responsibility of the government of the day. What choices are open, and when decisions must be made, should be matters of public knowledge and discussion. This implies that the preparation and publication of long-term studies as the basis for government decisions should normally be done by people other than a minister's own officials; they should be done by bodies which, while they may be subordinate to a minister in the sense that they work to his remit, are not under his direct day-to-day control and do not commit him to the views they express. Hiving off responsibility for future policy studies in this way would do much to ensure that the information on which government decisions are taken is available to Parliament and the public, even though the actual process of government decision-making remains confidential between ministers and their advisers. It would imply a more explicit distinction than today between the secretariat functions of the Civil Service on the one hand and its professional functions on the other. Such a distinction is a necessary element in the reform of government for other reasons too.

NEED FOR COHERENCE

The shortcomings developed by our system of government over the years—fragmentation of functions, confusion of responsibilities, excessive centralisation, excessive secrecy and lack of forward planning—affect both those who deal with the government and those who work for it.

Those who deal with the government find it difficult to cope with a multitude of authorities with different and sometimes inconsistent approaches to a problem. They are exasperated by what, at least to them, seems like muddle and delay: and, although they often suspect that confusion lurks behind the cloak of official silence, there is nothing they can do to sort it out–no-one they can go to for an answer or a decision. 'Nobody takes decisions in government', they feel; 'decisions just get taken–eventually.' The industrialist, especially the manager of a small firm, has been bothered by different unco-ordinated demands made upon him by the Board of Trade, Department of Employment and Productivity, Ministry of Technology, Inland Revenue, Department of Health and Social Security, etc., etc., and by the different unco-ordinated forms of assistance, advice, and exhortation which they have offered him. The sick, the badly housed, the poor, the unemployed, and those with family problems–who are so often the same people–are baffled at having to deal with different authorities with different, possibly conflicting sets of rules and regulations. In some areas of government work, such as the assessment and collection of taxes, the accumulation of complexity and delay has nearly reached the point where complete breakdown might occur.

From the point of view of those who work for the government the situation is no better. I have heard the Ministry of Defence described by one inhabitant as a comic nightmare, by Kafka out of the Marx Brothers; by another as a system cleverly designed to maintain itself in static equilibrium–as soon as one part moves, several others automatically move to counteract it! There is obviously an element of humorous exaggeration here. But there is more than an element of truth. The old theory of checks and balances has been working all too successfully, throughout Whitehall. It is a tribute to the energies of so many of the civil servants and professional men who work there that results so often emerge from the jungle of conflicting objectives, contradictory policies and opposing interests.

This state of affairs involves a growing misuse of valuable manpower in central government, which as a people we can ill afford; and it means, on the personal plane, that many of the individuals concerned do not enjoy an opportunity to develop their full potential. Their output–in terms of what actually happens in the real world as a result of their work–is much smaller than it should be. The vast majority of civil servants cannot expect to become the close confidential advisers of Ministers; but under the traditional system they cannot be given full managerial responsibility either. They are condemned to work in a sort of twilight zone, an ever-expanding no man's land, which cannot offer the satisfactions and disciplines either of the old administrative Civil Service or of professional work done according to professional standards. All in all, the situation is now very serious, and it has been deteriorating. Beyond a certain point muddle becomes self-generating; more and more people are brought in to unravel it, but in fact they succeed only in ravelling it further. We have now reached the point where some other solution simply must be sought.

The following chapters illustrate how this situation has evolved, and indicate some of the main problems that have arisen in particular fields of government activity. Much of what is said and many of the criticisms made are not new. It has for some time been accepted that the system of government we have in Britain today was not shaped by a conscious process of logic or design. It represents the unplanned accumulation of piecemeal solutions to a great multitude of different problems that have arisen over the years since Gladstone's day. Many people are already coming to recognise that the present working relationship between Parliament and the Executive, together with the organisation, the procedures and the methods of control that this involves, is still based on the assumption that Parliament's main task is to restrain the activities of the state–indeed of the Crown–in the interest of the laisser faire middle classes who achieved political supremacy in the nineteenth century. It is becoming commonplace that the stresses and strains in our system of government today stem largely from our attempts to pour the new wine of twentieth-century parliamentary democracy into the old bottles of a nineteenth-century parliamentary monarchy. Paradoxically, the advent of a supposedly right-wing Conservative Government may now enable us to transform this situation.

Fifty years ago, after the first world war, the Haldane Committee attempted comprehensive reforms of the machinery of central government. Nobody took any notice of what they said; everyone wanted to return to the pre-war 'normal'. After the second world war, although there was a flurry of structural change in government, no new Haldane Committee was set up to carry out a comprehensive review. Since then, although many suggestions for reform have been put forward, no attempt has been made to draw up a comprehensive programme of reform. Why, then, should this approach be any more acceptable today?

The reason, I believe, is that a new factor is entering the situation. Many of us do not want to go back to 'normal', and recognise that that is impossible anyway. We are coming to see that the nature of government now is altogether different from what it was in the past; it now belongs to *us*, not to *them*. And so we are beginning to realise that to understand the mechanics of government is a matter of close interest to us all, not just to the comparatively small number of politicians, government servants and academics who have traditionally regarded government as their own special preserve.

What is to be done? How is it to be done? Has it been done properly? Those three questions sum up the essence of government, in general and in each particular sphere. To improve the state of the art of government is to develop new and better methods of asking and answering these questions. To reform government is to reshape institutions and procedures so that they will be better able to help us in asking and answering them.

As we shall see in the following chapters, past changes in government organisation and procedures have, in fact, stemmed from dissatisfaction with the way the existing institutions were asking and answering the questions: what is to be done? how is it to be done? has it been done properly? But these changes often brought little permanent improvement because they were made without any sustained attempt to understand the logic of government decision and action or to develop a coherent philosophy (or methodology) of government. That is what we must now put right. We shall find that examination of past changes in particular areas of government activity suggests a number of principles on which such a methodology can be founded for the future, and then we shall try to pull these principles together into a coherent whole.

NOTES ON CHAPTER 2

General

In this chapter I have drawn fairly extensively on the evidence that I submitted to the Fulton Committee. Background information is to be found, for example, in Emmeline W. Cohen's *The Growth of the British Civil Service, 1780–1939*: Allen and Unwin, 1941–an excellent book. Also in John P. Mackintosh's *The British Cabinet*: Methuen, 1968; R. G. S. Brown's *The Administrative Process in Britain*, Methuen, 1970; and in many other publications.

Note 1. Lord Strang: *The Foreign Office* (page 146): Allen and Unwin (The New Whitehall Series), 1955.

Note 2. Lord Hankey: *Government Control in War* (page 73): Cambridge University Press, 1945.

Note 3. The Haldane Committee's Report was published by HMSO as Cmnd. 9230/1918.

Note 4. L. S. Amery: *Thoughts On The Constitution*: Hutchinson, 1947.

Note 5. Sir John W. Wheeler-Bennett: *John Anderson, Viscount Waverley* (page 168): Macmillan, 1962.

Note 6. Sir Henry Taylor: *The Statesman*: 1836.

3

Defence

Simple said, 'I see no danger'; Sloth said, 'Yet a little more sleep'; and Presumption said, 'Every vat must stand upon its own bottom'. And so they lay down to sleep again and Christian went on his way.

JOHN BUNYAN, *Pilgrim's Progress*

For many people defence is rather a boring subject. But it is of special interest in connection with the reform of government. Historically, it was the first sphere of activity in which the central government assumed direct administrative and executive responsibilities on a large scale. Running the Army and Navy involved much more than did the other classic tasks of nineteenth-century government—maintenance of law and order, conduct of external relations, and collection of revenue. In 1914, defence expenditure at £77 million was more than all the government's civil expenditure put together. The defence of the realm has always been a central feature of national policy.

This is no doubt why developments in defence organisation illuminate so many problems arising in other spheres. As the central government takes on increasing responsibility for health and social services, education, and economic management, we find problems arising that have already been encountered in the defence context, and we often seem to find in the development of defence organisation an evolving pattern which subsequently repeats itself elsewhere. From the secretariat of the Committee of Imperial Defence established in 1904 springs the first secretariat of the Cabinet in 1916. The unsuccessful Minister for Co-ordination of Defence appointed between the wars proves the fore-runner of unsuccessful co-ordinating Ministers in other spheres, such as Transport, Fuel and Power, and Economic Affairs. The decision to unify executive responsibility for the armed forces under a single Secretary of State for Defence in 1964 foreshadows similar developments in Education, Science and the Arts; External Affairs; Economic and Financial Affairs; Trade and Industry; and Heath and Social Security. Continuing inter-Service rivalry and reluctance to

33

co-operate sets the pattern for bureaucrats throughout Whitehall to fight their own little corners in the teeth of change.

At the same time, under the stimulus of two world wars, the armed forces have pioneered new methods of control and management (though it cannot be claimed that this has happened without strong resistance from the Service traditionalists). In particular the Services initiated the development of the mathematically based techniques of operational research which are now applied to control and management problems of all kinds. The Ministry of Defence imported programme budgeting from Mr Macnamara's Pentagon. In general, studies of military command and control systems have been one of the starting points for the analysis of organisational and administrative concepts in industry and the public service.

It would be wrong to imply that developments in defence organisation provide an example that ought to be followed elsewhere. Far from it. They provide a very good lesson in the pitfalls to be avoided–a lesson that has not so far been learned. The point is that defence is a well-defined sphere of government activity, in which a pattern of evolution common to other spheres can clearly be discerned. The process of organisational change in the defence sphere over the last fifty or sixty years brings out very clearly the lack of a coherent methodology in government and the practical difficulties that result.

The changes affecting the government's defence responsibilities have, of course, been very far-reaching indeed. A hundred years ago military questions could still be handled more or less exclusively by the State, without reference to and without very much direct impact on the people. That was true even of the Crimean and Boer Wars. Two world wars and modern weapons of mass destruction have altered all that. Even in peace-time today defence expenditure in the advanced countries is a major burden on national resources; defence industry is a leading element in national industry; and defence makes an important call on national resources of manpower, especially skilled manpower.

There are other changes to be considered too. Scientific developments have affected the task of managing the armed forces as much as they have affected any other aspect of government activity. This is most obviously true of military equipment; aircraft, other new weapons and much more complex military supply requirements generally have given rise to important problems of defence organisation. Social changes have also had a profound effect on the management of the armed forces.

34

DEFENCE

Except in war-time or a period of emergency serious enough to justify conscription, the Services have to compete for manpower against the counter-attractions of a society which affords its members a continually rising level of affluence, welfare and educational opportunity. The concept of the welfare state has imposed a wide range of new personnel management and welfare problems on the Services. Finally, although Britain's international position in terms of political, military and economic strength has declined, our military commitments have not declined proportionately. Our contribution to the Western nuclear deterrent, to the defence of continental Europe, to international peace-keeping and to defending our own interests overseas, has put a continuous strain on our resources ever since the second world war. We have been able to share some of these commitments with the other members of international defence organisations such as NATO, and to some extent with the other members of the United Nations. But, on balance, the emergence of international defence organisations has imposed additional new commitments which cannot easily be offset—witness the East of Suez controversy—by a corresponding reduction in the old.

The effect of these developments on government organisation for defence has been two-fold. First, within the sphere of defence itself, there has been simultaneously a tendency to create new departments to handle new tasks and a counter-tendency towards closer integration. Secondly, the defence functions of government have drawn closer to the civil functions, initially with the creation of the Committee of Imperial Defence at the beginning of the century, and subsequently with the development of Cabinet Office procedures for co-ordinating all central government departments. We shall return to the second point in Chapter 8. This chapter covers changes only within the defence sphere.

AIR-WARFARE AND DEFENCE SUPPLY

Before the first world war there were two defence departments, the Admiralty and the War Office. The history of the government's organisation for defence since that time has been shaped by three main considerations: the development of air-warfare; the problems of defence supply; and the problems of defence co-ordination.

The control of air-warfare was the subject of a great and continuing controversy between 1914 and 1924. Initially, a Royal Flying Corps had been set up in 1912 with separate naval and army wings but with common staff and facilities. By 1914, however, the two wings had

35

separated, the Royal Naval Air Service coming under the Admiralty and the Royal Flying Corps under the War Office. This reflected the assumption that air-warfare was simply an adjunct to sea-warfare or land-warfare. The air raids on London in 1917 demonstrated that this assumption was invalid. General Smuts drew attention to the possible strategic role of air operations carried out quite separately from naval or army operations, and after a good deal of controversy a separate Air Ministry and a unified Royal Air Force were set up in 1918. No sooner was the war over, however, than the controversy was reopened, and from 1919 to 1924 the Army and the Navy both sought to abolish the Air Ministry and divide the Royal Air Force between them. The attempt failed and the Salisbury Committee of 1923 came down in favour of a separate Air Ministry. The Air Ministry remained in existence until its incorporation in the Ministry of Defence in 1964.

The organisation of defence supply has been a vexed question for many a long year. For most of the time the issue has been whether each Service should be responsible for its own equipment and supplies, or whether they should rely on supply departments not under their control. Latterly the question has been whether supply arrangements not under the direct control of individual Services should be under the Ministry of Defence or under some other department of government such as the Ministry of Aviation or the Ministry of Technology.

At the beginning of the first world war the Admiralty and the War Office each had its own supply organisation. When it became clear that the War Office could not cope with the munitions problem, Lloyd George's Ministry of Munitions was set up and by the end of the war was providing the Army and the Royal Air Force with most of their military supplies. When Churchill, who was by that time Minister of Munitions, pressed hard for all the supply branches of the Admiralty and the remaining supply branches of the War Office to be transferred to him, the Cabinet took the view that *all* government supplies, civil as well as military, should become the responsibility of a single department and that the Ministry of Munitions should become a Ministry of Supply. What happened in fact was precisely the contrary! The Ministry of Munitions was wound up in 1921 and each Service resumed responsibility for its own supply.

With the second world war, the argument about military supplies blew up again. By 1940 responsibility was split between five ministries—the Ministry of Aircraft Production (responsible mainly for the RAF), the Ministry of Supply (responsible mainly for the Army), the Admiralty (responsible for the Navy) and the War Office and Air Ministry (with limited responsibilities for Army and RAF supply). Clearly some co-ordination was required between these five ministries, so a Minister of Production was appointed with a sixth co-ordinating ministry.

After the war ended the Ministry of Production was merged with the Board of Trade, and the Ministry of Aircraft Production was merged with the Ministry of Supply. The Minister of Defence, appointed for the first time in 1946 with a co-ordinating Ministry of his own, assumed some of the functions previously carried out by the Minister of Production. These arrangements lasted until 1959 when the Ministry of Supply was abolished. Its army production and supply functions returned to the War Office and its responsibility for aircraft production went to the new Ministry of Aviation, which also became responsible for the aircraft manufacturing industry and for civil aviation. In 1966 the Ministry of Aviation was abolished in turn. The question arose whether its defence functions should be transferred to the Ministry of Defence or to the newly created Ministry of Technology. Expert official advice at the working level favoured their integration with the rest of the defence effort under the Ministry of Defence. However, as a result of inter-departmental and ministerial horse-trading, shielded from any effective scrutiny by Parliament, they retained their separate existence as a semi-autonomous part of the Ministry of Technology. After the demise of that Ministry in 1970 they continued their separate existence, temporarily, in a new Ministry of Aviation Supply. They were finally absorbed in the Ministry of Defence in April 1971.

DEFENCE CO-ORDINATION

The development of air-warfare and the problems of military supply have tended towards increasing the number of departments concerned with defence matters. But other developments have tended towards greater unification. Advances in military technology have made it less and less realistic to handle sea-warfare, land-warfare and air-warfare as if they were separate activities. The nuclear armoury may consist of sea-borne missiles, land-based missiles or air-borne bombs and missiles; controlling the shape and size of this armoury, and its deployment and operation, is one task—not three independent Navy, Army and Air Force tasks. It is no longer realistic to organise the research, development, production and supply of military equipment and stores independently for sea-warfare, land-warfare and air-warfare. To maintain national forces of the required size and shape is one problem, not three independent problems; in making the best use of manpower resources it is becoming unrealistic to recruit and train men for a military career in only one of the elements. The allocation and control of expenditure for defence purposes as if part of it is reserved for sea-warfare, part for land-warfare, and part for air-warfare is no longer an adequate basis for policy-making or administration. These changes in the nature of national defence since the beginning of the twentieth century have led to a continuing series of organisational, administrative and procedural changes designed to secure closer co-ordination between the Services.

Co-ordination was a comparatively simple matter before the first world war, involving only the Admiralty and the War Office. The arrangements then made by the Committee of Imperial Defence undoubtedly contributed to our preparedness for war. But the Committee was only advisory and it could not take the centralised executive control which was required once war had broken out. This was assumed by the War Cabinet, established in 1916. Likewise the Committee had been unable to develop machinery for inter-Service planning or for inter-Service command in joint military operations. In this case the omission was not made good during the first world war.

The urgency of improving inter-Service co-operation was increased after the war by the emergence of the RAF as a third fighting Service. Among the proposals put forward was the creation of a unified Ministry of Defence, and even the unification of the three Services. After demands for a 'new Esher Committee' to propose improvements on the basis of experience in the 1914–18 war, as the Esher Committee had done after the Boer War, a batch of committees were appointed. The Geddes Committee of 1921 came out in favour of a unified Ministry of Defence, but the Mond-Weir Committee rejected any significant amalgamation even of supporting services common to the Navy, Army and Air Force. The actual course of events, however, followed the conclusions of the Salisbury Committee of 1923. This committee, as we have already seen, recommended the retention of a separate Air Ministry and Air Force. It recognised the possibility of a unified Ministry of Defence as an eventual solution to the problem of co-ordinating the Service Ministries, but concluded that the immediate need was to strengthen the existing machinery for co-ordination.

The Salisbury Committee recommended that a Cabinet Minister

should be appointed to be the Prime Minister's full-time deputy as chairman of the Committee of Imperial Defence, and that the three Chiefs of Staff should assume, in addition to their Navy, Army and Air Force responsibilities, 'an individual and collective responsibility for advising on defence policy as a whole, the three constituting as it were a Super-Chief of a War Staff in Commission'. These recommendations were accepted, and the Chiefs of Staff Committee was set up. About the same time, the sub-committee structure of the Committee of Imperial Defence was enlarged to include, in particular, new sub-committees on manpower and supply. The inter-Service committee system was further enlarged: in 1927 by the establishment of a Joint Planning Committee composed of the Directors of Plans of the three Service Ministries; in 1936 by the establishment of a Joint Planning Staff and a Joint Intelligence Sub-Committee; and in 1939 by the establishment of a Joint Intelligence Staff. These joint committees and staffs reported to the Chiefs of Staff. The principle of this joint system, both at the Chief of Staff level and lower down, was that inter-Service policies should be formulated by those who were responsible for carrying them out in each Service, and that those engaged in the work of inter-Service co-ordination should continue to be primarily responsible to their own Service. The main lines of authority and command from individual to individual should thus continue to run through single Service channels, from the Cabinet at the top down to the lowliest sailor, soldier or airman.

Thus was set the pattern for the future development of inter-departmental committees throughout Whitehall. The Salisbury Committee bears a grave responsibility!

The Salisbury Committee's proposal that a Cabinet Minister should be appointed as Deputy Chairman of the Committee of Imperial Defence, to supervise the co-ordination of defence policy by the Chiefs of Staff, lapsed between 1925 and 1936. The experiment had not been a success. The Minister had no authority over the Service Ministries and could not iron out differences between them; the status of the Committee of Imperial Defence was reduced when he, rather than the Prime Minister, presided; he was not necessarily in accord with the Prime Minister over the handling of an issue; he had no staff of his own; and the Secretariat of the Committee of Imperial Defence reported to the Prime Minister, not to him. The arrangement was revived in 1936 with the appointment of a Minister for Co-ordination of Defence. But this

D 39

was, at least to some extent, a piece of window-dressing by Chamberlain as Prime Minister to meet public and parliamentary demand for measures to co-ordinate the re-armament programme. In practice the new co-ordinating minister again had no authority over the Service Ministers or the Chiefs of Staff, no executive functions, no responsibility to Parliament, no staff and no money. When the war came in 1939 his position was recognised to be anomalous. He could not control the mobilisation and direction of the whole resources of the nation for total war, a task which necessarily fell to the Prime Minister, nor had he any specific responsibility for knitting together the activities of the three Services. The experiment of a co-ordinating minister had failed for the second time.

When Churchill became Prime Minister in 1940 he assumed the additional title of Minister of Defence. There was no need to define his duties in this capacity since there was no distinction to be drawn between his actions in it and in his capacity of Prime Minister of the nation at war. The main lines of command ran straight from the Prime Minister as Chairman of the War Cabinet and the Defence (Operations) Committee through each of the Chiefs of Staff, down to the three Service organisations. But when peace returned, the Prime Minister had other, more important, tasks than to act as Minister of Defence. Once again, as after the Boer War and the first world war, it was necessary to review the central organisation for defence.

The 1946 White Paper on this subject stressed one defect of the pre-war arrangements – the absence in the machinery of the Committee of Imperial Defence of 'a guiding hand to formulate a unified defence policy for the three Services'. This had not been remedied by the appointment of a Minister for Co-ordination of Defence, since he had no power to take executive action. The White Paper did not wholly reject the concept of amalgamating the three Services and placing them under a single Minister; like the Salisbury Committee before it, it recognised that at some stage in the future this might be found desirable. But the government did not wish to take that step at that time, and adopted the following arrangements instead. At the top level, a Defence Committee of the Cabinet, under the Prime Minister's chairmanship, replaced the Committee of Imperial Defence; next, a Minister of Defence was appointed to act as Deputy for the Prime Minister and to be responsible, with the help of a number of committees, for apportioning resources and settling common adminstrative questions between the Services; and, finally, the Service Ministers continued each to be responsible to Parliament for administering his own Service and Service Ministry. The basic changes from the pre-war arrangements were that the Minister of Defence had a small ministry, as opposed to a committee secretariat, to support him; that he was executively responsible for certain limited functions and expenditure; and that the Service Ministers were no longer members of the Cabinet. However, the Minister of Defence was not, in any effective sense, placed in authority over the Service Ministers. The Chiefs of Staff Committee remained unaffected, the chairmanship continuing to rotate among the three Service Chiefs.

The appointment of a Minister of Defence with his own Ministry, separate from the Service Departments, was a new departure. It was designed, as we have seen, to provide a guiding hand to formulate a unified defence policy. But, if it was to do this effectively, it could only do so at the expense of disrupting the lines of executive responsibility between the Cabinet and the Service Ministries. Otherwise, it would be ineffective.

It was in fact an ineffective arrangement. By 1957 it was recognised that the 1946 changes had not gone far enough towards unification and the Minister of Defence was given increased authority to take decisions on matters of general defence policy affecting the size, shape, organisation and equipment of the armed forces. In 1958 this arrangement was confirmed and certain further changes were made. The most important of these was the appointment of a fourth Chief of Staff, as Chairman of the Chiefs of Staff Committee and principal military adviser to the Minister of Defence. Just as the appointment of a Minister of Defence in 1946 had reduced the policy-making role of the Service Ministers, so the appointment of a Chief of the Defence Staff in 1958 reduced the policy-making role of the three Service Chiefs. But the Service Ministers and Service Chiefs were still expected to take responsibility for managing the armed forces. Largely for this reason, the 1957–58 changes also failed to secure the necessary degree of unified control over defence policy. It came to be recognised that, since policy and management could not be isolated from one another, the separation of the Ministry of Defence staff responsible for policy from the Service Ministries staff responsible for management was a major organisational defect. So in 1963 the decision was taken to integrate the Ministry of Defence and the three Service Ministries in a new, unified Ministry of Defence under a single Secretary of State, and the new Ministry was brought into existence in 1964. Once again the lines of command ran straight, from the Cabinet, through the Secretary of State for Defence, down to the Service Ministers.

Thus, in 1970 as in 1914, there were two ministries concerned with defence questions. But instead of an Admiralty and a War Office we had a Ministry of Defence relying on a Ministry of Technology for important aspects of defence supply. The process of unification at ministerial level had gone a long way but had not quite yet reached its logical conclusion. This came only in April 1971 with the absorption of those supply responsibilities in the Ministry of Defence itself.

RATIONALISATION

However, the process of unification at ministerial level only throws into sharper focus the need for rationalisation and reorganisation lower down the line. This need is urgent throughout Whitehall today. Again, the mistakes and failures of the Ministry of Defence since 1964 illustrate some of the pitfalls to avoid.

The Admiralty and the War Office were each run traditionally by a Board or Council whose chairman was the Minister and whose members were each responsible for a particular aspect of Service control and management. The Air Ministry adopted the same pattern. When the unified Ministry of Defence was set up in 1964 the three Boards or Councils continued to exist as the Navy, Army and Air Force Boards of the new Defence Council. The Secretary of State for Defence became chairman of all three Boards and the Service Minister and Parliamentary Under Secretary concerned with each Service continued to be members of their Service Board. Responsibility for managing their Service continued to be divided among the remaining members, civil and military, of each Board, as follows: Strategy and Operations; Personnel; Equipment;* Supplies; Civilian Management and Finance; Science. Thus, not counting ministers, the three Service Boards contained members responsible for a total of seventeen different functions, and additionally the Ministry of Aviation was responsible for equipment for the RAF. Above the three Service Boards the Defence Council was established. The Secretary of State became chairman and all three Service Ministers became members; the other members were the four Chiefs of Staff, the Permanent Under Secretary of State and the Chief Scientist. The Chiefs of Staff were the only military members of the

* Except for the Air Force Board, under the Ministry of Aviation.

Council; the functions for which the other military members of the Service Boards were responsible—personnel, equipment, and supply—were not represented on the Council at all. Thus the separation between policy and management still existed, though at one level lower than before.

The Service Departments supporting the three Boards were organised into sub-departments supporting each Board member, making seventeen sub-departments altogether. In the Central Department, the Chief of the Defence Staff, the Permanent Under Secretary and the Chief Scientific Adviser were supported by the Defence Staff, the Defence Secretariat and the Defence Scientific staff. Thus, taking its four Departments together the new Ministry of Defence contained no fewer than twenty sub-departments, each consisting of a very sizeable hierarchy of its own. Co-ordination between them was exercised by a large number of committees headed by the Chiefs of Staff Committee and Committees of Principal Personnel Officers, Principal Administrative Officers, Permanent Under Secretaries, and Chief Scientists. Many of these could trace their origin to inter-war sub-committees of the Committee of Imperial Defence.

Responsibility for executive control and administration of the fighting units of the three Services, and of the depots, dockyards, training centres and other establishments which support the fighting units, lies with *commands* outside Whitehall. When the unified Ministry of Defence came into existence, each Service retained its own command structure stemming down from its Department in the Ministry to its operating units and establishments in the field. Army commands were based on a geographic division—Southern Command, Northern Command, etc. Air Force Commands, at least in the United Kingdom, were based on a division of function—Bomber Command, Training Command, Maintenance Command, etc. The Navy had commands of both kinds, some like Portsmouth Command being responsible for a particular geographic area, others like Naval Air Command being responsible for a particular naval function. All three Services had commands overseas. In the early days of the new Ministry two 'unified' commands were set up in Aden and Singapore, and the unified Commander-in-Chief was made responsible for the control of all military operations in his area. But he had no responsibility for management or administrative support; he had to rely on individual Service hierarchies; and separate single Service commands remained in existence in his area, each with its own separate line of communication to its own Department in the Ministry of Defence.

It is hardly surprising that a Ministry which inherited this kind of organisational structure should have suffered from the outset from an overloaded administrative top-hamper. In 1964 the strength of the armed forces was around 450,000 and in addition there were about 400,000 civilian employees. Of these military and civilian staffs, no fewer than 25,000 were employed in the Ministry of Defence Headquarters, including over 550 senior staff (brigadier level and above). Another 40,000 were absorbed by Command Headquarters. There were seven ministers and five permanent secretaries.

In the last five years there has been, as officialese has it, a series of 'evolutionary changes towards a more stream-lined and closely integrated structure'.[1] In other words, the Ministry has muddled along in the general direction that was inevitable from the start, without any effective proper forward planning, in the face of continuing resistance from Simple, Sloth and Presumption!

Changes have been of two main kinds; areas of work previously handled by the Service Departments have been organised on a more unified basis; and those parts of the Ministry of Defence which formulate policy and co-ordinate its execution have been strengthened. In the first category are the abolition of the separate ministers, permanent secretaries, and deputy chiefs of staff in the Service Departments; the creation and subsequent abolition of ministers and second permanent secretaries responsible for administration (mainly personnel and logistics) and equipment; the creation of single organisations for civilian management services, contracts, accounts, statistics and finance; and inter-Service rationalisation, particularly in the supply field, where one Service undertakes a task on behalf of one or both of the others. The second category includes the improvement of the Chiefs of Staff organisation by appointing a Deputy Chief of the Defence Staff (Operational Requirements) to co-ordinate the Services' future requirements for weapons systems, and two Assistant Chiefs of the Defence Staff for Operations and Policy respectively; and the creation of the post of Chief Adviser (Personnel and Logistics) to give stronger central direction to the work of the Principal Personnel Officers and Principal Administrative Officers.

Outside Whitehall measures have been taken to cut down the 'tail', which in the recent past has absorbed so great a proportion of the resources that would otherwise have been available for strengthening the teeth arms. The command structure of the Services has been streamlined; and many supply and equipment depots, workshops, training establishments and other similar installations have been closed down. Some of these reductions in military support facilities are attributable to the general reduction in our defence effort and our military commitments overseas. But many have been made possible by the progressive integration under the unified Ministry of Defence of what previously were fragmented activities under different chains of command.

This process of evolutionary streamlining and integration continues. The 1970 Defence White Paper[1] reported that a committee had been appointed under the chairmanship of the Permanent Under-Secretary of State of the Ministry of Defence to look into these matters. The Committee included two members from outside the public service as well as senior representatives of all three Services. It was asked to examine critically all areas of activity in the Ministry of Defence to consider the extent to which the work still needed to be done; whether it required so complex a structure of consultation; whether it could with advantage be devolved or delegated elsewhere; and whether changes in organisation would aid efficiency. It was to draw on other valuable work which is already in hand in various areas, such as the studies of the committee under the chairmanship of Sir John Mallabar into HM Dockyards and the Royal Ordnance Factories, and by the Army Department into the future command structure in the United Kingdom.

The White Paper also reported that certain important recommendations of this committee were already being put into effect. 'The Chief of the Defence Staff is being given greater authority in his own right, as distinct from his position as the Chairman of the Chiefs of Staff Committee. The Chief Adviser Personnel and Logistics is being made responsible to the Chief of the Defence Staff, the senior military adviser to the Secretary of State, and is being empowered to initiate and co-ordinate studies and other action on matters affecting all three Services. In future he will be called the Chief of Personnel and Logistics.'[1]

When the Labour Government left office in June 1970, further ministerial changes were planned. Under the Secretary of State for Defence there was to be a single 'Minister of Defence for the Armed Forces', who would be responsible for all issues concerning personnel, logistics, and equipment, whether affecting one Service or all three. Similarly, at the Parliamentary Secretary level the three junior ministers were to lose their single Service function and be replaced by one or more Parliamentary Secretaries with responsibilities covering all three Services. It is true that the incoming Conservative Government reversed this last decision. But, even so, the trend towards further unification was continuing.

SOME INTERIM CONCLUSIONS

In this chapter we have dealt almost exclusively with the main organisational structure for defence. A number of other important questions, such as the division of responsibility between the civil servants for the financial aspects of defence and the military staffs for the planning and operational aspects, or the type of work imposed on civil servants by the nature of the organisation, are dealt with in other chapters. At this juncture we may merely draw the following interim conclusions.

First, unification at the top (in this case between the Admiralty, the War Office, the Air Ministry and the co-ordinating Ministry of Defence) is not only desirable for its own sake, when circumstances make it so. It also sets the stage for rationalisation and devolution down the line. It is one of the facts of organisational life that, while fragmentation leads to over-centralisation, integration is the first step towards devolution. The cycle is as follows: new organisational units proliferate to handle new tasks; the need to co-ordinate their activities leads to the centralisation of decisions; integration between previously separate organisational units then leads to the re-emergence of a unified decision structure; and that, in turn, makes it possible to decentralise decisions. Fragmentation of structure and centralisation of decision are the marks of a badly managed organisation in transition, whose leaders either lack the vision to see or the courage to declare where they are going. An organisation whose strategies and objectives are clearly mapped will have a simpler and more unified structure, in which decision-making is devolved.

Second, the power of organisational inertia is enormously strong, in the absence of lucid and courageous leadership. The changes that have taken place in the unified Ministry of Defence since 1964 have been little more than a continuation of the process of piecemeal evolution that has proceeded since the beginning of the century. The absence of any coherent strategy for organisational change has generated confusion

DEFENCE

and loss of morale among military and civilian defence staff, and means that the changes made have always been too little and too late. For both these reasons the capabilities and standing of the armed forces have suffered unnecessary damage over the last seven years, as over the fifteen that preceded them. Moreover, the administrative top-hamper is still heavily over-loaded. Total military personnel are now down to 385,000 and civilian personnel employed on defence work are down to 350,000. But the headquarters organisation still numbers 22,000; and, although the figures for senior headquarters staff in Whitehall are down to about 400, the reduction from 550 in 1964 appears to reflect a re-classification of posts as between Whitehall and various headquarters outstations rather than a genuine reduction in the weight of top brass.

Thirdly, and very importantly, the history of defence organisation during recent decades clearly shows that the size and cost of government activities do not depend solely on the scale of the tasks to be carried out. One standing joke about the Services is that they spend more time and energy fighting one another than preparing to fight a potential enemy. Another is that they are always able to demonstrate conclusively that if any cuts are to be made they must be made in the teeth arms rather than in the tail. The fact is that, in the absence of strategic leadership, bureaucracy feeds on itself; Parkinson's Law takes charge.* Part of the conventional wisdom, duly voiced by incoming governments, is that if you want to cut the size of government you have to cut its tasks. The recent history of defence organisation shows that there is a good deal more to it than that.

Finally, the absence of systematic Parliamentary scrutiny of defence expenditure and efficiency has undoubtedly contributed to organisational lethargy and bureaucratic inertia in the Ministry of Defence. It was a disillusioning experience to be at the receiving end of an Estimates Committee enquiry on defence supplies in 1964 and 1965. There were, without doubt, huge economies and improvements in efficiency to be secured by a radical re-appraisal of the existing organisation and procedures for handling defence supplies. But all I can remember of the parliamentary enquiry was that the Committee lighted on a cache of 20,000 old fezzes in one of the Army supply depots, and went off after these fezzes like hounds after a fox. The fezzes had not, so far as I

---

* One of the grotesque nude figures in stone above the north door of the main Ministry of Defence building is said – by the rude and licentious soldiery – to be a representation of Professor Parkinson!

47

recall, been deliberately planted in the parliamentarians' path to distract them from systematic analysis of defence supply organisation and procedures. But they could not have done the trick more successfully if they had been a deliberate red herring!

We shall find all of these conclusions emerging again in later chapters: unification as the prelude to rationalisation; the need for a strategy of organisational change; the propensity of the bureaucracy to feed on itself, in the absence of such a strategy; and the need for effective systematic scrutiny by Parliament. In all these ways, as in others, the lessons to be drawn from the recent history of defence organisation are very relevant to other areas of government.

NOTES ON CHAPTER 3

General

The Organisation of British Central Government, 1914–1964, written by F. M. G. Willson, edited by D. N. Chester, and published by George Allen and Unwin for the Royal Institute of Public Administration in 1968, is the standard account of changes in the machinery of central government in Britain in this century. Successive White Papers on *Central Organisation for Defence* (Cmnd. 6923 of October 1946; Cmnd. 476 of July 1958; Cmnd. 2097 of July 1963) give a reasonably clear account of developments in defence organisation, provided that one is equipped to read between the lines of bland official prose. (The word 'adjustment', for example, used twice in quick succession in the second of these documents, signifies that major changes are being made but that their importance is being played down. The words in the third document, 'The organisation must be capable of smooth and progressive development after the new Ministry has been set up', convey recognition that what is proposed does not make quite as much sense as it should and that there will be problems coming out in the wash over a period of years afterwards.)

Note 1. *Statement on the Defence Estimates,* 1970: Chapter 1: para. 50.

4

Industry and Commerce

If everybody minded their own business, said the Duchess
in a hoarse growl, the world would go round a good deal
faster than it does.
LEWIS CARROLL: *Alice in Wonderland*

The recent history of defence organisation illuminates the pattern of
proliferation and unification; it shows how integration at ministerial
level can prepare the way for rationalisation down the line, and it shows
how, even in a comparatively well-defined organisational situation,
failure of constructive leadership and creative planning and analysis
can occur. The developing pattern of government responsibilities for
industry, commerce and trade re-inforces those conclusions but also
throws up some rather different points.

It brings out clearly the changing relationship between the public and
the private sector. It raises the question of public accountability, both
as it affects the management of public enterprises like the nationalised
industries and as it affects the management of large firms in the private
sector. It raises important questions about the relationship between
Parliament and the Executive. Finally, it indicates the unreliability of
woolly concepts like 'economic growth' or 'productivity' as a basis for
organising the work of government.

PRIVATE OR PUBLIC ENTERPRISE?

The pattern of government a hundred years ago was based on the
assumption that industry, commerce and trade were the very stuff of
private enterprise. As John Stuart Mill said in his *Essay on Liberty*,
'Whoever undertakes to sell any description of goods to the public, does
what affects the interest of other persons and of society in general; and
thus his conduct in principle comes within the jurisdiction of society:
accordingly it was once held to be the duty of governments, in all cases
which were considered of importance, to fix prices and regulate the
processes of manufacture. But it is now recognised, though not till after
a long struggle, that both the cheapness and the good quality of

49

commodities are most effectually provided for by leaving the producers and sellers perfectly free, under the sole check of equal freedom to the buyers for supplying themselves elsewhere. This is the so-called doctrine of Free Trade, which rests on grounds different from though equally solid with, the principle of individual liberty asserted in this Essay.'[1]

This doctrine of *laisser faire*, supported by the growing political strength of the urban industrial classes in nineteenth-century England, formed one of the guiding principles of Gladstonian Liberalism and one of the basic assumptions which shaped the institutions of British government in the latter part of the century. There was no question then but that the coal industry and the railways should be in private hands. Similarly, it was accepted unreservedly that the provision of services like gas and water were matters for local, municipal control. Only in the case of postal services – and that purely by historical accident – was it accepted that central government had a direct responsibility to provide a public service.

The development of the government's functions in the industrial field during the twentieth century reflects our continually growing awareness that, with the increasing scale and increasing interdependence of industrial activities, the unregulated market economy is not, in fact, the 'most effectual' way of ensuring the provision of goods and services of acceptable quality at acceptable prices. The course of this development reflects a see-saw between two unsustainable political ideas – the first that unqualified private enterprise is the right answer, and the second (at the opposite extreme) that all industry should be brought under direct State ownership and control. It reflects the practical need, in two world wars, to mobilise the country's industrial energies and harness them to the national effort. And it reflects, since the second world war, dawning recognition that neither unqualified private enterprise nor wholesale nationalisation will give the right answer. In the 1940s and 1950s recognition of this fact took the form of the so-called Butskellite compromise: neither side should seek to press its doctrine unreasonably far. In the 1960s there have been signs that a more positive fusion between socialism and private enterprise may eventually emerge.

A number of major strands stand out over the last seventy years or so. There is the evolution of the nationalised industries. There is the growing government interest in manufacturing industry in the private sector, and in industrial research and development. There is the emergence of a whole new range of government activity in regard to employment and industrial relations. Measures taken in these spheres have been intertwined with measures in other emerging fields of government policy, for example on economic and regional questions.

The main strands stand out only in retrospect, of course. The actual process of evolution has been piecemeal and confused—perhaps more in this sphere of government activity than in any other. But, as we shall see, it now seems possible to detect a pattern: as new problems have arisen, detailed government intervention has proliferated, and has led to more and more centralisation in Whitehall and Westminster; but this unsystematic, interventionist, centralising phase is now giving way to a second more systematic phase, in which responsibility is again being devolved, but within a framework of central control. This pattern is most clearly seen in the development of arrangements for managing the country's industrial infrastructure through the nationalised industries. But it also seems likely to be the most effective approach to the exercise of public control over private industrial and commercial enterprise. The new Conservative Government's industrial relations legislation reflects a similar approach to public policy in the field of employment and industrial relations. It is even beginning to appear that a comparable approach, under labels like 'accountable management', is going to prove the right answer to the administrative problems of Whitehall itself.

INDUSTRIAL INFRASTRUCTURE

Since the early years of the twentieth century central government has concerned itself more and more closely with the country's industrial infrastructure. It has assumed responsibilities previously carried by private enterprise and local authorities—or previously non-existent altogether—for fuel and power, for the country's water resources, and for transport by land, sea and air. In each of these fields the problems of planning, development and operational management are infinitely greater and more complex than a hundred years ago. The same is true of posts and telecommunications, where the Crown's traditional function of handling the Royal Mail has developed into a truly massive industrial enterprise.

These developments have given rise to governmental problems of three main kinds:

What responsibilities for various aspects of industrial infrastructure are to be carried by the central government, and how are they

51

to be allocated between one minister (or one Whitehall department) and another?

What is to be the division of responsibility between Whitehall and the public corporations?

How are public corporations to be accountable to Parliament?

These questions are inter-related. They have never been asked and answered comprehensively. But they have arisen with increasing urgency over the last ten or fifteen years, and the outline of a coherent set of answers is now beginning to emerge.

Before the first world war, Whitehall's responsibilities for the country's industrial infrastructure were comparatively slight. The Board of Trade was responsible for regulatory legislation concerning the railways and shipping, electricity undertakings and private gas and water companies; the Local Government Board was concerned with municipal gas and waterworks, and with some aspects of roads and road transport; the Home Office was concerned with safety in mines and was regarded by the coal industry as its main point of communication with the central government; and the Home Office also had some interest in road transport, and was responsible for regulations governing civil flying.

By 1920, after the changes that took place during the war and its immediate aftermath, the situation had become rather different. The Board of Trade and its new Department of Mines were responsible for all the fuel and power industries except electricity, which belonged to the new Ministry of Transport; the new Ministry of Health was responsible for water; the Ministry of Transport was responsible for inland transport and docks, the Board of Trade for shipping, and the new Air Ministry for civil aviation; and of course the GPO was responsible for posts and telecommunications.

No further change of significance took place until 1939, but war again stimulated the process of structural change. By the end of the war the Ministry of Fuel and Power was responsible for all the fuel and power industries, the Ministry of Health for water, the Ministry of Transport was responsible for rail, road and sea transport, the Ministry of Civil Aviation was responsible for air transport, the GPO was responsible for posts and telecommunications. This pattern remained unchanged until 1951, when the Ministry of Civil Aviation was amalgamated with the Ministry of Transport.

Since then a number of further changes have been made. The

Ministry of Transport and Civil Aviation remained in existence only until 1959, when responsibility for civil aviation was once again hived off and given to the new Ministry of Aviation. Subsequently, the Ministry of Aviation was abolished in its turn and responsibility for civil aviation was transferred to the Board of Trade. Responsibility for shipping was transferred back to the Board of Trade from the Ministry of Transport, though the latter is still responsible for the docks. The Atomic Energy Authority, originally set up in 1954 under the ministerial supervision of the Lord President, was transferred to the Ministry of Technology. The Ministry of Power was abolished and its functions were transferred to the Ministry of Technology.

In early 1970, therefore, the situation was as follows. The Ministry of Technology was responsible for all types of fuel and power, including the development of nuclear power. The Ministry of Housing and Local Government was responsible for water. The Ministry of Transport was responsible for all forms of land transport. The Board of Trade was responsible for air and sea transport. The little rump Ministry of Posts and Telecommunications was responsible for supervising the Post Office Corporation. This situation could hardly sustain itself much longer. Organisational logic had been pointing for some time to a unified Ministry for Industrial Infrastructure. It was a pity that such a department did not emerge from Mr. Heath's reforms of October, 1970.

At this point, one episode should be mentioned which is significant for the methodology of government. In 1951 the Conservative Government, recognising the need for a coherent strategy for developing the country's industrial infrastructure appointed a Secretary of State for the Co-ordination of Transport, Fuel and Power. He was to be responsible for co-ordinating the Minister of Transport, the Minister of Civil Aviation and the Minister of Fuel and Power. Churchill, who was then Prime Minister, presented this arrangement (and the similar arrangement made at the same time for the Lord President to co-ordinate the Minister of Agriculture and the Minister of Food) simply as an extension of the system of co-ordination by Cabinet Committee. But the opposition were quick to point out the important difference between a minister who assumes a formal, publicly acknowledged responsibility for co-ordinating some of his colleagues and a minister who takes the chair of a confidential Cabinet Committee. What precisely are the functions for which the co-ordinating minister is answerable to Parliament? How are they distinguished from those of the ministers under

53

his supervision? These are, of course, the same questions which have arisen in respect of ministers appointed to co-ordinate defence and economic policy. In 1951 the opposition were able to press them home largely because the two co-ordinating ministers, Lords Woolton and Leathers, were not members of the House of Commons. The 'overlord' experiment was dropped.

THE NATIONALISED INDUSTRIES

Some nationalisation had taken place before the second world war. The Port of London Authority had been set up as early as 1908, the BBC and the Central Electricity Board were established in 1926, the London Passenger Transport Board in 1933, and the British Overseas Airways Corporation in 1939-and of course the Post Office had been operated as a state concern for hundreds of years. The first nationalisation measure after the war was the Bank of England Act, 1946. But the era in which a major sector of British industry was brought into public ownership and under some degree of Ministerial control really began with the nationalisation of the coal industry in 1946. Other industries soon followed-the air Corporations in 1946, several of the transport industries, the most important being the railways, in 1947; the remainder of the electricity supply industry in 1947; the gas industry in 1948; and the major part of the iron and steel industry in 1949 denationalised in 1953 but brought again into public ownership in 1967).

During the twenty years from 1950 to 1970 there was much discussion and controversy about how the nationalised industries should be controlled. Despite some initial confusion on the part of the 1970 Conservative Administration, gradually a coherent approach is beginning to evolve. This is based on the philosophy that the public corporations should be responsible for managing their industries efficiently within a framework of national policies laid down by ministers; and that, while ministers should account to Parliament for these national policies, the public corporations should themselves account to Parliament through a Select Committee for the efficiency with which they are carrying out the policies.

The way in which these arrangements for controlling the nationalised industries have evolved are very relevant to similar problems now arising in many other spheres of government activity, so it is worth spending a little time on them. The main landmarks have been as follows:

the statutes establishing the nationalised industries in the late 'forties;

the creation of the House of Commons Select Committee on Nationalised Industries in 1956;

The 1961 White Paper[2] on the *Financial and Economic Obligations of the Nationalised Industries*;

the 1967 White Paper[3] on *Nationalised Industries: A Review of Economic and Financial Objectives*; and

the 1968 report[4] from the Select Committee on Nationalised Industries on *Ministerial Control of the Nationalised Industries*.

The statutes establishing the nationalised industries generally gave ministers the power to appoint members of boards, to give general directions to boards in the national interest, and to approve the industry's investment and borrowing programmes. They laid down that boards should so manage their industries that 'taking one year with another', they would cover their costs, including the cost of servicing their capital.

The statutes gave very little guidance on the pricing and investment policies to be followed, and on the extent to which the industries should aim to finance capital development from accumulated revenue our pluses or from borrowing. The Select Committee on Nationalised Industries summed up the situation as follows. 'Indeed, one remarkable feature of the nationalisation statutes is the extent to which, as one witness put it, vital administrative questions, such as . . . the relationship between the managing boards and ministers and Parliament, remained subjects for disagreement and negotiations. Similarly, major economic issues, especially the pricing policies to be pursued by the industries and their overall financial obligations, were left imprecise. The Chairman of the Electricity Council, for example, referred to the lack of guidance given to Boards by the Statutes regarding breaking even; until the 1961 White Paper, some Chairmen interpreted it one way, some another. Hence it was inevitable that ministers and the industries—with Parliament also showing an active interest from time to time—have been forced to arrive at informal arrangements and understandings (or—all too often—misunderstandings) about the duties of the industries, the balance of powers, and the extent and nature of ministerial control.'[4]

E 55

The 1961 and 1967 White Papers on the Economic and Financial Obligations of the Nationalised Industries attempted to clarify this situation. The 1961 White Paper laid down that the industries would be required to meet precise financial objectives (in terms of a rate of return on capital) over a five-year period, and that these objectives should take account of unprofitable activities (such as the provision of loss-making railway services) carried out as a social service at the government's wish. The 1967 White Paper attempted to refine the 1961 method of control, by shifting the emphasis from a pre-determined financial objective to the adoption of efficient pricing and investment criteria. The Select Committee commented on this approach as follows. 'The Committee are convinced that one of the principal merits of adoption of the economic framework outlined in the 1967 White Paper . . . would be that it should enable ministers to concentrate on a proper exercise of broad strategic and policy control, and should leave the boards more managerial freedom. But this depends on clarity of purposes, policies and responsibilities. Pricing and investment policies must be unambiguous. The Committee accordingly recommend . . . *standard* policies for the economic control of the nationalised industries. Ministers should make this plain to the industries. And, unless otherwise requested, the industries would be expected to apply these policies as fully as possible. Where the use of marginal cost pricing does not appear appropriate, the proper pricing policy to be employed should be discussed by the minister with the board concerned, and their conclusions made public. Where extra social or wider public interest obligations are imposed on or undertaken by the industries, they should be publicly identified, quantified and appropriately financed by the ministers concerned. And where, for any reason, ministers require the industries to adopt pricing or investment policies different from the standard ones, they should make this fact public, they should justify their departure from the standard policies, they should explain the financial effects, and, where an industry suffers actual loss, they should normally negotiate financial compensation with the board concerned. These proposals may sound formal. But such an arrangement is essential for the proper public and parliamentary accountability of both boards and ministers. The taxpayer and consumer ought to know how and by whom their money is being managed.'[4]

The precise nature of ministerial control over the nationalised industries has been the subject of discussion and argument for many years. Herbert Morrison (the late Lord Morrison of Lambeth), who played a great part in the development of the public corporation as a new kind of government institution, put it as follows. 'A large degree of independence for the boards in matters of current administration is vital to their efficiency as public undertakings . . . Undue intervention by the minister would tend to impair the board's commercial freedom of action . . . The advantage of the public corporation is that we can combine progressive modern business management with a proper degree of public accountability.'[5] Some people have tended towards an even greater degree of commercial independence for the nationalised industries; others have claimed that ministers should intervene more closely in the day-to-day management of the industries.

The Select Committee summed up the situation as follows in their 1968 report. 'It was clearly intended by Parliament that ministers should, to some extent or other, exercise control over the nationalised industries: for this was one of the major purposes of nationalising them. On the other hand it was equally clearly intended that the industries should benefit from some degree of managerial autonomy, and that some limits should thus be set to ministerial control: otherwise there would be no point in establishing public corporations, with high-powered chairmen and their own independent staff; they could have been placed, like the Post Office in the past, under the direct responsibility of ministers. Hence the statutes imply a role for ministers, but not one that extends to what has come to be called 'day-to-day management'. They also imply a limited degree of parliamentary control; for example the industries' expenditure is not borne on the Estimates, and if the activities of ministers are limited their parliamentary accountability must be limited to a similar extent.'[4]

The Select Committee concluded that, 'to put it simply, ministers have largely done the opposite of what Parliament intended. They were supposed to lay down policies–in particular for the whole of their sectors of the economy–which would guide the operations of the individual industries, but not to intervene in the management of the industries in implementing those policies. In practice, until recently, they have given the industries very little policy guidance but they have become closely involved in many aspects of management. Much of the fault, the Committee believe, has sprung from confusion about responsibilities and about purposes.'[4] The Committee's report did much to clarify these responsibilities and to remedy the confusion.

As the Select Committee said, the division of functions between a minister and a nationalised industry implies a rather different relationship from the traditional relationship between a minister and the officials of his department. That in turn implies rather different relationships between Parliament, a minister, and the officials of a nationalised industry, from the traditional relationships between Parliament, a minister and his civil servants. In setting up the nationalised industries, Parliament in effect limited its own right to intervene through the minister in the day-to-day management of the industries. But in place of that right of intervention Parliament has evolved a new and very effective instrument of scrutiny, in the shape of the Select Committee on Nationalised Industries.

In the words of Mr David Coombes (Appendix 43 to the Select Committee's 1968 report), the Committee has 'proved a successful experiment in providing a measure of accountability for the nationalised industries, while at the same time respecting the statutory independence of the boards entrusted with the task of management. While the Committee has not subjected the industries to any sort of detailed or continuous accountability for their financial results or their services to the public, it has produced extremely full periodic reviews of the past results, the present difficulties, and the future plans of the different boards. So effective has the Committee been in working out a satisfactory relationship with the boards of the industries that it can now be said that the relationship of the industries to Parliament is far less controversial than it was ten years ago. It is in this respect that the public corporation seems to have proved most successful in combining features of independent business management with public scrutiny and criticism. Nevertheless, as I pointed out in my study of the Committee, this was only achieved by experimenting with the arrangements left by the nationalising statutes and by challenging the conventional view that management by public corporations was incompatible with direct Parliamentary accountability. In fact, the two have proved compatible, and the result has not been to hamper or weaken the boards of the industries. Indeed, the managers of the industries seem to have found inquiry by the Select Committee helpful and encouraging.'[4] The successful marriage between independent business management and effective parliamentary scrutiny achieved by the nationalised industries and the Select Committee, provides an example which Parliament, ministers and civil servants will sooner or later have to follow in respect of the managerial tasks of the civil service itself. It is also an example that may well prove relevant to problems of public accountability in the universities, scientific research, and the health service. But that is to digress.

The government, and therefore Parliament, are concerned with the nationalised industries from a number of different points of view. They are concerned with the interest of the *customers* of the industry in having an acceptable quality of service provided at an acceptable price. They are concerned with the interest of *taxpayers*, who must make good any deficit incurred by a nationalised industry. They are concerned with the interest of the *employees* of the industry. They are concerned with the *economic* implications of policy for the nationalised industries: how should resources be allocated between public and private sector investment? To what extent should investment in the nationalised industries be financed by higher prices and to what extent by higher taxes? And they are concerned to some extent with the impact of the industries' *activities at regional and local level*. The fact that the governmental and parliamentary interest is many-sided in this way has important implications for the way in which responsibilities for the nationalised industries should be organised and for the right procedures for examining their efficiency.

At ministerial level, as is now becoming fairly clear, there should be one minister responsible for the whole field of industrial infrastructure — that is to say Fuel and Power, Water, Transport and Communications. That minister should have supervisory responsibility for the investment programmes and for the efficient operation of all the nationalised industries within his sphere. He should be responsible for deciding investment priorities between one nationalised industry and another; and for ensuring, for example, that a decision whether or not to electrify part of the railway system is taken in the light of possible developments in the motorways or in the operations of internal airlines. His appointment should do something to reduce the 'vast network of committees on every conceivable subject' that, as the Select Committee[4] found, are required today for co-ordinating one nationalised industry with another. More broadly, this minister should also be responsible for considering the balance between private enterprise and the public corporations in the field of industrial infrastructure. In short, he would be responsible for the effective planning and management of the country's fuel and power, water, transport, and communications industries, and for providing the framework for the operations of public and private enterprise in this sphere.

This minister would not, however, be primarily responsible for slanting policy in such a way that the industries are managed in the interest of overall macro-economic policy as conceived by the Treasury; the Chancellor of the Exchequer would be responsible for that. Or that uneconomic services are provided in particular regions or localities, as a social policy; the local or regional authorities concerned would be responsible for that. Or that a subsidised service is provided for particular categories of people, again as a social service: the minister in charge of the social services would be responsible for that. The aim must be to distinguish clearly between the important function, for which a single minister should be responsible, of developing and operating efficient fuel and power, water, transport, and communications industries, and the equally important but different ministerial responsibilities for seeing that the industries' behaviour is influenced in the interest of economic and social policies that efficient commercial practice might not necessarily serve.*

This was the object of the proposal put forward by the Select Committee[4] in 1968 that there should be a single, unified Ministry of Nationalised Industries. That proposal itself was not correctly conceived, in my view, though in practice a Ministry of Nationalised Industries would be fairly similar to the Ministry of Industrial Infrastructure which is what is really needed.

There are two reasons against a Ministry of Nationalised Industries as such. The first is that it would give a spread of responsibility at once too narrow and too wide–too narrow because it would exclude the private sector oil industry and airlines, for example; and too wide because, if literally interpreted, it would bring in bodies like the BBC or the Bank of England whose functions fall much more happily into other spheres of government. The second reason is related to the first. There is nothing so special about the institutional form of the public corporation that all such corporations should be supervised by the same ministry. Quite the reverse, in fact. Very similar problems of public accountability and control as have arisen in respect of the nationalised industries in the last fifteen or twenty years are also arising elsewhere in Whitehall.

*Putting transport together with building, housing and local government in a department called Environment, as has been done in October 1970, seriously obscures this distinction.

One point remains to be mentioned—the need for an instrument to investigate the efficiency of the nationalised industries in greater detail than an unsupported Select Committee of Parliament can do, and to examine the justification for increases in prices on the one hand and salaries and wages on the other in a monopolistic (or at least oligopolistic) situation in which market forces do not act to restrain them. By 1970 such an instrument had been developed in the shape of the Prices and Incomes Board. We shall return to this point later.

THE PRIVATE SECTOR

At first sight, a clear pattern of development in the operating relationships between government and private sector industry over the last sixty or seventy years is difficult to discern. The evolution of the government's organisation and procedures in this sphere of its activity appears more than usually confused, and by 1970 the resulting apparatus of government had become more than usually cumbersome and complex.

This confused state of affairs reflected confused thinking. Industrial policies are closely related to economic policies, prices and incomes policies, consumer protection policies (or, more widely, policies aimed at preserving the rights of individuals), industrial relations and manpower policies, and regional and environmental policies. Although politicians have thought they understood what all those words meant, no government has in fact had a clear view of the range of practical activities they each embrace, and no government has yet succeeded in evolving a satisfactory organisational structure for them.

What is now required in this field of government as in all others, is a 'systems analysis'. In other words we need to examine the whole structure of government/industry relationships—the 'interface' between government and industry, in the jargon of the computermen—and see how the structure could more effectively match the pattern of decision-making and communication for which it is the vehicle. What are the decisions that government has to make, which bear on industrial and commercial firms? Into what different fields of ministerial responsibility should these various decisions fall? Which decisions should be taken by ministers themselves, as matters of high level national policy, and which (if any) should be delegated to non-ministerial agencies like the Monopolies Commission or the Restrictive Practices Court? Looking at it from industry's point of view, how are the various kinds of decision that firms have to take affected by various kinds of government action? How should industry organise itself to influence government policies in this regard? What channels of communication would best support the resulting interdependence of decision-making in government and in industry? Again, how should the managements of large corporations be accountable–to their customers, their employees and the public, as well as to their shareholders? How should the government account to Parliament for its activities in regard to industry and commerce? What role should the Courts play in the industrial sphere? Comparatively little effort has yet been made, either in government or outside, to analyse these questions systematically. As in other spheres, the present institutional arrangements have evolved in an unplanned, proliferative process over the years.

Before the first world war the government paid comparatively little attention to industry, but between 1914 and 1918 interest quickened. By the end of the war, in addition to the interest in industrial infrastructure described earlier in this chapter, and in addition to such internal house-keeping activities as government purchasing and taxation which affected industry, the situation was as follows. The Board of Trade had a general, predominantly regulatory, interest in industry as a whole and had assumed some responsibility for consumer interests. The Ministry of Labour (traditionally regarded as a social service department rather than an economic department) had been set up to take an active interest in matters connected with employment in industry, including industrial development in the Special Areas. In the field of industrial research, the National Physical Laboratory and the Department of Scientific and Industrial Research had been set up. Finally, certain ministries had begun to take a special interest in particular industries, agriculture being the most obvious but by no means the only one.

Between the wars the main problems were the very high unemployment of the twenties and early thirties and the need, as it was then seen, to help and protect the older, declining industries. On the outbreak of war in 1939 this situation changed. The main need then was to control and co-ordinate the industrial economy, including the deployment of manpower and the importation, production, allocation, and distribution of food, raw materials and manufactured products, in the interests of the war effort. The Ministry of Labour became the Ministry of Labour and National Service. The Food (Defence Plans) Department of the Board of Trade was hived off as a separate Ministry of Food, the Admiralty was made responsible for the ship-building industry, the

Ministry of Aircraft Production for the aircraft-manufacturing industry, the Ministry of Works and Buildings for the building and construction industry, the Ministry of Supply for the metal and engineering industries, and the Board of Trade was given special responsibility for industries which did not fall to any other Ministry. In short, each industry acquired a designated Ministry, its production authority or sponsoring department, whose task was to promote its efficiency, regulate its production, and represent its needs to the government. The whole range of productive industry was co-ordinated by the Minister of Production.

After 1945 the war-time concept of every industry having a sponsoring department was retained and to some extent it still existed in 1970. For example, the Ministry of Public Building and Works was still responsible for the building industry, the Ministry of Agriculture for the agricultural industry, and the Department of Health and Social Security for the pharmaceutical industry. At the same time, in the years shortly after the second world war the Board of Trade consolidated its position as the main ministry for industry, commerce and trade. It took over the remaining functions of the war-time Ministry of Production. It took over responsibility from the Ministry of Labour for distribution of industry when the concept of providing unemployment relief in Special Areas gave way to the more radical concept of distributing industry within the country as a whole in the interests of full employment. Since the war it has also tended to play an increasing role in the protection of consumers; the activities of the Consumer Council, and the measures taken or sponsored by the Board against monopolies, restrictive practices and resale price maintenance may all be instanced. Throughout, the Board of Trade has, of course, retained its regulatory responsibilities in regard to industry and commerce, as embodied for example in the Companies Acts.

In the conditions of full employment obtaining after 1945, the main emphasis of the Ministry of Labour and National Service shifted from the problems of unemployment to those of industrial relations. The Ministry remained responsible for a wide range of questions, such as safety, health and welfare, concerning the employment of people, but its main function during the 1950s—for example, under Sir Walter Monckton as Minister—was to act as a conciliatory force, intervening when required to settle disputes between employers and employees but not before. It was still regarded as a social service department rather

63

than an economic department. By the early 1960s, however, the climate had begun to change. In a managed economy a more active employment policy was becoming necessary, including measures for easing redeployment between different firms and different industries, and measures to promote industrial training. It was also becoming necessary to modernise the system of industrial relations, as well as to oil the wheels of the existing system. And a more active prices and incomes policy was introduced in 1961. One way and another the Ministry of Labour was gradually assuming a more active economic role. At the same time, as employment assumed growing importance in sectors other than industry, such as the public service, the Ministry's horizons began to widen and it became more than a purely industrial department.

By 1964 the two main departments concerned with industry were thus the Board of Trade and the Ministry of Labour, though other ministries still had sponsoring responsibilities for particular industries such as agriculture, steel, aircraft-manufacturing and building. The Board of Trade had been galvanised by Mr Heath into a flurry of activity on resale price maintenance and distribution of industry, and the Ministry of Labour was beginning to show signs of life. However, the two departments had a fairly well established reputation for a *laisser-faire* approach to life. Not many people really felt that between them they would be able to provide the necessary impetus to modernise British industry. In particular, many people thought that something else would be needed to put the new science-based industries like electronics and computers on the map. Moreover, the view was fast gaining ground that–so far as economic policy was concerned–effective action could not be achieved by macro-economic measures alone but would require government intervention at the micro-economic level, in particular to re-structure industry, to provide selective incentives to industrial modernisation, and to even out regional imbalances in the level of industrial activity.

This was the background–the somewhat confused background, as we can now see–against which the incoming Labour Government of 1964 set up the Ministry of Technology and the Department of Economic Affairs. The Ministry of Technology originally took over responsibility for the machine tools, telecommunications, computer and electronics industries, for the Atomic Energy Authority, and for most of the government's civil research and development establishments. Subsequently Mintech took over responsibility for the engineering and ship-building industries from the Board of Trade, the aircraft industry from the Ministry of Aviation, and the steel industry from the Ministry of Power, and became responsible for all the science based industries. The Department of Economic Affairs was given co-ordinating responsibility for improving industrial efficiency as a whole, within the broad context of economic policy. It recruited a staff of industrial advisers from industry; it took the lead in setting up twenty-three Economic Development Committees, or 'little Neddies', under the umbrella of the National Economic Development Council (originally established under the Treasury by the previous Conservative Government), to promote efficiency in particular industries; and it set up the Industrial Re-organisation Corporation to facilitate mergers in industry.

Apart from its responsibility for industrial matters, the Department of Economic Affairs had three other spheres of responsibility—national economic planning, regional policy, prices policy and incomes policy. These are discussed in Chapters 6 and 7. But the Prices and Incomes Board, which was set up to apply the principles of a productivity, prices and incomes policy, must be mentioned briefly here. Under Mr Aubrey Jones the Board developed a wide-ranging 'management audit' role, conducting efficiency enquiries and attempting to stimulate improved standards of performance in every corner of British industry. It made an effective contribution in this respect, whatever view is taken of the success or failure of the prices and incomes policy itself.

In fact by 1968 it seemed that the main *raison d'être* of the Prices and Incomes Board was the improvement of productivity, in the broad sense of output per man. Partly for this reason, no doubt, as well as for cruder political reasons, responsibility for prices and incomes policy and for the Board was transferred from the DEA to the Ministry of Labour, which was renamed the Department of Employment and Productivity. Mrs Barbara Castle took over the new department as Secretary of State, set up a new Manpower Productivity Service, set up a Commission on Industrial Relations as recommended by the Donovan Royal Commission, and prepared to modernise the whole industrial relations scene in the wake of Donovan.

Two problems now arose. First, the Government was defeated on *In Place of Strife*, and it became clear that a frontal assault on the modernisation of trades unionism and industrial relations would be shelved for the time being. Second, there was growing uneasiness about the overlap and possible conflict between the activities of the

65

Monopolies Commission under the Board of Trade, the Industrial Reorganisation Corporation under the Department of Economic Affairs (subsequently the Ministry of Technology), and the Prices and Incomes Board under the Department of Employment and Productivity. Just what were the functions of these bodies? How did they differ from one another and how did they relate to one another? If there were any defined criteria governing their activities and showing how they were expected to interpret the public interest, these criteria were not published, and the whole situation appeared to be very confused. In 1970 the Wilson government decided to resolve the problem, or partly resolve it, by merging the Monopolies Commission with the Prices and Incomes Board in a new Commission on Industry and Manpower under the Department of Employment and Productivity. But that proposal lapsed with the Labour Government's defeat in the General Election.

When the Labour Administration gave up the seals of office in June 1970, they left behind them a government organisation for dealing with industry which, in one way and another, might well lay claim to represent 'an aggregate of effort the most complex, confused, lacking in rationale and fertile in cross purposes that any administrative system in the world has possibly disclosed'.* We shall consider the remedy shortly. Meanwhile we turn briefly to the other side of the picture. How is industry organised in its dealings with government?

The main bodies representing industry are trade associations, employers' associations and trade unions. Trade associations are bodies formed by manufacturing and other firms to protect and promote their common interests. Employers' associations are similar bodies to enable firms to co-operate on matters concerned with the terms and conditions of employment in their industry. Trade unions are, of course, associations formed by employees to promote their common interests in dealing with their employers. A large number of these bodies have proliferated with the passing of the years. In 1956 there were estimated to be 1,300 national manufacturers' associations such as chambers of commerce. In 1965 there were estimated to be nearly 1,500 employers' associations. In 1966 there were estimated to be 574 trade unions. At the summit of this heap of representative bodies there are, of course, the Confederation of British Industries (CBI), representing trade associations and employers' associations, and the Trades Union Congress (TUC) representing the trade unions.

* See Chapter 5, Note 1.

Communication between government and industry is conducted either directly between the individual firm and the individual government department, or indirectly through one of the representative associations. There is also a third channel of communication, through a large number of advisory committees and councils. In February 1965 there were 240 such committees and councils, and in April 1965 it was announced that 63 new ones had been set up in the previous six months. The most important of these bodies in recent years have probably been the National Economic Development Council (Neddy) and its twenty-three industry Economic Development Committees (little Neddies), and the National Joint Advisory Council which is concerned with employment questions.

My own personal experience in this field—for example, as a member of a little Neddy and as a management consultant in contact with individual firms—left me in no doubt that by 1970 the whole structure of government/industry communication had become very muddled. A multitude of organisations dealing with one aspect of a firm's business or another imposes a very heavy burden on managements and seriously distracts them from their proper work—especially when the top men enjoy spending their time and energies on this kind of hob-nobbing! In particular, it bears very heavily on the smaller firms, as I discovered on one consultancy assignment for the Ministry of Technology, which involved visiting a large number of medium-sized and small companies and discussing their problems with them. The managing director of one small company would not allow 'the men from the Ministry' on to his premises. All the other managements we visited were delighted to find that we had actually come to seek their advice about how Mintech could help them, rather than to cause them trouble. Again, to take just one industrial sector as an example, consider the multitude of consultative, advisory, research and information bodies in the construction industries and the Ministry of Public Building and Works. They inevitably spend much of their time causing confusion to firms in the industries as well as getting in each other's way and taking in each other's washing. All in all, there is little doubt that the jungle of institutions and organisations that has grown up at the interface between government and industry involves a serious waste of human resources and human effort that could be more usefully employed. What is worse, it blocks initiative and strangles effective decision-making.

REFORM OF BRITISH CENTRAL GOVERNMENT

NEED FOR RADICAL RE-APPRAISAL

A radical re-appraisal of the whole system of government/industry relations is needed. It is necessary: to re-define the government's (in the broadest sense of the word) essential functions in relation to industry; consequentially, to re-define the functions of different ministers, Parliament and the Courts in this regard; and thirdly—and this will to some extent be up to industry itself as a result, for example, of the Devlin enquiry which has been put in hand by the Confederation of British Industries—to re-shape the existing structure of consultative and advisory bodies and services in the industrial and commercial field.

The essential functions of government that bear directly on firms include: taxation; government purchasing; the maintenance of an effective regulatory framework for companies' activities, including the regulation of monopoly and competition, consumer protection, and companies legislation generally; and an overall sponsorship responsibility for the well-being of the country's industrial and commercial sector as a whole. Successive governments have a poor record in these fields. They have been slow to modernise the tax system. They have been slow to develop positive government purchasing policies; as major users of industrially important products like computers, they have been slow to work out forward-looking policies of their own, from whose long-term spin-off British industry would benefit. They have been slow to modernise the Companies Acts and other legislation for protecting the legitimate interests of various classes of citizens, including consumers, workers, investors, creditors, inventors, and local residential communities. (Different people may take different views about the future of self-government in industry—'industrial democracy' or 'workers control' as it is sometimes called—and about the idea that company boards should contain representatives of employees, shareholders, customers and the community at large. But few would deny, especially after the Pergamon affair and other similar episodes in recent years, that there is much room for improving the accounting and reporting procedures of industry and the auditing procedures of the accountancy profession, so that the activities and performance of companies—including any merger proposals—are open to effective scrutiny by all concerned. It has become clear recently that the accountancy profession itself is preparing for an important and much needed step forward in this respect.) Finally, in recent years the responsibility for

68

'sponsoring' industry and commerce has been so fragmented between different ministries and departments that no minister has been in a position to take a coherent view of relative priorities as between one industry and another, or to assess their relative performance in the national interest.

To put the matter in a slightly different way, taxation, government purchasing and the regulation of industrial and commercial activities are tasks that government cannot escape. By tackling these tasks positively and effectively the government can create a framework that will stimulate companies to new levels of efficiency and oblige them to observe new standards of responsibility to the community at large. Recent governments have neglected these tasks. Conservative governments have thought they were boring and unimportant. All they cared about taxation was that it should be reduced; until quite recently Conservatives have seen no reason to try to plan it and manage it better. Government purchasing? a tedious chore, unworthy of a Conservative stateman's attention, that can safely be left to his Civil Service underlings and the market mechanism. And why bother overmuch with companies' legislation? the Conservative creed has been that private enterprise should be left free and unfettered. The reason why Labour governments have neglected these tasks is even simpler: they have been predisposed towards direct intervention; to put it more bluntly, they have always been happier minding other people's business than their own. But, in spite of traditional Conservative and Labour philosophies, the time has now come to recognise that only by doing its own job properly can government stimulate a higher standard of performance in industry. In the years immediately ahead the Treasury's progress in evolving strategies for taxation and public purchasing (and for prices and incomes) must be keenly scrutinised, as must the progress of the Department of Trade and Industry in modernising the Companies Acts and other instruments for regulating companies' behaviour and scrutinising their performance.

If these tasks of government are properly discharged, one consequence will be that commercial and industrial firms will find themselves operating in a much more open and competitive environment (the so-called gold-fish bowl); they will also find that they are much more effectively accountable to their share-holders, to their employees, to their customers and (in so far as may be necessary) to the public at large. This will reduce the need for special instruments of government consultation, action and investigation in regard to industry, such as the Neddies, and the former IRC and PIB. This in turn should go some way towards making it possible to restore, in the government's dealings with industry, the traditional distinction between: the 'executive' function, which consists essentially of doing things; the 'parliamentary' function which consists essentially of scrutinising what the government proposes to do or has done by way of general policies; and the 'judicial' function which consists essentially in deciding whether or not some particular action has been or would be in contravention of the laws.

This hypothesis is explored more generally in Chapter 9. The proposal is there discussed that there should be a system of Select Committees of Parliament covering the whole range of government activities, not to debate policies but to examine the efficiency with which policies are implemented. One of these Select Committees would be responsible for scrutinising government activity in regard to Industry and Commerce.

This Select Committee and others (notably the Select Committee on Fuel and Power, Water, Transport, and Communications, which would replace the existing Nationalised Industries Committee) will need the support of an investigatory staff with a more up-to-date capability than the present Exchequer and Audit Department. Before it was wound up by the Conservative Government that took office in 1970, the Prices and Incomes Board had developed methods of investigating the management of public corporations and private firms and scrutinising whether they were efficiently serving the interests of their customers, their employees, and the community at large. There appears to be a strong case for considering whether at least some of the former staff of the Prices and Incomes Board should become the servants of Parliament. They might be joined by some of the staff from the National Economic Development Office.

In so far as certain existing functions, for example those of the Monopolies Commission, are of a judicial rather than a consultative or scrutinising nature, they would more appropriately be transferred to a new commercial court than to a Select Committee of Parliament. This might be one element in a developing structure of commercial courts including, of course, the Restrictive Practices Court. Another structure of employment courts will be needed to handle employment ('industrial relations') proceedings. A structure of administrative courts will also be needed to handle proceedings arising from disputed acts of public administration–as discussed later in Chapter 9. In all three areas–commerce, employment, and administrative law–the existing court system is badly under-developed. It should be the Lord Chancellor's responsibility to put this right.

SUMMARY

We can now try to sum up what this re-definition of the functions of government towards industry might mean in terms of government organisation.

There should be one Ministry for Trade and Industry (in addition to a Ministry for Industrial Infrastructure as suggested above) responsible for the strength, efficiency and accountability of British industry. This ministry would take over responsibility for 'sponsoring' all industries (except fuel and power, water, transport and communications), including agriculture and building, and would be responsible for sponsoring the country's industry and commerce as a whole. It should also be responsible for companies legislation and more generally for the framework of regulation governing the activities of industry and commerce.

Another ministry would be responsible for manpower and employment questions including industrial relations, not just in industry but for the nation as a whole. Its role is further discussed in Chapter 8.

Another ministry (the Treasury) would be responsible for economic policy and for prices policy and incomes policy, not just as they apply to industry but as they apply to the country as a whole. The Treasury should also be responsible for public purchasing policy. The Treasury's role is further discussed in Chapter 7.

Another ministry would be responsible for the regional implications of industrial policy, along with the regional implications of other government policies. Its role is further discussed in Chapter 6.

Responsibility for the research and development activities of government would fall to the ministry responsible for the purpose of the R and D in question–industry, health, defence, transport, agriculture, etc., as the case may be. Any research and development activity carried out by government for no such specific purpose would be the responsibility of the Department of Education, Science and the Arts. This point is discussed further in the following chapter.

Consumer protection would remain the responsibility of the Ministry for Trade and Industry, so far as industrial products are concerned. But

Parliament, the Courts and the Press should also play a much more active role than at present in this sphere. The Lord Chancellor should be given special responsibility for improving the effectiveness of legal and judicial sanctions to protect consumers.

Finally, much of the consultative and investigatory apparatus that has grown up like a great blanket of cotton wool and blotting paper between government and industry could be scrapped. The necessary processes of consultation and investigation should in future be carried out in the open which is where they properly belong, partly under the auspices of Parliament and the Courts and partly by enlarging the area of public comment and discussion.

CONCLUSION

In this chapter we have dealt briefly with the way relations between industry and government have evolved during the last seventy years or more, as the country has become self-governing, and we have considered some of the main problems that have grown up. The theme that emerges is, in fact, very similar to that running through developments in other spheres of government. The time has come to clarify the government's functions towards industry, to simplify the jungle of institutions and procedures that have proliferated over the years and to redefine the responsibilities of different ministers, Parliament, public corporations, private enterprise and the courts.

Two ministries are needed, one to deal with industrial infrastructure and the other to deal with trade and industry. They should be responsible for the effective development of the country's industrial well-being. They should not be directly responsible for economic policy, nor for regional policy, nor for manpower, employment and industrial relations policies; three other ministries should be responsible for these. Meanwhile, Parliament and the courts must be strengthened if they are to carry out their functions effectively in the industrial and commercial field. So far as possible, public corporations and private firms should then be left free, within the framework of public policy and public accountability thus laid down by ministers, Parliament and the courts, to do their own jobs as best they can without interference or feather-bedding by the government. If direct intervention is required it should be carried out according to criteria clearly laid down, by a non-ministerial agency subject to effective parliamentary and public scrutiny.

So far, the signs are that Mr Heath's Conservative government are prepared, in principle, to pursue this line of approach. Only time will show whether, in practice, they will be able to develop a positive framework of parliamentary and judicial control, and of economic, regional, manpower and employment, and prices and incomes policies, in which private enterprise can then be allowed to flourish to the full.

NOTES ON CHAPTER 4

General

There is, of course, an enormous literature about what has been regarded with comfortable lack of precision as the 'economy' of the country and the government's 'economic' policies. Much of this is relevant to the government's handling of industrial questions, but if one began to refer to it one would hardly know where to stop.

For the nationalised industries the best source-book is the 1968 Report by the Select Committee on Nationalised Industries on *Ministerial Control of the Nationalised Industries* and the supporting evidence published with that report. There is no corresponding compendium of information, analysis and opinion about the government's relations with private industry, for the simple reason that economists, administrators, industrialists, politicians and other proponents of the conventional wisdom have only recently begun to recognise this as a definable field for study or government action.

Note 1. John Stuart Mill: *Essay on Liberty* (1859): Chapter 5.

Note 2. *Financial and Economic Obligations of the Nationalised Industries* (Cmnd. 1337): HMSO, 1961.

Note 3. *Economic and Financial Objectives of the Nationalised Industries* (Cmnd. 3437): HMSO, 1967.

Note 4. *Ministerial Control of the Nationalised Industries: First Report from the Select Committee on Nationalised Industries*: HMSO, 1968.

Note 5. House of Commons Debate, 4th December 1947: *Hansard*, Column 566.

5

A Common Pattern

We do not use a different scheme, a different framework,
on each occasion. It is the essence of the matter that we use
the same framework on different occasions.

P. F. STRAWSON:
Individuals: An Essay in Descriptive Metaphysics

This chapter suggests that past patterns of evolution and present
problems similar to those described in the two preceding chapters can
be discerned in a number of other spheres of government too. The
particular spheres covered are: External Affairs; Housing, Health and
Welfare; and Education and Science.

Developments in each of these activities of government display the
same rhythm of proliferation and subsequent re-integration which marks
the evolution of government organisation for handling defence and
industrial questions. But we also see how the external and domestic
responsibilities of government are now converging on one another. We
see the erosion of clear lines of demarcation between the local, regional
and national functions of government. We see problems of reconciling
the professional independence of doctors, scientists and university staff
with their public accountability, similar to the problem discussed in the
last chapter of reconciling managerial independence in industry with
public accountability. Finally, we see the need for a capability for
research and long-term planning under the Prime Minister himself, in a
Prime Minister's Department.

EXTERNAL AFFAIRS

The international scene has, of course, changed out of all recognition
in the last 100 years. The European powers no longer dominate the
world as they did in the nineteenth century and the early years of the
twentieth. Since then, the European world empires, including the
British Empire, have expanded and then exploded into a large number
of independent nations. The fragmentation is now being followed by a
process of re-integration at a different level, a trend towards one world.

74

A COMMON PATTERN

Developments in communication, especially air travel and telecommunications, are bringing the peoples of the world into continually closer contact with their neighbours in the global village. One result of this trend has been the emergence of international organisations; another is recognition by the advanced countries of an interest and a duty to help the less advanced.

Since the first world war the government's tasks in the field of external affairs have changed accordingly. The scale of our representation abroad has greatly increased, in commonwealth countries and with international organisations as well as with foreign governments. The scale of our administration of dependent territories expanded considerably until the period after the second world war, when it declined sharply—first with the independence of India, Pakistan and Ceylon and then with the independence of our colonies. The task of promoting overseas trade has continually become more pressing, and the long term importance of aid and technical assistance continues to grow also.

Changes in government organisation for handling external affairs reflect these developments. Before the first world war there were three departments of state involved, the Foreign Office, the Colonial Office and the India Office. By 1939 the number had grown to six, including the Dominions Office, Burma Office and Department of Overseas Trade in addition to the original three. By the early 1960s, although four of these had disappeared (India Office, Dominions Office, Burma Office and Department of Overseas Trade), there were still four overseas departments (Foreign Office, Commonwealth Relations Office, Colonial Office and Department of Technical Co-operation), or five if the short-lived Central African Office—set up under Mr R. A. (now Lord) Butler—is included.

But by then the writing was on the wall. As the world continued to shrink in size it was becoming less and less possible to deal with the various aspects of external affairs in separate compartments, and the unification of the various overseas ministries and departments became inevitable. In 1968 the Foreign, Commonwealth and Colonial Offices were merged in a single ministry. Only the Ministry of Overseas Development remained to be absorbed. But for some time it had been apparent that sooner or later its activities should be devolved to an executive Overseas Development Agency under the Foreign and Commonwealth Office. This was eventually done in October 1970.

This process of unification in the government's approach to external

75

affairs is comparable to that which has taken place in the defence sphere, not only because of its inevitability but because of the confused, piece-meal way in which it actually happened. Moreover, just as there has been a growing need to co-ordinate the defence and civil activities of government, so the need for co-ordination has grown between the external and domestic functions of government. The relationship be-tween external affairs and defence must be close, for obvious reasons; and since the turn of the century, special arrangements have existed for handling it. Overseas trade is also a matter on which it has been difficult to draw the right line between external and domestic responsibilities. But the same is now becoming more and more true of many other aspects of government business. The trend is accelerated by the emer-gence of international organisations, including the United Nations itself, functional bodies like the International Monetary Fund, the Food and Agriculture Organisation, UNESCO, and the World Health Organisation, and regional bodies like NATO. Finance and economics, defence, food and agriculture, labour, education, health, transport and communications – in all these spheres of government business, to men-tion only some of the more obvious, domestic and external policies are becoming more and more closely intertwined. This process is bound to continue. For example, if and when Britain eventually joins the Euro-pean Economic Community a whole range of government activities which now fall into the traditional categories of domestic or external affairs will become common to both. Or, to put it another way, those traditional categories will become increasingly meaningless for practical purposes.

This being so, it is ironical that the last half century should have seen the gradual separation of the government staffs handling external affairs from those handling domestic affairs, and that the institutional dividing line between them should have hardened. In 1914 the staff of the Foreign Office were members of the Home Civil Service; by 1946 they were members of a separate Foreign Service; and in 1965 they were joined in the new Diplomatic Service by the staff of the Common-wealth Relations Office, who until then had belonged to the Home Civil Service. The reason is to be found, of course, in the gradual unification of the government's functions in the field of external affairs under one major department of state, the Foreign and Commonwealth Office. Nevertheless, it is odd that it should have happened at a time when the dividing line between external and domestic affairs is breaking down.

A COMMON PATTERN

The change of emphasis from imperial administration to diplomacy is now beginning to be followed by a shift from traditional diplomacy to something much more like international administration. As this gathers momentum, the difference between the Home Civil Service and the Diplomatic Service will not be easy to maintain. The unification of the two services within a single public service is only a question of time.

HOUSING, HEALTH AND WELFARE

Since Gladstone's day it has come to be accepted that the community has a responsibility to provide a decent standard of housing and medical attention for all its members, and to see that the poor, the sick, and the unemployed and the elderly are cared for. We have come to regard the public welfare services as forming a more or less integrated system, the purpose of which is to provide every inhabitant of the country with a certain standard of personal welfare and security from the cradle to the grave. Changes in governmental responsibilities since the early years of the century reflect these changes of outlook in two ways. There has been a gradual shift of responsibility for social welfare from local authorities towards the central government, although the actual administration of many of the welfare services remains with local government. At the same time the emergence of the unified concept of the Welfare State has been largely, though not yet fully, reflected in unification of the central government's organisation for social welfare.

At the beginning of the first world war a large number of central government departments or agencies were concerned with welfare services. The Local Government Board supervised the local administration of the Poor Law, public health legislation, and legislation relating to the provision of personal health services, and was responsible for such municipal housing as was undertaken at the time. The Board of Education supervised the school medical service and encouraged voluntary maternity and child welfare services. The Privy Council had certain powers in respect of doctors and midwives. The Home Office was concerned with lunacy and mental deficiency, with 'infant life protection', and with workmen's compensation. The Admiralty and the War Office were responsible for administering pensions for disabled servicemen. The Treasury was responsible for Old Age Pensions and used the Board of Customs and Excise as disbursing agent. The Board of Trade was responsible for the Labour Exchanges which administered the

77

unemployment insurance scheme. Finally, Lloyd George's five Insurance Commissions, one each for England, Scotland, Ireland, and Wales and one Joint Commission were responsible for administering the health insurance scheme.

These arrangements were criticised for 'the labour, the waste of time, the inefficiency, the mutual jealousy, the ludicrous lack of co-ordination between departments in instances which might be indefinitely multiplied'. They were said to represent 'an aggregate of effort the most complex, confused, lacking in rationale and fertile in cross purposes that any administrative system in the world has possibly disclosed'.[1] In 1919, after a lengthy campaign in which Sir Robert Morant and Beatrice Webb were prominent, a Ministry of Health was established. It took over all the powers of the Local Government Board and of the English and Welsh Insurance Commissions (special arrangements were made for Scotland), and the powers of the Privy Council and the Home Office which related to health.

The establishment of the Ministry of Health thus represented the unification in a single Ministry of virtually all the central government's then existing responsibilities for health and housing. Throughout the 1920s and 1930s the medical services provided by local authorities expanded, but during the 1939–1945 war the Emergency Hospital Service, consisting of both local authority hospitals and voluntary hospitals, came under the direct administration of the Ministry of Health. This development led eventually in 1948 to the creation of the National Health Service, and thus to the removal of direct administrative responsibility for health services to the Ministry of Health, partly from the local authorities and partly from the private sector.

Until 1951 the Ministry retained most of its former functions in addition to the National Health Service, except those in respect of insurance, pensions and the Poor Law which had been transferred to the Ministry of National Insurance in 1945. In 1951, however, it lost its housing functions, together with its responsibility for planning and for exercising general supervision over local government, to the Ministry of Town and Country Planning, which in that year became the Ministry of Housing and Local Government. Thus the Ministry of Health became what it was until its recent incorporation in the Department of Health and Social Security, the Ministry responsible for the National Health Service and little else.

To trace the development of the organisation for handling pensions, insurance and assistance we have to go back to 1917. In that year, in order to meet the volume of work created by the war, the administration of war disablement pensions was unified under a New Ministry of Pensions. Although many of the functions of this Ministry were transferred back to the Service Ministries and to the Ministry of Labour and the Board of Trade after the war, it continued in existence with responsibility for war pensions and medical and hospital treatment for war pensioners. In 1939 its powers were widened to cover disablement pensions not only to servicemen, but also to civilians injured through enemy action. It continued to discharge these functions until 1953.

In 1916 the new Ministry of Labour took over responsibility for unemployment insurance together with the other labour functions of the Board of Trade. Although the number of people covered by unemployment insurance rose from two and a half million in 1914 to fifteen million in 1938, relief from mass unemployment between the wars had to be provided by assistance as well as by insurance. The separate Unemployment Assistance Board was set up in 1935 to meet this need.

In 1920 pensions for the blind were introduced and were administered on behalf of the Treasury by the Board of Customs and Excise, along with old age pensions. In 1925 a scheme of Old Age, Widows' and Orphans' Insurance was introduced and was administered as part of the system of National Health Insurance under the Ministry of Health. Pensions were supplemented where necessary by the Public Assistance Committee of Local Authorities until 1940. In that year the central government assumed direct responsibility for supplementary pensions through the Unemployment Assistance Board, which was renamed simply the Assistance Board.

By the early 1940s, therefore, a distinctly confused situation had developed in regard to pensions, insurance and assistance. The Ministry of Health was responsible for health insurance, for contributory old age and widows' and orphans' pensions administered by approved societies, for miscellaneous health and welfare services administered by local authorities, and for relief under the Poor Law administered by the Public Assistance Committee of local authorities. The Ministry of Labour was responsible for unemployment insurance. The Assistance Board was responsible for unemployment assistance and for supplementing contributory and non-contributory pensions. The Board of Customs and Excise was responsible for administering non-contributory old age pensions and pensions for the blind, on behalf of the Treasury. The Home Office was responsible for workmen's compensation. This was the background against which the welfare state was consolidated in the Beveridge Report of 1942.

Following the Beveridge Report a new Ministry of National Insurance was set up in 1945. It took over the insurance functions of the Ministries of Labour and Health, the Home Office's responsibility for workmen's compensation (which henceforth became known as industrial injuries), and responsibility for the new family allowances scheme. Thus a single Ministry became responsible for handling all questions concerning insurance for sickness, maternity, unemployment, industrial injury, retirement and death. It also took over the National Assistance Board. In 1953, when the Ministry of Pensions was abolished, its functions relating to the administration of pensions were transferred to the Ministry of National Insurance (which became the Ministry of Pensions and National Insurance), and its responsibility for administering pensioners' hospitals and for artificial limbs, etc., was transferred to the Ministry of Health.

The next step came in 1968 when the two ministries, Health and Pensions, were merged to form the Department of Health and Social Security. This clearly represented a further stage in the unification of central government responsibilities in the social welfare field. But housing still remained the responsibility of the Ministry of Housing and Local Government; and responsibility for child care continued to rest with the Home Office until 1970. So although developments in central government clearly reflect the emergence of the unified concept of the Welfare State, there is still one further step to take. Sooner or later housing policy will have to be transferred to a unified Ministry of Housing, Health and Welfare.

But it is outside Whitehall that some of the most important problems are now arising. These centre on: the future of the National Health Service; the development of the personal social services at local government level, following the Seebohm Committee's report[2]; the future of local government following the report of the Redcliffe-Maud Royal Commission on Local Government in England (whose recommendations were always subject to qualification by the Crowther Committee on the Constitution); and the proper relationship between the health and other social services. We shall explore further in the following chapter the general proposition that reform of government today is indivisible at central, regional and local levels. Here we concentrate on health and social questions.

The National Health Service has always been an odd animal, institutionally speaking. It has not been administered as a central government department; nor (with the exception of specifically local authority health services) as part of local government; nor as a public corporation. The hospitals have been administered by hospital management committees under fifteen regional hospital boards; and general practitioners have been administered by one hundred and thirty Executive Councils. Neither of these have been accountable in any real sense either to Parliament or to elected local authorities.

A major re-organisation is now required to bring together the separate hospital services, general practitioner services, and local authority health services. Two 'Green Papers'[3] were published by the 1960 Labour Government on the possible forms that this re-organisation might take, and the 1970 Conservative Administration is reviewing the question further. The main question is whether or not the National Health Service should become part of the general fabric of government at local and regional level. Strong arguments for this are put forward. In human terms, medical care should be provided as one component of a closely integrated range of personal social services. In professional terms, the demarcation lines between medicine and child care, care of the elderly, provision of special housing for the physically or mentally handicapped, and care of the chronic sick, are hard to draw. It is increasingly argued that the general practitioner should be the head of a community health service, rather than a specialist in an artificially narrow field of 'medicine'. If that were once accepted, it would follow that the health services should be fully incorporated in the structure of reformed government at all levels.

This does not mean to say that doctors would turn overnight into traditional Whitehall civil servants or local government officials. As the Redcliffe-Maud Royal Commission said (Report, paragraph 365): 'We do not think it necessary to assume that, if the national health service were brought within the jurisdiction of the new local authorities, this development would mean direct control of hospitals or general practitioners by local councillors in the way that is traditional in English local government. The Passenger Transport Act, 1968 prescribes a new relationship between elected representatives and those responsible for day-to-day running of the service, and this seems to us relevant. A similar relationship can be envisaged for the administration of the health service; the elected representatives would be responsible for general policy decisions and for co-ordinating the national health service with the personal social services; executive bodies consisting mainly of 'professionals' would be responsible, within that general policy, for building and running hospitals and administering the general practitioner service'.[4] A sort of public corporation at local government level is envisaged.

One difficulty, of course, has been that the medical profession has traditionally brought up its members to be individualists, whose sense of achievement depends primarily on their own personal proficiency and skill. Most doctors are not fired by the managerial challenge of running a good hospital or planning the optimal deployment of effort in a medical service. Moreover, most doctors nourish a fierce sense of independence from 'the State', which makes it difficult for them—even more difficult perhaps than for businessmen—to co-operate wholeheartedly in devising a system of administration which will give them a satisfactory working environment. And they sometimes appear to have little sympathy with the demand for effective public accountability, which will enable the community to appraise their performance in its service.

In the long run the health service will almost certainly have to be incorporated in the full range of social services at local, regional and national levels of government. This will be necessary if the use of resources is to be planned in the most effective way; for example, in achieving the right balance between the building of geriatric hospitals and old people's homes. It will also be necessary if those working in the social services are to be able to combine in providing the best everyday care for individual patients. But for this to happen three things will be necessary: wider understanding of the close horizontal links between the health services on the one hand and the social services on the other; better appreciation of the need for a comprehensive approach to the structure of government at local, regional and national levels; and recognition by the medical profession that it is possible to serve society, and be accountable for one's performance in its service, without necessarily becoming a traditional civil servant or local government official.

There is one further point to be noted under the heading Housing, Health and Welfare. Pressure will continue to grow for better co-ordination of the various financial relationships between the individual and the community. It should be possible to arrange matters so that all the various tax liabilities and social security provisions, taken together, add up to a coherent and sensible and fair sum-total payment in one direction or the other, between the community and each individual, appropriate to his or her particular circumstances. Hence the proposal for 'negative income tax' and a national minimum income. This proposal implies closer co-ordination between the Inland Revenue and the Department of Health and Social Security than exists today. We shall return to it in Chapter 7.

EDUCATION AND SCIENCE

It has been increasingly accepted for a long time that education and scientific research are of national importance, and not just of private and local concern, and the interest of the central government in them has grown continually.

Traditionally it was assumed that the central government should not engage directly in education or scientific research. School administration, including the provision of teacher training colleges, was for local authorities or independent bodies. Higher education was for the universities, whose 'academic freedom' has been jealously guarded. Scientific research was for the universities and, where their efforts need to be supplemented, for publicly financed Research Councils carefully insulated from direct political control. At the same time in practice, there has been a marked encroachment of central government influence over the local authorities, the universities and the independent bodies in this field since the beginning of the century, owing primarily to the increasing national importance of education and science and their increasing need for public funds.

The basis for a national system of state schools was provided by the Board of Education Act of 1899 and the Education Act of 1902. Two thousand five hundred separate school boards were abolished and the counties and county boroughs were made responsible for school administration. Arrangements were made for central and local government to subsidise the voluntary schools out of taxation and rates. The central government now had for the first time a department in Whitehall responsible for 'the superintendence of matters relating to education'.

The successive Education Acts of 1918 and 1944 made very little difference to the pattern of responsibility for school education within

83

the central government, though the Board of Education became the Ministry of Education in 1944. But they did signify a major shift in the balance between the local authorities and the central government. Under the 1944 Act the Minister of Education was made responsible for securing 'the effective execution by local authorities under his control and direction of the national policy for providing a varied and comprehensive educational service in every area'. Since then he has been empowered to issue statutory rules and orders, regulations and circulars laying down how the educational system should be organised and administered, and to over-rule a local education authority if he thinks fit. In recent years, to take one particular example, the political controversy over comprehensive education has been primarily a national issue and only to a secondary extent an issue in local politics.

When the universities began to receive financial assistance from the government on a substantial scale, a way had to be found of administering it which would not encroach on their freedom to decide their own research programmes and to teach what they wanted to teach in the way they wanted to teach it. The University Grants Committee was set up in 1919, reporting not to the Minister of Education but to the Chancellor of the Exchequer. The Committee's function was to receive the total grant from the Treasury and allocate it among the universities. It continued to discharge this function under the Treasury until 1964, since when an enlarged University Grants Commission has discharged it under the Department of Education and Science.

In the field of scientific research the counterpart of the University Grants Committee was the Research Council, several of which were established from 1915 onwards under the Privy Council. (Defence research, however, grew up largely within the Service Departments and the military supply departments like the Ministries of Supply and Aviation. In 1970 the various defence research establishments came under the Ministry of Defence and the Ministry of Technology.) By 1959 there were five major government Research Councils in the field of civil research, each of which was responsible to the Lord President of the Council as was the Atomic Energy Authority.

In that year a Minister for Science was appointed who took the place of the Lord President and assumed responsibility to Parliament for supervising the work of the Councils, for atomic energy, for space research, and for broad questions of scientific policy outside the sphere of defence. Meanwhile, various government departments (including the

84

Post Office and the Ministries of Agriculture, Aviation, Power, Transport and Works) had built up research efforts of their own, and central government was also providing the universities with very substantial grants for scientific research. Altogether the government's involvement with science was becoming closer and more direct.

The situation in the early 1960s thus was that three Ministers were directly concerned with education and science. The Minister of Education had responsibilities for school education which he discharged through the local authorities; the Chancellor of the Exchequer had responsibilities towards the universities, which he discharged through the University Grants Committee; and the Minister for Science had responsibilities for civil scientific research, which he discharged through the Research Councils and the Atomic Energy Authority. However, the march of events was bringing these spheres of responsibility closer to one another. It was becoming necessary to co-ordinate government policies on school education with policies on university education, and policies on university research with policies on government research, more closely than before.

Three main factors were bringing school and university education together. First, we were coming to accept that every young person had a right to receive education up to the level of which he was capable. All who had the ability should be given the opportunity to go on through the primary and secondary levels to a higher education. Moreover, this was coming to be regarded not just as an individual social right but also as a national economic need. So it became a matter of government policy to see that there was enough room on the higher rungs of the educational ladder for all those coming up from below, that what was being taught at each level bore some sort of relation to what was being taught at the others, and that the general balance of what was being taught at all levels bore some relation to the country's needs. Secondly, the large number of voluntary and local authority training colleges which had grown up to provide trained teaching staff for the schools were linked both to school and university administration. The schools depended on them for staff and they were mainly paid for by money which came ultimately from Ministry of Education Votes. On the other hand they had come to be administered since 1944 under the supervision of Institutes of Education established at the Universities. Finally, a number of the leading technical colleges established by local authorities and administered under guidance from the Ministry of Education

85

had become Colleges of Advanced Technology and were ready to assume the role of technological universities. In these various ways it was becoming apparent that a unified strategy was needed for developing our national system of education.

The main factor demanding closer co-ordination between research at the universities and government research work was the increasing amount of financial support required by both. The central government's support for university research had risen from about £1·5 million in 1945–46 to about £24 million in 1962–63, and expenditure on its own research work had risen from about £5 million in 1945–46 to about £125 million in 1962–63. Some arrangement had to be made to ensure that this research programme, costing £150 million a year and rising fast, was reasonably well balanced.

This was the background against which the Robbins Committee[5] on higher education and the Trend Committee[6] on the organisation for civil science reported in 1963. The upshot of their reports was the appointment in 1964 of a single Secretary of State for Education and Science, who assumed the responsibilities previously carried by the Minister of Education in relation to the schools, the Chancellor of the Exchequer in relation to the universities, and the Minister for Science in relation to civil science in government. (On the change of government later in 1964 some re-dispersal of responsibility for civil scientific research occurred. For example, elements of the DSIR specifically concerned with industrial research went to the new Ministry of Technology, and so did the Atomic Energy Authority.)

The emergence of a unified Department of Education and Science clearly follows the pattern of ministerial unification apparent in other spheres of government activity. The main problems outstanding now at central government level concern, first, the relationship between the scientific research sponsored by the Department of Education and Science and the research and development sponsored by other government departments; and, second, the relationship between educational policies and national manpower policies.

In principle, the proper division of ministerial responsibility for research is clear. Research activities should be financed by the ministry or department on whose behalf they are being carried out—defence research by the Ministry of Defence, transport research by the ministry responsible for transport, and so on. If it is necessary for government to carry out research on behalf of industry, that research should likewise be financed by the Ministry for Industry. Any research activity for which no other ministry or department is prepared to pay must, if it is worth doing at all, surely be pure research rather than applied research. Responsibility for it should therefore fall to the Department of Education and Science.

However, two questions now arise. First, who should be responsible for co-ordinating the research activities and scientific policies of the government as a whole? Secondly, is there not perhaps an intermediate kind of research into 'technologies', which is a proper function neither for the Department of Education and Science on the one hand nor for departments like Defence, Health or Transport on the other? The existence of Sir Solly Zuckerman in the Cabinet Office as the government's Chief Scientific Adviser reflected the view that the Prime Minister is responsible for co-ordinating the government's overall scientific effort. One argument for a Ministry of Technology was that there is a field of government activity which is properly called 'technology'.

The first of these views is sound, in my opinion, while the second is unsound. The right approach is probably as follows.

The research sponsored by each department of government, for example defence research or transport research, is properly regarded as an integral part of that department's long term planning Co ordination between the research activities of different departments is properly regarded as part of the long term planning for which the Prime Minister is responsible, as leader of the government as a whole. As will become apparent in Chapter 8, the Prime Minister needs a real department of his own (in which the Cabinet Office should be incorporated) to support him on this and other functions. The Prime Minister's Department should certainly contain officials, like the Chief Scientific Adviser, qualified to help him in co-ordinating long term planning, including research, for the government as a whole; and part of the Prime Minister's Department's budget should be available for financing research directed to long term problems which do not fall squarely into the field of any other department. It is in this context that any research and development activities should be considered which fall between the pure research carried out by universities under the ultimate sponsorship of the Department of Education and Science, and the applied research carried out or sponsored by other government departments.

The relationship between educational policies and national manpower policies needs to be much closer than it has been in the past. Again, in the research unit supporting the Prime Minister's Department there should be a small team responsible for considering how far the country's future manpower needs (as predicted by the Ministry of Employment and Manpower) match the future availability of qualified manpower (as predicted by the Department of Education and Science). This is likely to be one of that research unit's most important tasks.

PROFESSIONAL INDEPENDENCE AND PUBLIC ACCOUNTABILITY

The problem of reconciling professional independence with public accountability arises in the spheres of medicine, higher education, and science alike. Doctors, university teachers and scientists are all heavily dependent on public funds; conversely, medical services, universities and scientific research are all of great importance to the community and therefore to the government. Each raises complex questions of policy, management, and appraisal:

> What programmes of future development (in the spheres of health, higher education, and science) should be adopted, and how should resources be allocated between the various conflicting claims upon them?

> How can the work of running a hospital, a university, or a research establishment, best be managed?

> How can we judge after the event the success with which the programme of work has been planned and managed?

Parliament and the public are clearly interested in these questions and in the answers to them. Yet the professional independence of doctors, university teachers and scientists must be preserved from political interference in their work.

Just as a fruitful combination of business management with parliamentary scrutiny and criticism is now developing out of the relationship between the nationalised industries, ministers and Parliament, so it must surely be possible in principle to secure a fruitful marriage between professional independence and public accountability in the spheres of medicine, university teaching and scientific research. In outline this would consist of the following elements:

Ministers (or in certain cases their opposite numbers at regional or local levels) would be responsible for laying before the elected legislature plans for the future development of medical and health services, universities and scientific research, as a basis for making the strategic choices open to the country (or the region or locality) in these fields. (One element in these choices is, of course, the extent to which medicine, higher education and scientific research should be required–or permitted–to finance themselves in the market place. Except for the doctrinaire Conservative or Socialist there is no straightforward, once-for-all answer to this question.)

Within the framework thus laid down by the process of political decision, those responsible for running the medical services, universities and scientific research establishments should then be permitted and required to get on with the job to the best of their own ability.

These 'managers' of the medical services, universities and research establishments should discharge their public accountability by reporting annually to the legislature on the achievements of their enterprises.

Select Committees of Parliament, on the lines of the existing Nationalised Industries Committee, would be responsible for considering those reports and for examining any problems that seem to require closer attention. A similar arrangement would be made, as appropriate, at regional and local levels.

To the extent that this suggestion is at variance with our traditional notions of professional independence it may be because those traditional notions are wearing rather thin. Just as war is too important to be left to the generals, so medicine, science and the universities are now too important to be left to the doctors, the scientists and the dons. In fact, the introduction of arrangements broadly comparable to those for controlling the nationalised industries appears to be the next logical development from steps that have already been taken. For example, the accounts of expenditure by the universities and the University Grants Commission have recently been opened to scrutiny by the Public Accounts Committee of the House of Commons.[7] In a Green Paper[8] published in January, 1970 the Labour Government put forward proposals for a British Research and Development Corporation to be created from an amalgamation of the more important research establishments in Mintech and the Atomic Energy Authority. The Corporation would sell research to industry and the government and would in many ways be like a nationalised industry. The Conservatives seem

89

likely to press this approach even further. In one way or another, government research establishments seem likely to become self-financing to a greater extent than hitherto and their management seems likely to be brought under keener scrutiny.

Moreover, this sort of fusion between professional independence and public accountability accords with the movement away from the cottage industry mentality in medicine, the universities and science—the shift from an individualistic philosophy towards a collective or team approach to medical practice, university teaching, or scientific research. A growing emphasis on management is already discernible in these spheres as in others; as has been shrewdly said, doctors, dons and scientists will have come to terms with the modern world only when they recognise that policy-making and administration in their walks of life are matters for the ablest, not the weakest, of their professional brethren.

SUMMARY

We can now sum up the conclusions that emerge from this short survey of developments in several rather different fields of government.

The process of ministerial unification that emerged in earlier chapters has also been at work in the fields of External Affairs; Housing, Health and Welfare; and Education and Science. The logic of it is clear. It has led to the unification of the Ministry of Overseas Development with the Foreign and Commonwealth Office in a single ministry handling external affairs; it points to the transfer of responsibility for housing to the Department of Health and Social Security, which would thus become a unified Ministry of Housing, Health and Welfare; and it has recently led to the incorporation of the industrial research responsibilities of the Ministry of Technology in the new Department of Trade and Industry.

We have seen that the problems of professional independence and public accountability affecting doctors, academics and scientists in the public sector are similar to those affecting the managers of industry in the public sector. We conclude, therefore, that the ministerial and parliamentary arrangements for planning and controlling the national effort in medicine, universities and science should develop in a similar direction to those for handling the nationalised industries which were discussed in the last chapter.

The need for an integrated approach to government organisation as between central, regional and local levels has become clear, especially in relation to health and associated social services. This will be discussed further in the next chapter.

The eventual unification of the Home Civil Service and the Diplomatic Service in a single public service comes up again in Chapter 8. That chapter also explores further the impact of the 'management revolution' on the institutions and style of central government generally, and considers further the need for a research capability in the Prime Minister's Office.

Finally, the function proposed in this chapter for Select Committees of Parliament in the spheres of medicine, the universities, and government sponsored research activities – as also discussed in the last chapter in respect of the nationalised industries – is considered further in Chapter 9, in its general application to all fields of government.

NOTES ON CHAPTER 5

General

Recent changes in the organisation of government in the field of external affairs are reasonably well documented in the reports of the Plowden Committee on the Overseas Representational Services (Cmnd. 2276: HMSO, 1964) and the Duncan Review Committee on Overseas Representation (Cmnd. 4107: HMSO, 1969). Lord Strang's *The Foreign Office* in the New Whitehall Series (George Allen & Unwin) is interesting and helpful. There is, of course, a vast literature on British foreign and colonial policy in the twentieth century.

Similarly, there is no question of providing here a proper reading list on the massively documented subjects of Housing, Health and Welfare. Among the books that I have found helpful and stimulating are Richard Titmuss' *Essays on the Welfare State* (Unwin University Books) and Rosemary Stevens' *Medical Practice in Modern England* (Yale University Press).

The same is true of Education, Science and the Arts. The Report of the Robbins Committee on Higher Education (Cmnd. 2154: HMSO, 1963) and its supporting volumes of evidence are still the major official source of information and opinion on that subject. The Royal Commission on Local Government in England (Cmnd. 4040: HMSO, 1969) throws interesting light on the organisation of education services. But these are merely two important sources among a multitude. On government organisation for science, F. M. G. Willson's *The Organisation of British Central Government, 1914–1964* (George Allen & Unwin) is very clear and helpful.

Note 1. These criticisms, published in 1917 respectively by the *New Statesman* and by a Conservative party report on 'The Health of the People', are quoted by P. R. Wilding in his article on 'The Genesis of the Ministry of Health' in *Public Administration*, Volume 45, Summer 1967.

Note 2. *Report of the Committee on Local Authority and Allied Personal Social Services*: Cmnd. 3703: HMSO, 1968.

Note 3. (a) *National Health Service: The Administrative Structure of the Medical and Related Services in England and Wales*: HMSO, 1968. (b) *National Health Service: The Future Structure of the National Health Service*: HMSO, 1970.

Note 4. Cmnd. 4040: HMSO, 1969.

Note 5. Cmnd. 2154: HMSO, 1963.

Note 6. Cmnd. 2171: HMSO, 1963.

Note 7. See the very illuminating report, and the evidence published with it, of the Public Accounts Committee on *Parliament and Control of University Expenditure*: HMSO, 1967.

Note 8. *British Research and Development Corporation*: HMSO, January 1970.

6

Local and Regional Government and Environmental Planning

A place for everything, and everything in its place.
SAMUEL SMILES

So far we have been talking about Defence; Industry; External Affairs; Housing, Health and Welfare; Education, Science and the Arts—all of these being spheres in which the government has specific activities to perform and specific services to provide. In this chapter and the following two we come to functions of a rather different kind, second-order functions or (as some might say) meta-functions, the object of which is to make sure that all the various activities of government fall into a consistent pattern, or in other words make sense, in respect of certain important characteristics or dimensions of the total picture.

In this chapter we consider the task of:

supervising the pattern of central, regional and local government;

regulating the siting of national, regional and local activities, both public and private; and

controlling these activities in relation to the interests of those in the vicinity.

This is the task of ensuring that all the other activities of government make sense in relation to a particular geographical area, and thus of providing a geographical dimension to other fields of policy-making. Other comparable second order functions include financial planning, meaning that various activities of government must together make sense in relation to total available expenditure; and manpower planning, meaning that they must make sense in relation to the manpower available. We find that the financial dimension (discussed in the next chapter) involves reference to tables of figures such as estimates and accounts; the manpower dimension (discussed in Chapter 9) involves reference to manpower inventories; while the geographical dimension involves reference to maps. (For example, the report of the recent

93

Royal Commission on Local Government in England is based on maps.) The question of the right geographical pattern of government and the problems of regional and environmental planning are, of course, very closely related to one another. We find that, as the central government's functions in these fields have grown, what were originally separate spheres of responsibility have tended to converge upon one another–following the broad pattern of unification that we have come to recognise in earlier chapters.

Local government, like university teaching, scientific research, the Bank of England, and the medical profession, is one of the areas of British national life supposedly regarded as sacrosanct from direct interference by the central government. In practice, of course, the central government has always found it necessary to intervene from time to time in local government matters, and this has happened on an increasing scale.

The nineteenth century saw an explosion of services provided locally to meet the needs of an industrial population. Boards of health; poor law unions; authorities for highways, street paving, street lighting, police and schools; burial and sanitary boards–all these grew up separately, each with their own areas of jurisdiction, alongside the existing vestries, boroughs and justices of the peace. 'To modern eyes the picture of local government in the middle of the nineteenth century is an administrative nightmare, a tangle of authorities, unrelated to one another either in area or function, and with little coherence or uniform direction from above'[1]–much like our whole system of central, regional and local government in the middle of the twentieth century! The administrative nightmare became unsupportable, and in 1871 the Local Government Board was created with responsibility for supervising local government matters. Under its guidance, a whole succession of measures was taken during the next thirty odd years, dividing the country into urban and rural sanitary areas (subsequently urban and rural district councils), re-organising the boroughs, creating county boroughs, administrative counties and metropolitan borough councils, and transferring responsibility for education from the school boards to the county councils and other local government authorities.

The late 1930s probably saw the high-water mark of the system of British local government which came into existence towards the end of the nineteenth century. After the second world war local authorities acquired a number of new functions, such as housing and town planning, but they lost a number of important functions to the nationalised industries, the National Health Service and the Ministry of National Insurance. Moreover, their increasing financial dependence on the central government for the functions which they retained, such as education and police, inevitably affected their standing and confused their image in the public mind.

This led to renewed pressures for organisational change in local government all through the 1950s and 1960s. In 1951 supervisory responsibility was transferred from the Ministry of Health to the Ministry of Housing and Local Government. In 1958, the Local Government Commission for England was set up to review boundaries between local authorities and to suggest changes in the interest of greater efficiency. In 1963 the London and Middlesex County Councils were abolished, together with the Metropolitan Borough Councils and other local authorities in Greater London, and were replaced by the Greater London Council and thirty-two London Borough Councils. During the mid-1960s the Maud[2] and Mallaby[3] enquiries were carried out into the management and staffing of local authorities, and eventually in 1966 the Redcliffe–Maud Royal Commission on Local Government[4] was appointed. We shall return to its findings later.

Environmental planning as we know it today can be traced back to before the second world war. Between the wars certain powers had been taken by the Minister of Health and the Minister of Transport to control the physical development of towns, and some steps had been taken to encourage industry to go to special areas of high unemployment. Then in 1939, just before the outbreak of war, the report of the Barlow Commission[5] on the geographical distribution of the industrial population included a minority recommendation for a new Ministry to be made responsible for 'promoting and supervising the planning of the country for industrial, agricultural, residential and recreational requirements'.

In October 1940 Lord Reith, then Minister of Works and Buildings, was asked to work out machinery for handling the reconstruction problems following the London blitz. He formed a Reconstruction Group, appointed the Uthwatt and Scott Committees[6] on compensation and betterment and on land utilisation in rural areas, and encouraged the local authorities to think about their post-war reconstruction plans. In 1942 the Ministry of Health's town and country planning powers were transferred to the Ministry of Works, which then became the Ministry of Works and Planning. In the following year, however, this unified responsibility both for town and country planning and for reconstruction planning was transferred to a new Ministry of Town and Country Planning, and the Ministry of Works and Planning reverted to plain Ministry of Works. Responsibility for housing, sewage and water supply and for general supervision of local government remained with the Ministry of Health, which kept them until 1951. It was then transferred to the Ministry of Town and Country Planning, which was changed to the Ministry of Local Government and Planning and subsequently became the Ministry of Housing and Local Government. The functions of environmental planning and the supervision of local government had merged in a single ministry.

The development of *regional government* contains the following related strands:

the special arrangements which have been made for Scotland and Wales (and Northern Ireland);

the arrangements made by central government ministries individually to co-ordinate their local offices region by region, and the wartime arrangements made by the central government as a whole to co-ordinate the regional activities of the various ministries;

the arrangements which developed first under the Ministry of Labour and then under the Board of Trade for encouraging and co-ordinating industry region by region; and

finally the arrangements for regional economic planning which developed in the 1960s.

Since the first world war special administrative arrangements have been developed for Scotland and, to a lesser extent, for Wales. The Secretary for Scotland became a Secretary of State in 1926, exercising his powers through the Scottish Home, Health, Agriculture, and Education Departments in Edinburgh, these functions being regarded as predominantly local or regional in character. In 1962, largely in response to the need to set up regional planning machinery in Scotland, the functions of the four departments were re-allocated between a new Scottish Development Department, a new Home and Health Department, and the Agriculture and Education Departments. The other functions of the central government in relation to Scotland, including those connected with finance, industry, trade, transport and communications, have been discharged throughout by ministries in London with a

United Kingdom (not just an England and Wales) jurisdiction. These functions have been regarded as national, as opposed to regional or local, in character and, although as Scotland's Minister the Secretary of State takes a close interest in them as they affect Scotland, he has no statutory responsibility for them. This supposed distinction between local or regional functions on the one hand and national functions on the other has been the source of much confusion. The fact is that *every* function of government increasingly involves activities at central, regional and local levels. The organisational problem is two-fold: to distinguish 'horizontally' between different functions; and to distinguish 'vertically' between different (central, regional and local) levels of government.

There have been no separate administrative arrangements for Wales on anything like the Scottish scale, and throughout the period since 1914 England and Wales have been treated as a single unit for administrative purposes. But most ministries have regarded Wales as a single region, and the Ministry of Housing and Local Government has had a Welsh Office since 1951. During the 1950s and 1960s there was a definite trend towards special regional arrangements for Wales: in 1951 the Home Secretary was made Minister for Welsh Affairs and given a general responsibility for supervising the central government's activities in Wales; in 1957 this title and this responsibility were transferred to the Minister of Housing and Local Government; and in 1965 a Secretary of State for Wales was appointed with a Minister of State and a Welsh Office (under a Permanent Secretary) to support him.

Since the first world war almost every major ministry, except the Treasury and the external affairs ministries, has set up regional offices to co-ordinate its activities within the regions. During the second world war, Regional Commissioners were appointed, by the Minister of Home Security, to co-ordinate the civil defence activities of *all* the central government departments operating within each region. Machinery grew up under these Commissioners for co-ordinating other responsibilities of the central government, such as manpower, production and transport, and for co-ordinating the central government's activities with those of the local authorities in the region. But the idea that some such regional machinery of government should be permanently established in peacetime to deal with economic or social activities as opposed to defence activities was slow to take root. The central government ministries were anxious to maintain their autonomy at the regional level, and the local authorities were reluctant to accept a unified central government presence between themselves and Whitehall. Largely for these reasons the Regional Commissioners were disbanded in 1945 and, although attempts were made between 1945 and 1950 to consolidate and stream-line the other regional administrative arrangements which had grown up during the war, these tended to lapse during the 1950s. As a result, by the early 1960s the regional arrangements made by each individual ministry did not add up to any coherent pattern of regional administration. There was a vacuum at the regional level between local government and central government.

We turn now to *regional planning*.

The powers taken by the central government to encourage the distribution of industry to areas of high unemployment rested with the the Ministry of Labour until 1944. The Special Areas were then re-named Development Areas, reflecting the view that the rescue of depressed areas was only one facet of the wider task of regulating the distribution of industry, and administrative responsibility was trans-ferred from the Ministry of Labour to the Board of Trade. Regional Boards for Industry were also set up during the second world war under the Ministry of Supply to stimulate production in the engineering trades. After the war no-one quite knew how they fitted in. They were first taken over by the Ministry of Labour, then by the Board of Trade, next by the Ministry of Economic Affairs in 1947, then by the Treasury later in the same year, and again by the Board of Trade in 1952!

By the early 1960s a number of factors were stimulating pressure for regional planning. An alarming drift of population to the South East of England from other regions appeared to be aggravating the internal economic imbalance of the country. This imbalance was already such that stop-go economic policies were stopping economic expansion in some regions before it had even started to go. From the social point of view, wide differences in employment levels between one part of the country and another were becoming unacceptable. Unemployment was now recognised to be a regional problem rather than a local problem; the development *district* concept was out of date. Finally, it was apparent that the physical planning of urban renewal in the great conurbations, and the siting of new towns, airports, motorways, docks, hospitals and universities, were more than merely local matters. They must be planned on a regional and inter-regional basis.

Through the 'sixties, the economic and industrial aspect of these

problems seemed the most acute. Under the Conservatives in the early
'sixties the top regional priority was industry. In 1963 the Board of
Trade's responsibility for distribution of industry was expanded and a
new President of the Board of Trade (Mr Heath) was appointed with
the additional title of Secretary of State for Trade, Industry and
Regional Development. However, when the Labour Government came
to office in 1964 they regarded the 'economic' rather than the strictly
industrial aspect of regional planning as paramount, and decided that
responsibility for regional planning should be transferred to the new
Department of Economic Affairs. Eight regional economic planning
councils were set up under the Department of Economic Affairs, composed of representatives of various interests in the region, to advise on
the broad strategy of regional development and the best use of the
region's resources. Each council was supported by a regional planning
board, composed of officials from the various Whitehall ministries with
interests in the region.

The development of machinery for regional planning in this form
raised a number of awkward problems. How was it to be related to the
growth of regional arms of government in Scotland and Wales? Was it
correct to suppose that regional co-ordination was primarily concerned
with economic and industrial questions? Would the economic planning
boards be able to act without the unanimous agreement of the ministries
represented on them? If the answer was 'No', they would be virtually
powerless; if it was 'Yes', they would disrupt the chain of command
between the ministries and their regional and local staffs; in either case
an unsatisfactory situation. Finally, how would the regional councils
and boards impinge on the local authorities? If the answer was 'Very
little', it would mean that they were largely ineffective; if it was 'A lot',
it would lead to confusion of responsibility between central and local
government. It was clear from the beginning that the internal contradictions of these arrangements for regional economic planning would
make themselves felt.

To summarise so far, developments in three originally separate fields
of government (local government; environmental planning; and regional government, including regional economic planning) had by the
middle 1960s progressed to the point where responsibility for local
government and environmental planning was unified under the Ministry
of Housing and Local Government, partial responsibility for regional
government in Scotland and Wales was devolved to special Secretaries

of State for those two countries, and regional economic planning came under the Department of Economic Affairs. At the same time the relationships between local, regional and central government responsibilities were giving rise to increasingly awkward questions. During the later 1960s, moreover, a number of new pressures began to make themselves felt. The first was the proposed reform of local government. The second was a reaction against a primarily economic approach to government. Thirdly, the problems of urban transport became so acute that for the time being they became the dominant factor in urban planning. Fourthly, there was a rising sense of alienation and political discontent, especially during the years 1966 to 1968, in the regions and particularly in Scotland and Wales.

The reaction against a primarily economic approach to government can be seen as part of a wider reaction against the claim that economists had the solution to every social problem.* The effect of this reaction on regional and environmental planning was particularly marked. The *Torrey Canyon* disaster and growing anxiety about the extent of oil pollution; the Aberfan disaster, and growing recognition of the dangers and the waste created by a too narrowly defined approach to industrial objectives; the saga of the third London airport, the early stages of which appeared to demonstrate that the government's own approach to planning was based on too narrow a calculation of the public interest; the siting of new reservoirs and motorways without sufficient regard to the interest of amenity; growing disquiet about the problems of noise and pollution generally; and a whole host of similar problems in which a narrow economic approach appeared to lead unfailingly to the wrong answers—all these developments created increasing pressure for a shift of emphasis towards a wider social and environmental approach in regional policy and local planning.

In 1969, in response to these pressures, Mr Anthony Crosland was appointed Secretary of State for Local Government and Regional Planning. The new Secretary of State took charge, as 'overlord' of the Ministry of Housing and Local Government and (in recognition of the immediate urgency of the problems of urban traffic) the Ministry of Transport. The Ministry of Housing and Local Government took over the regional planning functions of the (now abolished) Department of Economic Affairs, thus becoming something like a Ministry of Regional

* To be fair, economists themselves played a leading part in this reaction. See, for example, E. J. Mishan's *The Costs of Economic Growth*.

and Local Government. Regional and local government in Scotland and Wales, however, remained under the supervision of the Secretaries of State for Scotland and Wales.

Mr Crosland immediately faced an awkward problem. The Redcliffe–Maud Royal Commission on Local Government published its report in June 1969.[4] The Royal Commission's terms of reference, unfortunately, had restricted it to considering the structure of local government only *in relation to its existing functions*. It was not allowed to consider the possibility of re-allocating functions between central and local government, nor of establishing a new intermediate level of government for the regions. Thus the Commission's recommendations that its proposed 61 new local government areas should be grouped in eight provinces, each with its own provincial council, and that these provincial councils should replace the existing regional economic planning organisation, were tantamount to saying that we should co-ordinate the interest of *local* authorities at the regional level and therefore stop co-ordinating the *central* government's activities there. It was rather like saying that you should buy some trousers and therefore throw away your shirt! Surely the body politic needs to be clothed all over.

Mr Senior, who dissented from the other members of the Royal Commission, put his finger on the point. 'The need for an intermediate or provincial level of government activity arises from the existence of problems which cannot be comprehended (and therefore cannot be solved) except by bodies operating at that level—problems which stand in the way of the proper discharge by both central and local government of their respective responsibilities. I therefore agree with my colleagues that some kind of provincial organisation is necessary to bridge the gap—to take a synoptic view of the combined effects of departmental policies over as wide an area as possible, to bring local needs and aspirations to bear on decisions that have to be made nationally but cannot rationally be made from Whitehall, and to give local planning authorities a long-term strategic context for structural plan-making. But I cannot agree that this organisation must necessarily, or even should preferably, be an integral part of local government. The bridge must be built from both sides, and in such a way that the two halves meet in the middle.'[7] Quite so.

However, that is not the end of the story. The problem was further complicated by the fact that the Commission on the Constitution (the Crowther Commission) had been set up at the beginning of 1969 to take some of the steam out of Scottish and Welsh nationalism and discontent in the English regions. The Constitution Commission's terms of reference required it:

'To examine the present functions of the central legislature and government in relation to the several countries, nations and regions of the United Kingdom:

To consider, having regard to developments in local government organisation and in the administrative and other relationships between the various parts of the United Kingdom and to the interests of the prosperity and good government of our people under the Crown, whether any changes are desirable in those functions or otherwise in present constitutional and economic relationships:

To consider, also, whether any changes are desirable in the constitutional and economic relationships between the United Kingdom and the Channel Islands and the Isle of Man.'[8]

This further enquiry clearly cut right across the work of the Royal Commission on Local Government. As the Royal Commission recognised in its report (paragraph 439), if the Constitution Commission recommended that 'provincial councils should be called upon to assume functions now concentrated in an overworked system of central government' and 'there were a substantial devolution of central government functions to the provincial councils', this would give these councils a significantly different character.

The basic point, in fact, is very simple. There are certain activities of government that need to be carried out at the national level; there are certain activities that need to be carried out at regional (or provincial) level, including Scotland and Wales; and there are certain activities that are best carried out locally. (There are also certain activities that are best not carried out by government at all!) It is time that we defined them all. We shall not get a sensible form of central government, regional government, or local government, until (with Morant) we look comprehensively at the structure of government as a whole.

For the future, the right developments seem likely to be on the following lines:

1. A Secretary of State for Local Government and Regional Planning should assume supervisory responsibility for Scotland and Wales, whose Secretaries of State should be abolished. Why should we Scots and Welsh be regarded as second-class citizens, who need special nannies at Westminster, like the Colonies in the old days?

2. Responsibility for transport should fall within a unified Ministry of Power, Transport and Communications (the Ministry for Industrial Infrastructure proposed in Chapter 4). Transport should certainly not be muddled up with local government and regional planning. It is just as short-sighted, and will lead to just as much distortion, to suppose that local government and regional planning are mainly about transport, as to suppose that they are mainly about industry or economics. There is a local and a regional dimension to *every* aspect of government activity, whatever the economist or the transport planner says.

3. Responsibility for housing, which is a social service, should be transferred to the Department of Health and Social Security which would become a fully fledged Ministry of Housing, Health and Welfare as proposed in Chapter 5.

4. The new Ministry of Local Government and Regional Planning, covering the country as a whole and stripped of its inessential functions, will then be able to get to grips comprehensively with the pressing problems of local government, regional government and environmental planning.

5. In spite of the Redcliffe–Maud Royal Commission, and in spite also of the alternative proposals recently put forward by the Conservative Government, the right pattern of government that will eventually emerge will almost certainly be three-tier: central, regional, and local; one central government, about twelve (including Scotland and Wales) regional authorities, and perhaps about 200 local authorities.[9] In that way, the piecemeal developments of the last hundred years will be consolidated in a clearly intelligible structure of government over the country as a whole.

In this chapter we have seen once again the emergence of a number of separate functions of government and their gradual unification into a single field of central government responsibility—in this case for local government and regional planning. Part of the same process of evolution has been the gradual growing together of local, regional and central government activity to the point where it is now necessary to systematise and define comprehensively the relationships between them. That should in fact be the first major task of the proposed Ministry of Local Government and Regional Planning.

NOTES ON CHAPTER 6

General

Again, F. M. G. Willson's *The Organization of British Central Government, 1914–1964* is an invaluable source-book. *The Devolution of Power* by J. P. Mackintosh (Chatto & Windus and Charles Knight & Co., 1968) provides an excellent survey, and has not – in my view – been invalidated by the subsequent publication of the Redcliffe-Maud Royal Commission's Report (Cmnd. 4040/1969). That report and the supporting documents published with it are, of course, essential to any study in depth of the questions dealt with in this chapter.

Note 1. W. Eric Jackson: *Local Government in England and Wales* (p. 37): Penguin Books, 1964.

Note 2. *Management of Local Government:* HMSO, 1967.

Note 3. *Staffing of Local Government:* HMSO, 1967.

Note 4. *Report of the Royal Commission on Local Government in England, 1966–1969*: Cmnd. 4040: HMSO, 1969.

Note 5. *Report of the Royal Commission on the Geographical Distribution of the Industrial Population*: Cmnd. 6153/1940: HMSO, 1940.

Note 6. Cmnd. 6378/1942 and Cmnd. 6386/1942: HMSO, 1942.

Note 7. Cmnd. 4040: HMSO, 1969: Vol. II, *Memorandum of Dissent by Mr. D. Senior*, paragraph 454.

Note 8. *Hansard, Written Answers*: Col. 290, 11th February 1969.

Note 9. This solution is convincingly argued by J. P. Mackintosh in *The Devolution of Power*.

7

Financial and Economic Affairs

The age of chivalry is gone. That of sophists, economists
and calculators has succeeded.
EDMUND BURKE:
Thoughts on the Present Discontents
You pays your money, and you takes your choice.
Anon.

MONEY: A SOCIAL CALCULUS

Of all the spheres of government activity the financial is perhaps the one
in which it is easiest to see the effect of the government's changed role
in society. The course of events has taken broadly the following lines.

Two centuries ago the monarch, that is to say the Crown, raised
money by taxing the people and borrowing from the merchants and
banks to support his kingly needs. Parliament's task, in the long series
of Economical Reforms begun by Burke in 1780, was to keep taxation
down and to bring expenditure into some sort of reasonable order. As
Burke himself said in Parliament, 'neither the present, nor any other
first Lord of the Treasury, has ever been able to make a survey, or even
make a tolerable guess of the expenses of government of any one year,
so as to enable him with the least degree of certainty, or even proba-
bility, to bring his affairs into compass'.[1] We find that the task of 'bringing affairs into compass', of providing a clear picture of the activities
and plans of government (or more recently of the incomes of all the
people) and seeing that in totality they make sense in relation to the
amount of money available, is a constantly recurring theme in the annals
of financial reform. It represents the application of a financial dimension
to the affairs of government and society, corresponding to the geographical dimension discussed in Chapter 6.

The next stage in the evolution of public finance is represented by
the Gladstonian financial reforms of the 1860s. Gladstone's objectives
were in fact very similar to Burke's—to set limits to government
expenditure, to ensure that these limits were observed, and to establish
'general order and regularity'[2] in regard to the government accounts.

Economy and propriety were the watchwords. A balanced budget was the mark of financial probity in public as in private affairs. The notion that public expenditure, taxation and borrowing could be planned and manipulated for economic and social purposes, or that public expenditure could be efficiently or productively managed, hardly arose in the Gladstonian philosophy.

Two factors mark the third phase in this story: the enormous growth of public expenditure; and the rise of Keynesian economics.

Because they have grown so large, the total effect of government spending, government borrowing and taxation has become one of the main factors determining the commercial activity of the community and influencing the spending and investing behaviour of companies and individual citizens. In other words government spending, government borrowing and taxation have become one of the main instruments available to the government for steering the economy. In 1870, government expenditure was running at only £18 million a year, and managing it could be regarded as an internal housekeeping function of interest to the government alone; the community's interest was limited to keeping the total figures down. In 1970 when public expenditure is several hundred times higher and represents something like half the country's gross national product (depending on how you do the sums), controlling the government's finances has become largely synonymous with regulating the economic and financial activities of the community as a whole. By learning how to do its own job properly, the government can thus influence the behaviour of industry and individual citizens in accordance with the needs of economic policy. As we have become self-governing, the task of managing the government's finances has broadened into the task of managing the economy as a whole.

Under the Keynesian type of approach to economic policy that became steadily more fashionable from the 1930s onwards, the government's instruments of economic management were mainly used to regulate the economy in the short term, that is to say not more than about one year ahead. The main object of the exercise was to maintain full employment. In the last two decades, as the problems of unemployment eased, other goals have grown in importance—a stable balance of payments, stable prices, and economic growth.

By the late 1950s and early 1960s lack of success in the pursuit of these goals, especially economic growth, led to dissatisfaction with the short-term mechanism of control exercised by the Treasury and to the search for a different kind of approach to 'economic' policy. It was supposed, especially by the Labour party and their economic advisers, that economic policy should be directly concerned with real resources and was therefore in some way different in kind from the government's financial policies. It was this idea–allied to justifiable impatience with the Treasury–that led to the creation of new and separate machinery for economic planning under the Department of Economic Affairs. Unfortunately, this institutional development diverted attention from the real problems: how to use for strategic purposes the financial flows controlled by the government; how to use financial controls to regulate the use of real resources; and how to turn the country's financial system into a more effective mechanism for implementing our social choices and reflecting our values as a community.

The stage of development we are now entering appears likely to mark a departure from any previous approach to economic and financial problems. It will be based on recognition of the fact that money can indeed be used effectively as a social calculus; that financial flows (see Figure 1) are indeed the control system of the economy; and that government spending, government borrowing and taxation are instruments by which the government can steer the strategic development of

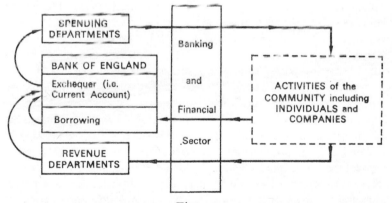

Figure 1

Note: In most years the government is a net borrower, as Figure 1 shows; tax revenue is less than total spending and the difference has to be met by borrowing. But in some years tax revenue exceeds total spending; it is then possible for the government to pay back some of the money it has borrowed and so reduce the total amount of the national debt.

the economy over the longer term as well as regulate it in the short term.

INSTITUTIONAL DEVELOPMENTS

It is illuminating to consider briefly, as in the other fields of government discussed in previous chapters, how the present institutional pattern has evolved. Just as, for example, the evolution of British defence organisation during this century now appears as inevitable, if slow and largely unconscious, progress towards the unified Ministry of Defence which was set up in 1964, so in the sphere of economic and financial affairs events appear in retrospect to have led inevitably to the transformation of the traditional Treasury into a unified Ministry of Economic and Financial Affairs, with overall responsibility for all the government's work in that sphere.

As it happens, the arrangements originally adopted for economic co-ordination in the 1920s were explicitly based on those which had evolved for co-ordinating defence. The Committee of Civil Research was set up in 1925 as a parallel to the Committee of Imperial Defence, 'with the duty of giving connected forethought from a central standpoint to the development of economic, scientific and statistical research in relation to civil policy and administration'.[3] In 1930 this Committee was replaced by an Economic Advisory Council under the Prime Minister's chairmanship. This, like the Committee of Imperial Defence, was a standing body attached to the Cabinet, advisory and without executive responsibilities, consisting of government officials and outside experts, supported by sub-committees, and served by the Cabinet Secretariat. Following a similar pattern to that adopted for defence, the Economic Advisory Council was replaced on the outbreak of war in 1939 by a Ministerial Economic Policy Committee of the Cabinet. This was merged after a time with the Lord President's Committee which, first under Sir John Anderson and later under Mr Herbert Morrison, handled the whole range of domestic policy during the war. The Committee was supported by the Central Economic Information Service. This was a staff of economists and statisticians which was established in the Cabinet Office in 1939 and was subsequently divided into the Economic Section and the Central Statistical Office.

The post-war Labour Government retained this arrangement until 1947 when Sir Stafford Cripps, who had been President of the Board of Trade, assumed the new post of Minister for Economic Affairs and took over the responsibilities for economic policy hitherto held by the Lord President. He was supported by a new Economic Planning Staff, under a Chief Planning Officer, and an Economic Information Unit, in addition to the existing Economic Section and Central Statistical Office. He also took over from the Board of Trade responsibility for the Regional Boards for Industry. With his small personal staff and the various planning and information bodies which supported him, the new Minister for Economic Affairs in 1947 was in a somewhat similar position to the Minister for Co-ordination of Defence between 1936 and 1939. He had important planning and co-ordinating responsibilities without executive authority over the instruments of economic and financial administration, which remained under the Treasury and the Board of Trade.

However, this arrangement did not last for long. When Mr Dalton resigned as Chancellor of the Exchequer after his Budget leak in November 1947, Sir Stafford Cripps succeeded him, and the duties of Minister for Economic Affairs were merged with those of Chancellor of the Exchequer. The Economic Planning Staff, the Economic Information Unit and the Regional Boards moved over to the Treasury, but the Economic Section and the Central Statistical Office were left in the Cabinet Office. In 1952 under the Conservative Government the Economic Section was transferred to the Treasury and its head became Economic Adviser to the Government, while the Regional Boards for Industry were transferred from the Treasury back to the Board of Trade. Thus in 1952 the Treasury appeared to have consolidated its position as the ministry primarily responsible for economic as well as financial affairs.

During the next twelve years the internal organisation of the Treasury adapted itself step by step to these new responsibilities. In 1956, the post of Permanent Secretary to the Treasury was split in two. One of the new Joint Permanent Secretaries was left free to concentrate entirely on economic and financial affairs while the other, Sir Norman Brook, who was already Secretary of the Cabinet, became the official Head of the Home Civil Service and took charge of the Treasury's personnel management and machinery of government responsibilities. In 1962 the Treasury itself was reorganised to reflect this separation of tasks. Previously, the same division had often been responsible for the control both of finance and of personnel in a particular sphere of government. Under the 1962 reorganisation responsibility for economic and financial matters was concentrated in one side of the Treasury, reporting to one of the two Permanent Secretaries, and responsibility for personnel management and machinery of government was concentrated in the other side of the Treasury (the fore-runner of the Civil Service Department), reporting to the other Permanent Secretary. At the same time the economic and financial side was divided into three groups dealing with public expenditure, finance and economic co-ordination.[4]

However, the 1962 reorganisation of the Treasury came too late, and probably placed too little emphasis on the importance of economic co-ordination and economic growth, to carry conviction that the Treasury was capable of discharging the full responsibilities of economic policy-making. Moreover, the Labour party and its economic advisers at that time took the view that 'economics' was an activity of government that ran much wider than the activities covered by the Treasury. So when the Labour Government came to power in October 1964 they set up a separate Department of Economic Affairs. In addition to taking over responsibility for economic co-ordination from the Treasury the new department absorbed a considerable number of professional economists from the staff of the National Economic Development Council (which had been set up in 1961 under the Conservative Government), and recruited more from the universities. In the sphere of industrial development, as we have seen already, the new department appointed advisory staff to stimulate modernisation of industrial practices; and it assumed co-ordinating responsibility for regional economic planning. The situation was much as it had been in 1947: on the one hand, a Minister for Economic Affairs with wide co-ordinating responsibilities in the sphere of economic policy, together with some of the Board of Trade's traditional policy-making responsibilities for industrial efficiency and regional planning; on the other hand, executive authority over the instruments of economic and financial policy retained by the Chancellor of the Exchequer and the President of the Board of Trade.

The position of the Minister in charge of Economic Affairs between 1964 and 1969 was thus comparable to that of the Minister of Defence between 1946 and 1957. The arrangement could not be permanently satisfactory for two main reasons. First, since a co-ordinating minister has no authority over the actual instruments of government action he is not in a position to decide or to do anything; and since the essence of government is decision and action, this means that in the long run the co-ordinating minister will have comparatively little influence. The second reason is more specific to this particular case. For practical purposes the three fields of government activity called 'economic and financial affairs', 'industry' and 'regional development' are not necessarily related more closely to one another than they are to other fields of government activity. To construct the machinery of government on the assumptions that economic and financial affairs are largely about industry and that regional development is largely about economic and industrial matters begs a lot of important questions. It distorts the mechanism for making decisions and is bound to lead to trouble. For these reasons the eventual demise of the Department of Economic Affairs was inevitable right from the start. It was wound up and its economic functions were transferred to the Treasury in 1969.

The Treasury is organised in three main groups under the Chancellor of the Exchequer.

The Public Expenditure Group means just what it says. One of the government's tasks is to plan and control public expenditure, both in total and in its allocation between different public purposes. (The actual expenditure is incurred, of course, by all government departments, including especially the big spenders like the Ministry of Defence and the Department of Health and Social Security.)

The Finance Group covers public borrowing and the management of the national debt, the control of credit and the regulation of interest rates, and whatever other action may be thought necessary to regulate the country's mechanisms for making payments and carrying out financial transactions. (Executive action in this field, as in the field of overseas finance,* is mainly in the hands of the Bank of England.)

The National Economy Group covers three main functions; first, economic forecasting; second, the economic aspects of industrial policy and incomes policy; third, taxation. Executive responsibility for raising taxation rests with the Revenue Departments, in particular the Board of Inland Revenue and the Board of Customs and Excise.

*We shall not be discussing overseas finance, not because it is unimportant—the balance of payments has been a critical factor for many years —but because we are concentrating on the domestic functions of government. However, see Chapter 11.

Of the government agencies that take executive action in this field, the most important are the Bank of England, the Board of Inland Revenue, and the Board of Customs and Excise.

The Bank of England was nationalised in 1946. Under the Bank of England Act of that year the directors of the Bank ('the Court') are appointed by the Crown, and the Chancellor of the Exchequer has power to give instructions to the Governor. This recognises the fact that the Bank of England is, in effect, a public corporation and that it should be under the ultimate control of the elected government of the country. But the Bank does not come under the direct control of the official Treasury, on the ground that its staff should preserve, and be known to preserve, their professional integrity as bankers. The most important recent development has been the enquiry into the Bank's affairs by the Select Committee on Nationalised Industries in the 1969–1970 session of Parliament.[5] This enquiry subjected the activities of the Bank to very much the same sort of parliamentary scrutiny as has been developed for the nationalised industries generally. The Select Committee also recommended that 'it is a matter for consideration whether in those areas where the Bank operates as an arm of government its activities, along with those of the Treasury, should be subject to examination by a Select Committee on Economic Affairs'.[4]

The two revenue departments also report directly to the Chancellor. Although, unlike the staff of the Bank of England, their staff are civil servants, they are not part of the Treasury or in any way subject to Treasury officials. The Inland Revenue are responsible for direct taxation (including income tax, surtax, profits tax, corporation tax, capital gains tax, estate duty and stamp duties), while Customs and Excise are responsible for indirect taxation (including duties on drink and tobacco, purchase tax, and petrol tax). It is strange that so little has yet been done to bring taxation policies under keener public scrutiny and to bring the two revenue departments closer together. A clear distinction between direct and indirect taxation is becoming less easy to maintain as new forms of taxation develop, such as Selective Employment Tax and Value Added Tax. Efficient management of the national economy certainly demands a more coherent approach to taxation policy than seems to have been possible hitherto.

This is, in fact, only one of a number of criticisms that can be made of the present procedures for planning and controlling the three main flows of government money–expenditure, taxation and borrowing.

Another is that until recently, these flows have all been managed on a short-term basis; only in the last fifteen years, and even now only in the case of public expenditure, are plans made more than one year ahead. A further point of criticism is that the three flows have been managed as if they represent three quite separate activities. Only quite recently has it been realised that it is their combination that largely determines the economic activity of the community. Sir Richard Clarke made this point in relation to taxation and expenditure (though not explicitly to government borrowing) in his 1964 Stamp Memorial Lecture, as follows: 'One may look at taxation as the means by which the Government raise the money to pay for public expenditure. Or one may look at taxation as the instrument by which the Government restrain the growth of private consumption and private investment to the extent necessary to make room for the growth of public services on the one hand and exports on the other. But whatever one's approach, this is the strategic point to which the long term review of public expenditure and resources is bound to lead.'[7] None the less, the institutional arrangements, that is to say the organisation and the working procedures of the Treasury, the Bank of England and the Revenue Departments, are still based on the assumption that the three flows of government money can be managed separately.

The Treasury can also be criticised for knowing so little about the precise effect on the economy of changes in government spending, borrowing and taxation—in other words, about the effects of the government's financial planning and management on the allocation and use of real resources. However, this reflects the backwardness of our economic understanding generally. The present state of the art can be judged from the current argument between those economists who claim that monetary policy (i.e. government borrowing) is all that really matters and those who claim, on the contrary, that fiscal policy (i.e. government spending and taxation) is all that really matters. This is as if the medical profession were split between one school of doctors believing that health depends entirely on eating and another believing that, on the contrary, it depends entirely on breathing. No wonder the patient suffers!

Now that the Treasury are unequivocally responsible for planning and controlling the three main flows of government money in the best interest of the long-term economic well-being of the country, their ability (and that of the executive agencies they supervise) to develop the present rather primitive state of the art of national economic and financial management will undoubtedly come under keen scrutiny. And rightly so. Some idea of what this is likely to mean can be got from looking at developments over the last fifteen years in the procedures for controlling public expenditure. These developments, besides being of interest for their own sake, suggest how the present procedures for controlling taxation and government borrowing can also be improved.

PUBLIC EXPENDITURE

Historically, as we have seen, it was Parliament's job on behalf of the people to regulate the amount of money raised by the Crown in taxation and spent by the Crown on its own purposes. The system of financial control which evolved was designed to enable Parliament to prevent abuses; to prevent the Crown taking too much of the people's money; to prevent the Crown spending this money on undesirable objects; and to prevent malpractice, speculation and corruption by servants of the Crown. The system was not designed to give Parliament powers of constructive management; the power to decide how much of the people's money it would be best to spend on public purposes; or the power to ensure that, having been allocated, it was spent to best effect by the servants of the Crown. Traditionally, Parliament did not think of itself as representing the interest of the share-holders in the national business, but as representing the interest of the subject people against the Crown. It was not concerned with the efficient management of public affairs on behalf of the people, but with protecting the people against the Crown. The Gladstonian reforms of the late nineteenth century systematised, but did not basically alter, Parliament's traditional procedures in this sphere.

The system of financial control applied by the Treasury to satisfy Parliament had a profound effect on the organisation and methods of work of government.

First, it led to a very simple method of cash accounting. The government was given specific sums of money to spend on specific items in specific years. The accounts were designed to show that these sums had been spent faithfully on the items for which Parliament voted them. They were not designed to show that the money had been spent usefully and productively.

Second, it led to the estimates and the accounts being constructed so as to show what the money was being spent on (things like staff salaries as opposed to travelling expenses), rather than what it was being spent for (things like the Singapore military base as opposed to bases in Europe, or primary education as opposed to secondary education).

Third, it led to expenditure being authorised only one year ahead, in accordance with the parliamentary annual budget and annual estimates procedures.

Fourth, it led to piecemeal decisions on expenditure. As the Plowden Committee on Control of Public Expenditure said in 1961:

> In the traditional system in this country, as it developed in the nineteenth century and has continued through the life-time of successive Governments to the present day, the tendency is for expenditure decisions to be taken piecemeal. The individual departmental Minister asks the Chancellor of the Exchequer for the money he needs for a new proposal of policy. If the Chancellor is content, and the new proposal is agreed by the Cabinet, the Minister can then proceed. If, on the other hand, the Chancellor says 'No', the Minister may appeal to the Cabinet. Discussion among Ministers is likely to centre on the merits of the particular proposal, in relation at most to a general background of the financial situation rather than upon the competing claims on the present and future resources of the country which are represented by the aggregate of the spending policies of the Government. There are exceptions to this, notably in the handling of public investment; and at the same time of the year when the Estimates are being examined, the financial background is usually brought out more sharply than at other times. But in general over the whole of public expenditure throughout the year the system is one of piecemeal decisions.[8]

As Burke might have put it, this system of financial control did not enable the Chancellor of the Exchequer to bring his affairs into compass.

Fifth, the system of Treasury control imposed a sharp division between managerial responsibility and financial responsibility. Ministers were supposed to be responsible for carrying out the functions allocated to them, but as Parliament's watch-dog the Treasury was responsible for authorising the necessary money. Within ministries the professional staff were mainly responsible for the professional work of the department, such as building roads or enforcing safety regulations in factories, but financial responsibility rested with a separate cadre of administrators acting as the watch-dogs of the Treasury. There could be very little delegation of financial responsibility to the person actually in charge of, say, the employment exchanges or the Navy dockyards. There always had to be a financial watch-dog at the manager's elbow ready to bark at him, or even occasionally to bite him if need arose. Under these arrangements no-one could ever be fully responsible for the success of any government activity.

In all these ways the arrangements for financial decision-making and control exercised on behalf of Parliament by the Treasury and the Comptroller and Auditor-General were at variance with the modern approach to financial planning and management. The modern approach is based on three very simple principles which apply respectively to the future, the present and the past.

> You need to be able to decide what things you are going to do, and how much each of them is going to cost.

> You need to put someone in charge of each of these tasks, and give him a budget for it.

> You need a method for assessing how well he has carried out his task.

In order to understand the changes that are now taking place in the procedures for controlling public expenditure we must consider briefly how these principles can be applied in practice. In order to achieve the first principle it is necessary to adopt a procedure of the kind variously described by such terms as 'programme budgeting', 'output budgeting', 'objective estimating', or 'functional costing'. One should not be misled by these jargon phrases into supposing that anything very mysterious is involved. They simply mean that expenditure is divided up according to the purposes for which it is required as opposed to the items on which it is to be spent. In the hypothetical example at Table 1, we would use the first set of figures as the basis for decisions about future expenditure, rather than the second. In this way it is possible to discuss priorities intelligently and to allocate the total funds available accordingly. (This is the context in which cost/benefit studies have a part to play, by helping to elucidate the benefits to be expected from various alternative choices, each of which may be expected to incur a certain cost.)

FINANCIAL AND ECONOMIC AFFAIRS

Table 1
(Figures are hypothetical)

1. Education Expenditure by Outputs

	£m
Primary Education	100
Secondary Education	175
Further Education	30
Higher Education	195
Total	500

2. Education Expenditure by Inputs

Staff	375
Buildings	75
Equipment	50
Total	500

3. Education Expenditure by Outputs and Inputs

	Primary	Secondary	Further	Higher	Total
Staff	82	143	20	130	375
Buildings	8	20	7	40	75
Equipment	10	12	3	25	50
Total	100	175	30	195	500

In order to achieve the second of the three principles—that someone should be in charge of each sphere of government activity who can be called to account for his performance—it is necessary to adopt a procedure of the kind described in the jargon of the experts as 'accountable management' or 'management by objectives'. This means that the task must be defined: what precisely is the job that the individual concerned is required to do? It also means that there must be some way of measuring his performance: how well has he done it? In the private sector, accountable management operates mainly by the yardstick of profitability. The person responsible for a 'profit centre' (corresponding to a task) can be given a defined budget and profit target, and his performance can be judged by his success or failure in achieving this target. In the public sector it is more difficult to define the target and to find yardsticks to judge success or failure. But the attempt can usefully be made, as we shall see.

Of course, accountable management implies a good deal of delegated responsibility or decentralisation. You cannot be held accountable for the way you carry out a task if your instructions pre-determine in detail

117

how you must do it. In particular, you need some freedom to decide for yourself, within the budget you have been given, precisely what resources you can best use and how you can best deploy them to achieve your task. Thus, to go back to Table 1, accountable management would again be based on the first section of the Table rather than the second or the third. This means that as accountable management is introduced more widely in government it will inevitably involve much badly needed clarification and devolution of responsibilities.

Turning now to methods of assessing how well a task has been performed we find another set of jargon phrases such as 'performance measurement', 'administrative productivity', 'efficiency audits', and 'management ratios'. These terms refer to methods of assessing administrative or managerial performance in situations where the simple yardstick of profitability is either inapplicable or insufficient. They imply the development of quantitative indicators relating to various kinds of costs, and to the various kinds of output that may be appropriate in each particular case. These indicators can then be used as a basis for looking at trends between one year and another, and at comparisons between one organisation and another. An organisation's performance in a certain respect can be compared against its performance the previous year, against the performance of a comparable organisation in the same year, or against a standard or average performance.

In the private sector, management ratios are now widely used as indicators of performance to supplement the simple profit and loss account and balance sheet. The Centre for Inter-firm Comparison, for example, has developed management ratios as a basis for comparing the performance of one firm against other comparable firms, and many firms use similar ratios to assess current performance against that in previous years. In the public sector it is less easy to develop performance indicators of this kind, because often no straightforward quantitative measurement of output can be made; in other words there can be no figures directly comparable to the value of sales or profits in the private sector. The Treasury has begun to develop performance indicators,[9] but the most ambitious attempt in the field so far has probably been a study by the US Bureau of the Budget, published in 1964 under the title 'Measuring Productivity in Federal Government Organisation'. Five organisations were involved: the Post Office; the Treasury's Disbursement Division, which produces bills and savings bonds on behalf of other government organisations; the Insurance Department of the Veterans

Administration–a life insurance organisation; the Systems Maintenance Service of the Federal Aviation Agency; and the Bureau of Land Management in the Department of the Interior. In every case except the last it proved possible to develop meaningful measures of productivity.

Perhaps this all seems a little technical. But the point is that, now we live in a self-governing society, we need to know whether our government is thinking out priorities properly, managing its work effectively, and accounting properly for the results. So we have to insist on the government adopting this kind of approach to public expenditure. Indeed, this approach, must not only be used by the Executive for its own purposes; it must be used as the basis for scrutiny by Parliament. Certain things follow as regards government organisation and procedures.

Financial control that focuses on objectives and results is applicable at each level. At the top it is necessary to divide the whole span of government activity into, say, a dozen broad categories of work such as Defence, External Affairs[10] and so on. That makes it possible to consider whether the balance of expenditure between these broadly defined spheres of activity correctly reflects the priorities we give them and whether we are getting good value for money in each of them. Then at the next level down, it is necessary to subdivide each of these broad categories into a further set of, say, a dozen sub-categories. For example, Defence will be divided into such sub-categories as Nuclear Strategic Forces, European Theatre Ground Forces, General Purpose Combat Forces, and so on.[11] That in turn makes it possible to consider whether we have got the priorities right within the total Defence effort. And so on down the line. At each level of this hierarchy we structure the work in such a way as to enable us to plan, to manage and to account, with an eye to what we are aiming to achieve.

There is also the point that, whereas a hundred years ago it was not necessary to plan most government activity more than a year ahead, it has now become necessary to plan it many years ahead. Most government decisions on expenditure of any importance today involve commitments stretching far into the future. The old system of annual budgeting one year ahead is not enough. This is why, since the late 1950s, the Ministry of Defence has prepared 'functional costings' for forward planning and why the Treasury has found it necessary to set up the Public Expenditure Survey Committee, affectionately known as PESC. As the Plowden Report said, 'regular surveys should be made of public expenditure as a whole, over a period of years ahead, and in relation to prospective resources; decisions involving substantial future expenditure should be taken in the light of these surveys'.[12]

Finally, the new approach to financial control requires us to think about planning for the future, managing present activities, and accounting for past achievements as parts of a single process. We cannot plan for the future without considering how the plans are to be carried out when the time comes; we cannot usefully account for past achievements without regard to the plans we were trying to carry out; we cannot judge the achievements of those responsible for managing government activities if we cannot compare the out-turn shown in their accounts with the targets shown in their budgets. As time's ever-rolling stream turns expenditure projections (for the future) into budgets (for the present) and budgets into accounts (for the past), we must monitor progress. We must use feedback from the present and the past to help us to plan for the future. We need a fully integrated circle of control as shown in Figure 2.

As we have seen, this new approach to financial control is inconsistent with the traditional system in many ways. It concentrates on outputs instead of inputs; it looks several years, not just one year, ahead; it unifies and delegates responsibility instead of dividing it and centralising it. Because it is so much at variance with the existing system, anomalies arise as it comes to be applied piecemeal and partially. For instance, the Treasury has felt able from time to time to delegate a little more financial authority to departments than they had before; but because this runs against the grain of the existing system it cannot be taken very far; until delegation becomes part and parcel of a new system of control, delegated authority will tend to be snatched back and over-ruled by the Treasury in times of financial crisis. Again, we find that when departments engaging in trading activities were required to produce trading accounts of the normal commercial type, or when departments began to introduce costing for management purposes, these were regarded as totally separate activities – carried out by different staffs and using different sets of figures – from the normal government estimates and accounts.

The same is true of the Ministry of Defence's forward projections of expenditure and of the PESC projections. The defence functional costings, originally prepared for forward planning during the 1950s and subsequently developed on lines similar to Mr Macnamara's Planning,

Programming and Budgeting System (PPBS) for the United States
Pentagon, had very little connection with the expenditure figures used
for practical administration and parliamentary accounting by the
Ministry of Defence. Different staff were responsible for them, and the
figures were used for planning purposes only. They could not, and still

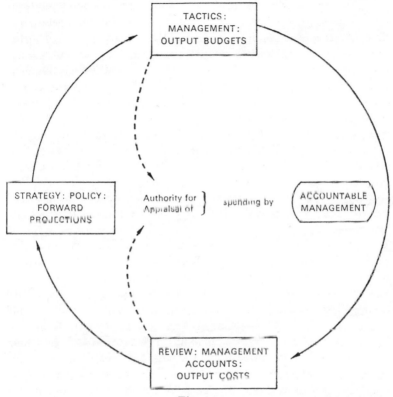

Figure 2

cannot, be used to see how the plans work out in practice. Similarly
with the Treasury's PESC surveys. Partly because the surveys were
originally regarded as providing only background material for forward
planning rather than an actual basis for decisions, and partly because it
was not expected that any government would feel able to place these
surveys before Parliament and the public, they were developed as a
separate exercise from the annual estimating, budgeting and accounting
procedures. In other words, there was no way of seeing what happened

when the time came for the projected figures to turn into actual ones. Indeed, it has been unkindly said of the Treasury economists and planners that they were only interested in drawing up projections and plans and not at all interested in the actual results of those projections and plans when the time came for them to be put into practice. However that may be, when in 1969 the forward survey of public expenditure was eventually published in a White Paper, it became apparent that the categories of expenditure used could not easily be related to the form in which the annual estimates and accounts of government expenditure are submitted to Parliament for approval and scrutiny. The situation bore an uncanny resemblance to that which the Commissioners of Public Accounts noted towards the end of the eighteenth century: 'Most of the Accounts are made up Twice; first in common Figures, that they may be added together; and then turned into Latin, and the same entered into Exchequer figures.' As the Commissioners then remarked, 'It does not seem reasonable that (these) Proceedings are to remain in Mystery and Obscurity. Simplicity, Uniformity, and Perspicuity, are Qualities of Excellence in every Account, both Public and Private; and Accounts of Public Money, as they concern all, should be intelligible to all.'[13]

Much useful progress has, in fact, been made in improving the government's procedures for controlling expenditure over the last ten or fifteen years. Further progress will no doubt stem from the new Conservative Government's 'programme analysis and review' (PAR) procedures. But, as usual, the advances have been made unsystematically and piecemeal, not as elements in any new philosophy of government. New methods of financial planning, management and accounting have been grafted on to traditional methods based on conflicting principles. The time has now come to consolidate these advances into an integrated system of planning, management and review—forward projections, annual estimates, and accounts—a new circle of control, orientated towards objectives and results. In a self-governing country the government should know, and Parliament and the public should be told, how the government's present dispositions (as reflected in annual expenditure estimates) and past achievements (as reflected in annual accounts of past expenditure) are related to the strategy originally put forward as expenditure plans. Furthermore, the systematic introduction of this new approach to expenditure control will clarify the responsibilities of officials and ministers alike. As we shall see in the next chapter, this will provide the financial element in a new approach to the organisation and work of government as a whole.

TAXATION AND GOVERNMENT BORROWING

So much for recent developments in expenditure control. What lessons do they have for taxation and government borrowing?

The fact is that where taxation and borrowing are concerned, the state of the art in the Treasury stands today much as it stood fifteen years ago in relation to public expenditure–in a rather primitive condition. A list of various central government taxes in force in 1970 is at Table 2. It is true that radical reforms were announced in the 1971 Budget, but–though important–they leave the main point unaffected.

Table 2. Various taxes (June 1970)

Taxes on Income
Income Tax
Surtax
(Post-War Credits)   } Inland Revenue
(Tax Reserve Certificates)
(National Insurance Contributions)   Department of Health and
    Social Security

Company Taxation
Corporation Tax
(Initial Allowances)   } Inland Revenue
(Annual Writing Down Allowances)
(Investment Grants)   Ministry of Technology

Taxes on Capital
Capital Gains Tax
Tax on Short Term Gains   } Inland Revenue
Death Duties

Taxes on Expenditure
Customs Duties on Imports
Excise Duties on Home Products
Purchase Tax   } Customs and Excise
Betting and Gaming Tax
Selective Employment Tax   Department of Health and
    Social Security
(Repayments)   Department of Employment
    and Productivity
Stamp Duties   Inland Revenue
Motor Vehicle Duties   Ministry of Transport
Various Licences   Post Office
    Customs and Excise

There is no effective system for building all these different taxes into a deliberately constructed tax programme for a given year, and for presenting alternative possibilities to ministers for decision and to Parliament and the public for debate and discussion. Still less is there any effective system for projecting a tax programme of this kind forward over a period of years. The House of Commons Estimates Committee said of public expenditure in 1958, 'it is really an abuse of language to speak of a "system" of Treasury control, if by the word "system" is meant methods and practices that have at one time or another been deliberately planned and instituted. What is called "Treasury control" is better described as a complex of administrative practice that has grown up like a tree over the centuries, natural rather than planned, empiric rather than theoretical. The question here at issue is whether a "system", many features of which emerged in times when public expenditure played a relatively small part in the national economy, is appropriate to the middle of the twentieth century.'[14] The same is true of taxation today, and much the same could be said of the government's borrowing programme.

The next few years will undoubtedly see great changes in the Treasury, the Revenue Departments and the Bank of England. They will have to construct, as the Public Expenditure Survey Committee originally did, comprehensive projections of taxation and government borrowing some years ahead as *background* to the shorter-term annual decisions. Then they will find–lo and behold!–that these projections indicate the need for and provide the basis for longer-term decisions about priorities. They will then find, as in the case of public expenditure, that a feedback system is necessary–a circle of control–so that it is possible to see how the taxation and borrowing projections actually turn out, as the future turns into the present and the present into the past. And eventually, before we are all dead, God willing, they will be able to combine these separate systems for planning, managing and reviewing expenditure, taxation and borrowing into a unified system for controlling them in combination. Only then shall we be able to talk realistically about steering the economy in the desired direction.

INCOMES POLICY

The vexed question of a prices and incomes policy throws a good deal of light on the methodology of government. Bertrand Russell once said that 'every proposition which we can understand must be composed wholly of constituents with which we are acquainted'. This is not unlike Professor Ayer's verifiability principle, according to which a statement is meaningful only if one knows what observations would lead one to accept it as true or reject it as false. Whatever the philosophical validity of these principles, they certainly have their counterpart in the methodology of government: a policy is meaningful only if we have a clear and precise idea of the measures that would be necessary to carry it out.

The fact that politicians have had no precise idea of the measures involved in carrying out a prices and incomes policy largely explains why responsibility for it has been shunted from the Treasury, to the Department of Economic Affairs, to the Department of Employment and Productivity, and back again to the Treasury, all in the space of ten years. It also explains the failure, at least so far, to achieve anything resembling a long-term solution to the problem, and to halt the prices and incomes spiral except temporarily during a 'freeze'. And, of course a freeze on incomes could never amount to an incomes policy. A freeze can be no more than a short-term emergency measure in a critical economic situation.

The prices and incomes problem arises from the simple fact that the *laisser-faire* approach is no longer viable, but that so far we have failed to find an effective substitute. Prices and incomes cannot now be left to find their own levels in the market place; the result is chaos. On the other hand it is not feasible to decide prices and incomes by detailed government intervention in every case. A self-governing community has to evolve institutions and measures which will contain the rise in total incomes to the rising level of goods and services produced and which will at the same time provide for relative changes in prices and incomes as needed to stimulate efficiency, to enable those who cannot provide for themselves to lead a decent life, and to reflect fairly differences in the value of the work done by different members of the community. On this last point, if money is to be an effective calculus of social value, people's incomes should reflect—among other things—the value that society places on their work. One only has to compare the pay of people doing different jobs to realise how far this is from being the case today—say, occupational therapists with shorthand typists, teachers with engineering workers, nurses with dockers, or policemen with stockbrokers. As a country our most important resource—from every point of view—is people. Apart from any other consideration we ought to price it in accordance with our priorities.

Clearly an incomes and prices policy involves a wide variety of measures. No one department of government can be responsible for them all, even in a co-ordinating role.

The Treasury is required to take the necessary action to keep the availability of national purchasing power (i.e. money) from rising above the level of the gross national product. This it must do by planning and regulating the national financial flows outlined in Figure 1 on page 107. What the Treasury is also required to do–and this will be a new departure–is to compile a national incomes budget. This will be a comprehensive statement, showing how total national income (i.e. the total cake) is divided among different categories of people (nurses, dockers, teachers, policemen, stockbrokers, and so on) and how many of us fall into each of these categories. This would begin to show us how the national cake really is divided up. It would provide a basis for us to debate how it might be more fairly divided, and divided in such a way as would make for greater economic efficiency. The argument for a regularly published national incomes budget is the same as for any other budget. It enables one to 'bring one's affairs into compass'. Nelson, writing to the Secretary of the Treasury in 1787 before proper budgetary procedures had been adopted in government, complained about the fraudulent behaviour of victualling contractors to the Navy in the West Indies and said, 'The only emulation I can perceive is, who could cheat the most.'[15] Today the division of the national income would take place more fairly and efficiently if the whole picture was more clearly set out.

The Treasury, then, must be responsible for seeing that the economic and monetary framework is such that total national money income does not rise faster than total real income, and also for compiling a comprehensive picture of the way in which the total national money income is divided among different categories of people. That sets the essential scene within which specific procedures and mechanisms can operate for effecting relative changes in incomes and relative changes in prices.

In a pure market economy it would be possible for the government merely to hold the ring and let competition determine whatever changes in incomes and prices were necessary. But we do not have and never again will have a pure market economy. The strength of large firms and the monopoly position of most nationalised industries and of all the public services; the strength of organised employees; and the existence of social security and social welfare services–these conditions will always be with us, and between them they effectively neutralise the discipline of the market so far as the economy as a whole is concerned.

From this it follows that we have to ensure in respect of each sector of the economy either that the market mechanism is working effectively within that sector or that some other discipline is imposed on it. In every case openness and effective scrutiny appear to be prerequisite.

Take prices first. In the monopoly situation of the nationalised industries effective scrutiny is needed to demonstrate that prices are not unjustifiably high; in the government sector comparable scrutiny is needed to demonstrate that operations are efficient and that costs are being kept down; and in the private sector large companies similarly must publish enough information about their activities for the general public (as well as shareholders and employees) to be satisfied of their efficiency. In the first case we have the system of parliamentary scrutiny by the Nationalised Industries Committee described in Chapter 4; for the Civil Service we shall have to make comparable arrangements for accountable management and parliamentary scrutiny, in the way suggested in Chapter 9; for companies in the private sector we must rely on strengthening the regulatory framework for industry and commerce on the lines suggested in Chapter 4. The efficacy of these arrangements should be the responsibility of a Ministry for Industrial Infrastructure, a Prime Minister's Office, and the Department of Trade and Industry respectively.

Similarly, on the incomes and employment side, where mercifully the rise of trade unionism has greatly softened the rigours of a free 'labour market', we have to develop effective ways of seeing that fair and economically efficient dealings take place between employers and employees. Whether we do this by developing a legal framework to regulate relations between employers and employees, as in the new industrial relations legislation, or whether there is some other way of focussing the spotlight of scrutiny on them, backed by the ultimate sanction of public opinion, is really a secondary question. What we have to do is to make employers and employees publicly accountable for the way they deal with one another. This is a matter that falls fairly and squarely in the field of employment and manpower, and will have to be the responsibility of the Department of Manpower and Employment that will emerge eventually as the modern equivalent to the old Ministry of Labour.

Finally, we come to those who for one reason or another—old age, sickness, or incompetence–cannot provide themselves with an adequate income by their own unaided efforts. The community must provide them with an income, related both to their own needs and to the incomes earned by other members of society. Social security is an important element in an incomes policy. Social benefits and taxation have to be considered as complementary instruments for regulating incomes, within the total income budget of the nation. It will be for the Treasury as the department in charge of financial policy to secure the co-operation between the Inland Revenue and the Department of Health and Social Security in developing a workable system of 'negative income tax' on the lines described briefly in Chapter 5.

There is one last point to be made about economic and financial policy. Money is one of our main mechanisms of social choice. The efficiency of the country's financial system, in the public and the private sector together, determines the efficiency of this mechanism for allocating resources one way or another, for choosing one priority or another. As suggested earlier in this chapter, there is scope for considerable reform in the government's methods of handling expenditure, revenue and borrowing. There is also undoubted scope for reforming its present methods of regulating the activities of the banks and other financial institutions in the private sector, so that these institutions can compete more freely with one another and so improve the efficiency of the country's financial system as a mechanism of choice, both for the individual citizen and for society as a whole.

SUMMARY

In this chapter we have seen how the domestic financial control function of nineteenth-century government has developed into the job of steering the economy of our twentieth-century industrial country. Slowly, in a gradual series of small steps, the financial function of government has disengaged from the function of controlling government personnel. Arrangements have developed slowly and piecemeal for managing government expenditure in a more positive way–forward planning, management costing and delegation of financial responsibility. Arrangements have grown up zigzag for dealing with the country's economic problems.

This process of change has been marked by inevitable conflicts and contradictions: conflicts of organisations when, for example, a new Department of Economic Affairs was set up to handle the problems in a new way, alongside the Treasury which was still expected to handle them in an old way; and conflicts of procedures, when new methods of financial planning and management were introduced alongside the old ones based on opposing purposes and principles.

However, now at last the unified function of national economic management and government financial control is the undivided responsibility of one minister, the Chancellor of the Exchequer, and one department, the Treasury. Hitherto, stemming naturally from the Gladstonian system of financial control laid down by Parliament, the Treasury has exercised its functions in the manner of the amateur back-seat driver. Its main job has been to intervene in the work of departments and tell them not to do it, or how to do it better. But the Treasury now has a professional job of its own to do. It will need to make a sustained effort to develop effective, systematic procedures for planning and controlling the flows of public money—expenditure, taxation and borrowing—in pursuance of long-term as well as short-term national economic objectives. It will be up to Parliament and the public to scrutinise very keenly how the Treasury shapes up to this new responsibility.

NOTES ON CHAPTER 7

General

Samuel Brittan's *Steering the Economy* (Secker & Warburg, 1969) and its predecessor *The Treasury Under the Tories, 1951–1964* (Penguin Books, 1964) provide an excellent account of the development of economic policy and the government organisation for handling it over the last twenty years.

Peter Jay, the Economics Editor of *The Times*, has been a protagonist of financial reform in government for a number of years. His ideas are always stimulating, whether in writing or conversation. He, like Sam Brittan, has played a major part in generating the pressure which has now gathered behind the movement for financial reform in Whitehall and Westminster.

Two distinguished Treasury officials, Sir Richard Clarke and Sir William Armstrong, have pronounced on important problems in this field in Stamp Memorial Lectures, published by the University of London, the Athlone Press. Sir Richard Clarke's subject in 1964 was *The Management of the Public Sector of the National Economy*, Sir William Armstrong's in 1968 was *Some Practical Problems in Demand Management*.

A number of recent parliamentary reports are of particular interest. These include the Select Committee on Procedure's important report on Scrutiny of Public Expenditure and Administration published in September 1969 and the reports of the same Committee's enquiry published in May 1970 and February 1971 on Scrutiny of Taxation. It is perhaps natural that I should refer the reader to my own memoranda of evidence submitted to the Procedure Committee in the course of these enquiries. The report of the Select Committee on Nationalised Industries published on 5th May 1970 contains much interesting and relevant information about the Bank of England.

Of the enormous literature on economic and financial policy-making, the only other publications I shall mention are *The Treasury* (George Allen & Unwin) by Lord Bridges, the former head of the Treasury; and *The Politics and Economics of Public Spending* (Brookings Institution, 1968) by Charles L. Schultze, the former head of President Johnson's Bureau of the Budget. They are two very different books but both are well worth reading.

Note 1. *Parliamentary History (1780)*, vol. 21, page 29.

Note 2. Quoted in Epitome, H. C. 154 of 1937–38, page 190.

Note 3. Treasury minute published as Cmnd. 2440/1925, quoted by Willson in *Organisation of British Central Government*.

Note 4. An internal Treasury Organisation Committee prepared the proposals on which the 1962 reorganisation was based. Its Chairman was Sir Norman Brook; one of the main contributors was Sir William Armstrong (subsequently head of the Treasury and now head of the Civil Service); the secretaries of the Committee were Mr Ian Bancroft and myself.

Note 5. *First Report from the Select Committee on Nationalised Industries, Session 1969–70*. HMSO, 1970.

Note 6. *Op. cit.*, paragraph 281.

Note 7. *The Management of the Public Sector of the National Economy*, University of London, the Athlone Press, 1964.

Note 8. *Control of Public Expenditure*, Report by the Plowden Committee; Cmnd. 1432: HMSO, 1961, paragraph 8.

Note 9. See, for example, *A Selection of Unit Costs in Public Expenditure*, published by HMSO for the Management Accounting Unit of the Treasury.

Note 10. The Public Expenditure White Paper, now published annually, goes some way in this direction but the categories of expenditure now used are not particularly helpful.

Note 11. See, for example, Annex D of the *Statement on Defence Estimates, 1970*; HMSO: Cmnd. 4290.

Note 12. *Op. cit.*, paragraph 12.

Note 13. *8th Report from the Commissioners of Public Accounts*, vol. ii, pages 37 and 38.

Note 14. *Report of the Select Committee on Estimates, Session 1957–58*, paragraph 94.

Note 15. *The Life and Services of Horatio Nelson*, vol. i, page 96; J. S. Clarke and John McArthur. Quoted by E. W. Cohen in *The Growth of the British Civil Service*, page 23; George Allen & Unwin, 1941.

8

The Central Direction of Government and the Management of the Civil Service

As the scale and complexity of government activities have grown, new arrangements for co-ordinating and managing them have become necessary. This chapter shows how the Cabinet Office, the Treasury and now the Civil Service Department have evolved step by step to meet this need. It suggests that their rationalisation as a fully fledged Prime Minister's Office is now desirable and indeed inevitable. It suggests also that the central government's responsibilities for civil service personnel and more generally for public service personnel, should not fall to the Prime Minister's Office, but should be merged with the government's responsibilities for national employment and manpower questions in a single Ministry of Employment and Manpower.

THE CABINET

Parliament gives powers by statute to individual ministers and individual ministers are formally responsible for the actions of the departments of government under their control. The Cabinet was originally an informal body that grew up as ministers began to meet regularly to discuss their policies and take collective decisions about them. In due course the convention was established that every member of a government should be prepared to defend the actions of his colleagues. The British Cabinet system thus came to embody the twin constitutional doctrines of the individual responsibility of each minister and the collective responsibility of the Cabinet as a whole. In recent years both these doctrines have come under serious strain. Many people would now regard them as constitutional myths or fictions. Mr Crossman, for example, has said that 'with the coming of Prime Ministerial government, the Cabinet in obedience to the law that Bagehot discovered, joins the other dignified elements in the Constitution'.[1]

131

So long as the business of government remained comparatively simple and the number of ministers remained comparatively small, the Cabinet could continue to work informally and the arrangements could continue to be handled by the Prime Minister's private secretary at 10 Downing Street. There are signs that the strain began to tell towards the end of the nineteenth century. There were occasions on which lack of a written record led to confusion. In 1882 one Minister's private secretary wrote to the Prime Minister's private secretary:

> My dear Eddy,
>   Harcourt and Chamberlain have both been here this morning and at my chief about yesterday's Cabinet proceedings. They cannot agree about what occurred. There must have been some decision as Bright's resignation shows. My chief has told me to ask you what the devil was decided for he be damned if he knows. Will you ask Mr. G. in more conventional and less pungent terms.[2]

As early as 1841 there is a nice story of Lord Melbourne as Prime Minister leaning over the banisters at 10 Downing Street and shouting to his Cabinet colleagues as they left a meeting on the Corn Laws: 'Stop a bit. What did we decide? Is it to lower the price of bread, or isn't it? It doesn't matter which, but we must all say the same thing.'[3]

However, it was the expansion of government work resulting from the social reforms of the 1906 Liberal Government and the first Lloyd George Insurance Act in 1911, followed by the vast increase in government activity in the first world war, that broke the back of the informal Cabinet system. In 1916 the Secretariat of the Committee of Imperial Defence, under Maurice Hankey, 'the little Colonel of Marines', was transformed into the Cabinet Secretariat. Cabinet business submitted to the discipline of written agenda, memoranda and minutes.

The development of the Cabinet system since 1916 reflects the increase in the number of ministers and ministries and the need for closer and closer co-ordination between them. The size of the Cabinet itself has steadily grown. (We are talking here about peace-time Cabinets; special war-time arrangements have been made.) The peak may have been reached with twenty-three members under the Wilson Labour Government and the Conservative Government of the early 1960s. The number of ministers in charge of departments who have to be left out of the Cabinet has also grown. In theory, the doctrine of collective responsibility is maintained by circulating Cabinet documents to all ministers in charge of departments and by appointing them to serve on Cabinet Committees dealing with their work.

The number of these Committees has grown very rapidly. It is not possible to be at all precise about them since the fiction is still preserved that they are merely an internal arrangement made by the informal group of ministers called the Cabinet, and they are therefore kept confidential. Usually a senior minister, often one of those without a department of his own, takes the chair of these committees. Sometimes, exceptionally, he may be given responsibility publicly for this. Sometimes he may be given a small ministry to help him; as we have seen in earlier chapters, Defence and Economic Affairs have been examples. Sometimes he may be an 'overlord', like the pre-war Minister for Co-ordination of Defence, Lords Woolton and Leathers in 1951, or Mr Anthony Crosland in 1969. In no case has such an arrangement been a success. Organisational logic and human psychology combine to ensure that there can be no satisfactory half-way house between the individual responsibility of a minister for the activities of his department and the collective responsibility of the Cabinet for the activities of the government as a whole.

Also reflecting the growing task of central co-ordination, the staff of the Cabinet Office now exceeds the 500 mark. This figure includes over 100 members of the secretariat and about 150 staff in the Central Statistical Office. It has also included a number of co-ordinating staffs, such as the staff of the Secretary of State for Social Services and the staff of the government's Chief Scientific Adviser. In the past there have been occasions when co-ordinating staffs of this kind have hived off from the Cabinet Office to become the nucleus of another ministry. Perhaps this may happen again. But, even making allowances for this, the Cabinet Office has now grown into a sizeable little department in its own right, under the ministerial control of the Prime Minister. It is misleading to think of it today as a small secretariat, whose status is in some way less formal than the rest of the machinery of central government, and whose activities and efficiency need be of no concern to Parliament and the public.

CIVIL SERVICE MANAGEMENT

The growing need to co-ordinate the activities of government under the Cabinet has been paralleled by a growing need for more effective management of the Civil Service. As we shall see, central responsibility for Civil Service questions was traditionally regarded as an element of financial control. It disentangled itself only slowly as a separate function in its own right, and it is really only in the last fifteen years that it has begun to gravitate towards the closely related Prime Ministerial function of Cabinet co-ordination.

The demand which arose during the late eighteenth century for reforms in the organisation and staffing of government departments stemmed primarily from the desire to save money, as originally voiced by Burke in the context of his 'Economical Reforms'. Thus it was the Treasury that took the lead in Civil Service questions and took responsibility for supervising the implementation of the famous Northcote–Trevelyan Report. Even so, as late as the first world war the various ministries and departments still retained a very large measure of autonomy. So much so that it is unrealistic to think of a unified Civil Service at all at that time.

Between 1914 and 1939 all this began to change, largely at the instance of Sir Warren Fisher, who was Permanent Secretary to the Treasury for twenty years from 1919 to 1938. Immediately after the first world war the standard three-tier administrative/executive/clerical staffing structure was introduced throughout the Service. The Permanent Secretary to the Treasury was appointed Head of the Civil Service, and became the formal channel of advice to the Prime Minister on all senior civil service appointments. The rise of Service-wide staff associations led to closer Treasury co-ordination of pay and conditions of service. These growing responsibilities for Civil Service pay and management were marked by an internal Treasury reorganisation in 1919, when for the first time a group of separate 'establishments' divisions came into existence alongside the divisions responsible for controlling expenditure.

During and after the second world war the trend towards a unified Civil Service continued, and the Treasury's responsibilities expanded into all aspects of personnel management, including Training and O and M (Organisation and Methods). Both these last tended to be considered rather tedious activities, to be carried out at a very routine level and to be practised mainly by the lower orders (i.e. the executive and clerical classes) on one another. Indeed the traditional Treasury administrators tended to regard any 'establishments' posting as a form of banishment from proper Treasury work.

THE MANAGEMENT OF THE CIVIL SERVICE

Nevertheless, the continually growing importance of the Treasury's task of Civil Service management and its recognition as a separate function from financial control led to further reorganisation in the 1950s and 1960s. In 1956 two joint Permanent Secretaries were appointed, one—Sir Roger Makins, now Lord Sherfield—to take charge of economic and financial affairs, and the other—Sir Norman Brook, who was already Secretary of the Cabinet—to be Head of the Civil Service and to take charge of Civil Service management. Then in 1962 the Treasury was reorganised as we have seen in Chapter 7, into two quite separate sides—one to deal with economic and financial affairs, the other to manage the Civil Service. Between 1956 and 1962 Sir Norman Brook, as Head of the Civil Service and Secretary of the Cabinet, was in effect the Prime Minister's Permanent Secretary even though he was responsible for functions being carried out in two separate departments, the Cabinet Office and the Treasury. Since 1962 the Head of the Civil Service and the Secretary of the Cabinet have been two separate people, now Sir William Armstrong and Sir Burke Trend, but that should be regarded only as a temporary regression. The need for the Prime Minister to have a single senior official and a single Prime Minister's Office, fully responsible for supporting him across the whole range of his work, cannot be ignored much longer.

ORGANISATION OF GOVERNMENT

Oddly enough, it is the Treasury (now the Civil Service Department) rather than the Cabinet Office that has been responsible for advising the Prime Minister on how the government should be organised—'machinery of government' to use the civil servants' term of art. This arrangement reflected the traditional notion that organisational questions were either a form of O and M and thus within the Treasury's sphere, or that they concerned the personal distribution of tasks between the members of the informal Cabinet group and were best decided informally without official help.

The net result is that there have never been effective arrangements for keeping the high level organisation of government under review. (This must be abundantly clear from the process of organisational change described in previous chapters!) Most changes in machinery of government have reflected the immediate pressures of the hour; they have been decided by Prime Ministers (over a cup of coffee or during a

K   135

taxi-ride,* for example) on the basis of their own personal experience and prejudices and with short-term political considerations uppermost in their minds. Sometimes, it is true, a committee or commission studying some aspect of government organisation makes recommendations for change, and sometimes these recommendations are accepted. But they are only partial and piecemeal. On one occasion only has a committee been set up to look at the whole organisation of government—the Haldane Committee on Machinery of Government of 1917–18. It was a powerful body, containing Beatrice Webb and Sir Robert Morant as well as Lord Haldane himself. But little attention was paid to its report. In the aftermath of the war everyone wanted to 'go back to normal'. In 1918 the attempt to create a new synthesis, recognising that government had become different in kind from what it had traditionally been, was premature.

In 1942 during the second world war a ministerial Cabinet Committee called the Machinery of Government Committee was established to keep the organisation of government under review. It remained active until 1945, but in subsequent years it met infrequently and was eventually wound up in 1950. A committee of senior officials called the Government Organisation Committee remained in existence for some years thereafter, supported by a small branch in the Treasury led by Mr William Armstrong—now Sir William Armstrong, the Head of the Civil Service. But organisational changes are so closely linked with policy that they must be questions for ministers; where the whole organisation of government is concerned, they are questions for the Prime Minister himself. If the Prime Minister and his ministerial colleagues are not interested in organisational planning, there is very little that officials can do.

For this reason, some academic students of government draw the conclusion that a rational approach to major questions of government organisation is impossible. These are usually people who have had a little first-hand experience of Whitehall; they regard themselves as initiates of the corridors of power, privileged to reveal some hint of their mysteries to the profane. They will tell you solemnly that they know the game; personal knowledge of politicians would soon convince you that Prime Ministers will always be swayed by short-term political pressures;

*We are told that the Department of Economic Affairs was conceived in a taxi taking Mr Harold Wilson and Mr George Brown to the House of Commons one afternoon.

so it is no use trying to take a long view of the government's organisational problems. It apparently fails to occur to these pundits that it might be a good idea to alter the balance of these pressures, to change the rules of the game. And, in fact, that is just what needs to be done. During the last ten years the temptation to play ducks and drakes with the Whitehall departments, to re-shuffle the organisation of government hither and thither with no proper strategic planning or consultation, has become too strong. Any business tycoon who handled important industrial mergers in this way would soon be in trouble. The time has come to subject the Prime Minister's performance as organiser of the government to some effective form of scrutiny.

There were signs in 1970 that, as Prime Minister, Mr Heath would handle the problems of government organisation not just with an eye to short-term tactical advantage but also with proper regard for the needs of strategic planning. Whether this would extend to the development of really effective means of public and parliamentary scrutiny in this field remained to be seen. What these might be is discussed in the next chapter.

SUPPORTING SERVICES

We now turn very briefly to the way that central arrangements have developed for providing the government with supporting services. These have been the concern of the Ministry of Public Buildings and Works, the Stationery Office, the Civil Service Commission, the Central Statistical Office, and the Central Office of Information.

Before 1940 the Office of Works was a comparatively minor department under a First Commissioner. It was then transformed into a Ministry of Works and Buildings and was recognised as the government's main building agency, even though the Service Ministries retained their own works organisations. Apart from its old Office of Works functions and its new responsibilities for constructing and maintaining government buildings, the new Ministry also became the government's channel of communication with the building and civil engineering industries. In 1962 it became the Ministry of Public Building and Works, took over from the Service Ministries responsibility for military building, and was given a more positive responsibility to modernise the country's building industry—a function that properly belongs to a Ministry for Industry (see Chapter 4). It has always exercised its responsibilities for government building under fairly close supervision from the Treasury (and now the Civil Service Department), especially where important inter-departmental projects are concerned. In October 1970 it was incorporated uneasily in the Department of the Environment.

The Stationery Office is responsible for government stationery and printing, and for the provision of office machinery and computers. Its responsibilities for the efficiency of office services in government should be closely linked with those of the Ministry of Public Building and Works for providing, furnishing and maintaining government accommodation. The Stationery Office's work as government publisher links it closely with the Central Office of Information. It does not make very much sense for these three closely linked agencies of government to be responsible to three different ministers.

The Civil Service Commission is responsible for recruitment to the Home Civil and Diplomatic Services. Its personnel are civil servants, but it has traditionally preserved the same kind of independence from political interference as do the Bank of England and the Board of Inland Revenue in their spheres. This reflects the Commission's origin in 1855, when one of the main reasons for setting it up was to limit the scope for political patronage in civil service appointments. The Civil Service Commission was attached to the Treasury until 1968, when it was transferred to the new Civil Service Department.

The Central Statistical Office came into existence in 1941, at the same time as the Economic Section, and has remained in the Cabinet Office ever since as the co-ordinating unit for all central government statistics. After the critical report[4] on Government Statistical Services by the House of Commons Estimates Committee under Dr Jeremy Bray's chairmanship in 1966, Professor Claus Moser was brought in as Director of the Central Statistical Office and under his guidance important developments have been taking place. These are based on two new factors: first, the rapidly growing need in industry and government alike for large quantities of accurate and up-to-date statistical data; secondly, the rapidly developing power of computers to handle data of this kind. These trends imply highly streamlined flows of information between various government departments and between government and industry. They require close co-operation by all the parties concerned in the design of the required information-handling systems. They demand careful analysis of the objectives of government policy and the purposes for which statistical data are required. They bring into sharper focus the need for 'systems analysis' in the whole organisation of government.

138

THE MANAGEMENT OF THE CIVIL SERVICE

By the middle 1960s, then, the arrangements for co-ordinating the activities of central government as a whole, for controlling its organisation, for managing the Civil Service, and for providing central supporting services, were scattered among the following offices and departments:

10 Downing Street
Cabinet Office
Central Statistical Office
Treasury
Stationery Office
Central Office of Information
Civil Service Commission
Ministry of Public Building and Works.

The Prime Minister no longer had a single senior official, as Mr Macmillan had had in Sir Norman Brook, to support him across the whole span of his work as the government's chief executive. There were no effective arrangements for planning organisational change.

During the previous ten years or so there had been rising dissatisfaction with the way the central government was being run. This dissatisfaction stemmed, not so much from a negative desire to save money and to limit the abuse of government power and patronage as had the corresponding pressures for reform in the nineteenth century, as from a growing sense that the system was ill-equipped for the positive tasks of mid-twentieth-century government. In particular, since it is always easier to blame people than institutions, criticism centred on the quality of the Civil Service and its work. A spate of books, pamphlets and articles appeared. Some of these, like Professor Chapman's *British Government Observed*,[5] may not have seemed very constructive; others, like Dr Balogh's 'Apotheosis of the Dilettante',[6] may have appeared to concentrate rather spitefully on the supposed shortcomings of civil servants as individual people. However, just as the ancient Romans were once alerted to danger by squawking geese, so now, even if the precise diagnoses were not always sound or the proposed remedies always constructive, the growing volume of criticism effectively warned the British public that all was not well with their institutions of central government. And, of course, there were more

139

constructive contributions like, for example, the Fabian pamphlet *The Administrators*.[7]

SHORTCOMINGS OF THE CIVIL SERVICE

What were the shortcomings of the Civil Service and how had they arisen?

Changes in the activities of government since the 1870s had changed the nature of Civil Service work, as described in Chapter 2. This had had important effects on the Civil Service itself.

For example, there had been marked changes in the structure of the staff. Take the administrative class. Before the first world war there were three working grades–Permanent Secretary, Assistant Secretary and Principal. In some ministries the Permanent Secretary might have a deputy; and there was also the training grade of Assistant Principal. In his life of Sir John Anderson (later Lord Waverley) Sir John Wheeler-Bennett has described what the Home Office was like fifty years ago.

When Anderson took charge of the Home Office in 1922 it comprised only seven administrative divisions. These dealt with a wide range of differing subjects which might indeed have been handled by seven different Departments . . . Each of these divisions was in the charge of an Assistant Secretary. Between these heads of divisions and the Permanent Secretary there were only two superior administrative officers; neither of these was a genuine Deputy–each had a rather specialised role . . . Thus for the most part Anderson dealt directly with the heads of various divisions– devolving on them a much larger measure of responsibility than is enjoyed by Assistant Secretaries nowadays. They were men of mature experience, with detailed knowledge of their own subjects; and he allowed each of them to run his own division, though he encouraged them to go to him for guidance and advice.[8]

By the 1960s the situation had become very different. Between the Assistant Secretary and the head of his department two, and in some cases three, new grades had blossomed: Under Secretary, Deputy Secretary, and Second Permanent Secretary.

Perhaps even more important than the vertical lengthening of the hierarchy had been its expansion horizontally. The number of administrative divisions had grown enormously so that, for example, there were about 35 assistant secretaries in the Home Office in place of the original seven. Moreover, they were now flanked by a multitude of scientific and professional cadres which did not exist at all in 1870 and hardly at all until much more recently—agricultural and veterinary advisers and investigators, statisticians, economists, lawyers, scientists of a wide variety of types, inspectors of education, doctors, engineers, architects, inspectors of constabulary, housing and planning inspectors, information officers—about 1,400 classes in all, each with its own self-contained hierarchy and career structure.

The cumulative effect of these changes had been very debilitating. As the vertical chain of command had lengthened, the work had been down-graded right down the line. As the work had become more and more fragmented horizontally, responsibility had further diminished. As it happened, the Colonial Office and the Cabinet Office (the two departments in which I had the good fortune to spend most of my time as a civil servant) had been largely unaffected. A young man in the Colonial Office in the 1950s, as the desk officer in charge of one of the colonial territories (or two small ones such as Mauritius and the Seychelles) still had a clear responsibility of his own. In the Cabinet Office in the early 1960s he could still carry well-defined responsibility for useful work not far from the centre of the action. During that spell I had heard about the 'soggy middle layer' as one of the personnel problems of the civil service, but it was only when I went to the Ministry of Defence in 1963 that I met it personally.

It was a profound shock to discover after ten years of rewarding—indeed exciting—work in Whitehall that so many of the stock criticisms of it were justified. There appeared to be literally thousands of people— real, live, individual people like oneself, many of them potentially able or once able—whose energies were being wasted on non-jobs (most of which would be done all over again by someone else and most of which would in any case make no difference whatsoever to anything of importance in the real world), whose capabilities and aspirations were being stunted, and who were gradually reconciling themselves to the prospect of pointless work until retirement. Of course, one recognises that something like this (or worse!) has been the lot of most men and women down the ages—and still is. But surely we can do better. I am convinced that if in 1964 the Ministry of Defence headquarters' staff of 25,000 could have been cut down to one tenth of that number, it would have done its work far better and its morale would have been infinitely higher.

This sort of situation was, in fact, steadily becoming endemic in most of the big Whitehall departments. It was not eased by the division of responsibility for Civil Service management between the Treasury and the other departments. Senior staff were being shifted around between different departments more and more frequently by the Treasury, while at the same time each department maintained its own separate promotion ladder. This represented a sort of half-way house between the traditional pattern of decentralised Civil Service management by separate, autonomous departments, and a new pattern of centralised management of a unified Civil Service whose members worked temporarily in one department and then another. It was – and indeed still is – an unsatisfactory situation. It inevitably weakens any real sense of responsibility for staff management on the part of senior officials. It makes it difficult to take a constructive approach to questions of machinery of government, management services, training and personnel management in general.

Another problem was that the status of civil servants in relation to the rest of the community had changed. Their numbers, as also the numbers of other public servants in local government and public corporations, had grown out of all recognition. At the same time, the differences between the work of civil servants, other public servants, and people employed in private enterprise, had lost much of their former significance. Many of the officials in a ministry like the Ministry of Defence, a nationalised industry like the Coal Board, or an industrial firm like ICI, now do much the same type of work as one another, in much the same type of organisational environment. They make much the same sort of contribution to the general welfare of the community. So, whereas civil servants had once been a comparatively small number of people doing work distinctly different from that done by the rest of the community, they had now become a large body of people doing work very similar to that done by anyone else in a big organisation.

The service had slowly adapted itself to these changes in an unplanned, piecemeal way. There had been concern that recruitment both to the Home Civil Service and the Diplomatic Service should be more widely based and should more accurately reflect the standpoint and attitudes of the country at large than was necessary a century ago. It had become accepted in principle that there should be interchange of staff between the Civil Service and other walks of life. None the less the Service was still founded on the principles of the Northcote–Trevelyan reforms of a century earlier.

The most important of these principles was that civil servants should form a specially selected cadre of honest, competent, non-political officials. They should be appointed by competitive examination rather than by patronage. They would have a permanent professional career in the service of the Crown. They should enjoy a degree of security in their jobs and special superannuation arrangements which were not available in most other walks of life. (Non-contributory pensions had been introduced primarily to remove the temptation to corruption; but, since they were also non-transferable, they encouraged civil servants to continue their service until retiring age and, since dismissal would result in loss of pension rights, they fostered amenable behaviour and good discipline.) Thus in the old days civil servants enjoyed a privileged position close to the centre of affairs, a special status as servants of the Crown, and a high degree of security in comparison with their fellow citizens. They cheerfully accepted the restraints on their private and political behaviour, and on their career mobility, which went with their special position. But a hundred years later all this was changed, along with the changes that had taken place in the role of central government in society. The underlying principles on which the Civil Service was based were now obsolete. Its very foundations had crumbled.

What *was* a civil servant, anyhow? Civil servants were still defined as 'servants of the Crown, other than holders of political or judicial offices, who are employed in a civil capacity and whose remuneration is paid wholly and directly out of monies voted by Parliament'.[9] This mumbo-jumbo had meant something in the 1860s, but what on earth did it mean in the 1960s? Why should people who worked in employment exchanges be civil servants, while people who worked in post offices were not? Why should the scientists who worked at Farnborough be civil servants, while the scientists who worked at Harwell were not? Why were Inland Revenue officials civil servants, while Bank of England officials were not? There were historical reasons for all these and a host of similar oddities, but no logical reasons. No-one could draw a clear line between what sort of work civil servants were supposed to do and what sort of work other public servants were supposed to do. The traditional idea of the Civil Service had become meaningless. It was no longer capable of definition in terms of practical activities.

REFORM OF BRITISH CENTRAL GOVERNMENT

This was the background against which the Fulton Committee on the Civil Service was appointed in 1968. It was asked in its terms of reference 'to examine the structure, recruitment and management, including training, of the Home Civil Service, and to make recommendations'.[10] The Prime Minister, Mr Wilson, in announcing the Committee's appointment said that the time had come to ensure that the Civil Service was properly equipped for its role in the modern state. But unfortunately the Committee was precluded from considering what that role should be. The Government's willingness to consider changes in the Civil Service did 'not imply any intention to alter the basic relationship between ministers and civil servants'.[10] Moreover, the Committee was not allowed to look at the machinery of government. As they said rather plaintively in their report, they 'found at many points of our enquiry that this imposed limits on our work; questions about the number and size of departments, and their relations with each other and the Cabinet Office, bear closely on the work and organisation of the Civil Service'.[10] The understatement of the century!

Three explanations were current at the time for the limitations placed on the Fulton Committee's terms of reference. First, it was said that the Prime Minister (Mr Wilson) insisted on narrow terms of reference so that the overall effect of the Committee's eventual report would be to focus criticism on the Civil Service; this would provide a useful let-out for the Labour Government when they came to give an account of their stewardship. Secondly, it was said that senior civil servants in the Treasury insisted on narrow terms of reference because they hoped–poor innocents!–to limit the enquiry to comparatively routine matters like recruitment and training procedures and internal staffing structures. Thirdly, it was said that all the parties to the matter–politicians, civil servants, and the chairman and members of the Fulton Committee themselves–genuinely missed the point: they did not see that it would be impossible to lay down a blue-print for a modern Civil Service, without clarifying the role of the Civil Service in a modern society and its relation to other parts of the government system. It seems difficult to believe any of these explanations! Only the opening of the relevant public records in about 25 years time will show which is correct. But, whatever the explanation, the Fulton Committee's terms of reference could hardly have been allowed to take the form they did if they had been the subject of intelligent parliamentary and public discussion at the time. Perhaps that is the main lesson for the future.

When the Fulton Committee's report came out in 1968, it was necessarily something of a hotch-potch. For example, it was extremely critical of the 'amateurishness' of the Civil Service, especially in the report's notorious first chapter; but because the Committee was unable to define the role of the Civil Service in modern society it was unable to shed any light on the true professionalism of a modern civil servant. The only suggestion that came through was that Civil Service administrators should really be professionals of another kind, economists or sociologists for example! Again, the report concentrated, quite rightly, on the need for many civil servants to be skilled managers, and it made important recommendations for improving management training and management services; but it was unable to recommend changes in the structure of government which would define the managerial role of civil servants and differentiate it from the secretariat role of those civil servants directly assisting ministers. 'We see no reason', the Committee said, 'to believe that the dividing line between activities for which ministers are directly responsible, and those for which they are not, is necessarily drawn in the right place today. The creation of further autonomous bodies, and the drawing of the line between them and central government, would raise parliamentary and constitutional issues, especially if they affected the answerability for sensitive matters such as the social and education services. These issues and the related questions of machinery of government are beyond our terms of reference. We think, however, that the possibility of a considerable extension of "hiving off" should be examined and we therefore recommend an early and thorough review of the whole question.'[11] The Committee forebore to mention that the results of such a review might completely alter our conception of what the Civil Service is and what it is for! Again, the Committee recommended, quite rightly, that greater emphasis should be placed on long-term forward planning and research and that each department should have a Planning Unit; but they were unable to suggest the right relationship between these Planning Units and a comparable unit for the central government as a whole. They recognised that some central direction of the departmental Planning Units would be necessary, but 'the status and location of this central direction, whether by the Cabinet Office, the Treasury or the development of other machinery, is a question of machinery of government and therefore beyond our terms of reference'.[12] Again, they were unable to look at the heart of the problem.

The Fulton Committee's three main recommendations were that:

a new Civil Service Department should be set up and the Civil Service Commission should be integrated with it (the precise opposite of 'hiving off'!);

a new Civil Service College should be set up;

and a unified grading system should replace the existing staffing structure of 1,400 different 'classes'.

They also recommended that:

in order to encourage mobility into and out of the Civil Service, the pension scheme should be reviewed;

management services units and planning units should be set up in all departments;

the principles of accountable management should be applied to organising the work of departments;

the possibilities of 'hiving off' and related changes in the machinery of government should be examined;

ways and means should be examined of getting rid of unnecessary secrecy in government;

a new pattern of joint consultation between management and the staff side should be considered; and

recruitment procedures should be speeded up.

The general tenor of these recommendations was undoubtedly progressive. As the Head of the Civil Service, Sir William Armstrong, said at the time, publication of the Fulton Report undoubtedly helped 'to break the log-jam'.

Virtually all Fulton's recommendations were accepted by the government. The Civil Service Department, incorporating the Civil Service Commission, came into existence on 1st November 1968. It was directly under the ministerial control of the Prime Minister. Its Permanent Secretary was the Head of the Home Civil Service. Its tasks were stated to be as follows:[13]

personnel management – policy and central arrangements for selection and recruitment, the selection process itself, training, promotion, personnel management, posting and general career management of civil servants, including problems of staff wastage together with welfare, security and retirement policy; responsibility for advising on 'top level' appointments;

the development and dissemination of administrative and managerial techniques; general oversight of departmental organisation, inter-departmental arrangements and the machinery of government, the working environment of civil servants and the provision of central services, including O and M, computers and operational research;

the supervision of departmental administrative expenditure generally and departmental manpower requirements in terms of both numbers and grading;

the control of rates of pay, procedures for reimbursing expenses incurred in the public service, and allowances in the Civil Service, and of its structure in terms of grades and occupational groupings; the co-ordination of government policy in relation to pay, etc. in the public services generally, including the approval of salaries, allowances etc. for the members and staff of non-departmental bodies;

the development and execution of policy on Civil Service superannuation; co-ordination of pension arrangements throughout the public sector.

It is arguable, and indeed I shall argue later in this chapter, that of these five tasks only the second is really part of the central direction of the government and that the remainder should not be under the direct ministerial control of the Prime Minister.

The new Civil Service Department set to work with a will 'to implement Fulton', as its task was interpreted by many of the staff serving in it. Progress was made in following up the recommendations on training, recruitment, terms of service (including superannuation), and grading of staff. Studies were put in hand on the scope for accountable management and 'hiving off'. The government's central capability in the field of management services was strengthened. All this was pulled together in a co-ordinated programme of development covering the Civil Service as a whole, in close consultation between the official side and the staff side of the Service. Even if it had achieved little in the way of tangible results (apart from the establishment of the new Civil Service College) by the time the Labour Government left office in June 1970, it must have been a very educative experience for all concerned. And certainly the greatly increased training facilities in the fields of computing and management science can have done nothing but good.

NEXT STEPS

Separating the management of the Civil Service from the Treasury and making it the responsibility of a department directly under the Prime Minister established that the management of the government machine was a central function in its own right. That was a very important step forward. But, unfortunately, because the Fulton Committee's terms of reference were too narrowly drawn, the scope and nature of this central function were not properly understood. Two important mistakes were made.

The first mistake was to create yet another new department, the Civil Service Department, to take over and develop *only* the existing responsibilities of the Treasury for Civil Service pay and management. The opportunity should have been taken to rationalise all the overlapping functions of the various departments and agencies concerned with managing and servicing the central government machine under the Prime Minister's overall supervision.

The second mistake was the converse of the first. It was to suppose that *all* the activities that had evolved in the Treasury in connection with Civil Service pay and management constituted a single function. In fact, these activities were an amalgam of what are now coming to be recognised as two separate functions: on the one hand, the central function of supervising the organisation and management services of the government as a whole; and, on the other hand, the function of personnel management, including such tasks as recruitment, training, pay, pensions, conditions of service, staffing structures and grading, and negotiations with the staff. The first of these two functions is a vital responsibility of the Prime Minister as managing director or chief executive of the government; the second should be the responsibility of another minister, corresponding to the government's personnel director.

By 1970 it already seemed that these two distinct functions of the

148

Civil Service Department would have to be disentangled from one another. The first would have to be brought together with the functions of the Cabinet Office (and Central Statistical Office). With it would also have to be associated responsibility for the central supporting services provided by the Ministry of Public Building and Works, the Stationery Office and the Central Office of Information. A new Central Policy Studies Unit would have to be added. All these functions would then have to be made the responsibility of a properly constituted Prime Minister's Office, organised as shown in the diagram at Figure 3 (p. 150). The Office itself should be small and high powered; not more than 300 staff in all should be needed. The supporting units and offices shown on the diagram would naturally be larger.

It was not known whether Mr Heath's thinking in opposition, and the studies that were then made by the Conservative Research Department, pointed in the general direction of a Prime Minister's Office. It now seems clear that they did not; certainly Mr Heath's reforms so far fall well short of what is needed. The creation of such an Office would be a major step forward in our conception of government, in that it would explicitly recognise the nature of the modern Prime Minister's job as leader and organiser of the government. In practical terms, however, it would represent little more than a rationalisation of the Prime Ministerial functions now dispersed in various offices and departments of Whitehall.

What of the personnel functions now carried out by the Civil Service Department? As we shall see later in this chapter, there appear to be increasingly good reasons for bringing together the government's responsibilities for its own internal staffing problems with its wider responsibilities in respect of employment and manpower in the country as a whole. This would be analogous to the way in which the Treasury's traditional responsibilities for the internal financial affairs of the government have now merged with the wider responsibilities of government in respect of the economy as a whole, as described in Chapter 7. It would be achieved by:

> merging the personnel functions now carried out by the Civil Service Department with the closely related functions of the Diplomatic Service Administration Office in a new Public Service Commission;
>
> putting this Commission in charge of other public service appointments and staffing, such as the growing number of public appointments now made by the Prime Minister and by other ministers; and

REFORM OF BRITISH CENTRAL GOVERNMENT

PRIME MINISTER'S OFFICE

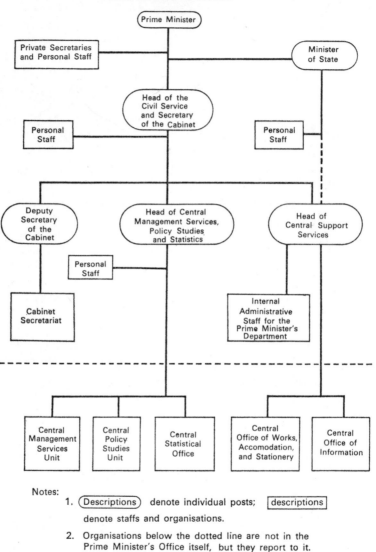

Notes:
1. (Descriptions) denote individual posts; [descriptions] denote staffs and organisations.

2. Organisations below the dotted line are not in the Prime Minister's Office itself, but they report to it.

Figure 3.

THE MANAGEMENT OF THE CIVIL SERVICE

taking the Public Service Commission out of the Prime Minister's direct sphere of responsibility, and making it one of the semi-autonomous supporting agencies of the new Ministry of Employment and Manpower proposed in Chapter 4. The organisation chart for that ministry would then be on the lines of Figure 4.

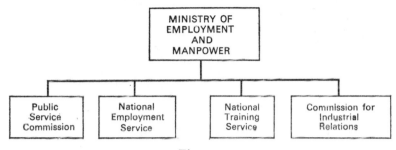

Figure 4

Again, this would be a comparatively small policy-making ministry, supported by larger executive agencies to administer:

public service recruitment and training;

the employment exchange service;

government training centres, industrial training schemes, and government-sponsored business education schemes; and

an industrial relations and personnel advisory service.

The new Office of Manpower Economics would, in effect, constitute parts of its research and planning capability.

ADMINISTRATIVE DEVOLUTION

As in other spheres of government activity, the unification of ministerial authority in a Prime Minister's Office will be the starting point for important developments down the line. One of its main functions will be to carry forward (with the support of its Central Management Services Unit) the work now being done in the Civil Service Department on 'accountable management', 'management by objectives', and 'hiving off'. These terms of art sound rather formidable to the layman, and there is a natural tendency for the experts to pretend that they are more mysterious than they really are. So it is important to stress that they embody certain simple basic ideas.

L   151

The Fulton Committee described these underlying ideas in three paragraphs of their report, as follows:

> To function efficiently, large organisations, including government departments, need a structure in which units and individual members have authority that is clearly defined and responsibilities for which they can be held accountable. There should be recognised methods of assessing their success in achieving specified objectives.
>
> Accountable management means holding individuals and units responsible for performance measured as objectively as possible. Its achievement depends upon identifying or establishing accountable units within government departments – units where output can be measured against costs or other criteria, and where individuals can be held personally responsible for their performance.
>
> Work of this kind should thus be organised into separate commands. The manager of each command should be given clear-cut responsibilities and commensurate authority and should be held accountable for performance against budgets, standards of achievement and other tests. Within his unit he should set up sub-systems of responsibility and delegated authority on similar lines.[14]

These ideas are recognisably similar to those described in Chapter 4 on the nationalised industries. The operating framework for the nationalised industries should be such that ministers take responsibility for setting objectives and targets for the industries, and the heads of the industries take responsibility for meeting these objectives and targets. The heads of the industries have a 'command' of their own. They have clearly defined authority and clear-cut responsibility at a different level of decision from the minister to whose remit they work. Similarly, as we have seen in Chapter 7, there is a close link between the concepts of accountable management and such financial control concepts as output budgeting. If he is to be accountable, a manager must be given a budget of his own and be required to show what he has achieved with it.

These ideas are now well understood by progressive civil servants in Whitehall. In this respect the evidence given by Sir William Armstrong and other officials from the Civil Service Department[15] to the Select Committee on Procedure in 1968–69 contrasted favourably with that given by some (though not all) of the Treasury officials who appeared before the Committee. Unfortunately, however, these ideas are not yet at all well understood by many politicians, political commentators and academic students of government. There is a tremendous task of education here.

The concept of accountable management leads on to another very important point. If the process of defining and devolving responsibility is to be effective, it must extend not only to finance but also to staff. The accountable manager will have to be given and will have to accept very much greater responsibility for managing his own staff than civil servants have had hitherto. He may have to be given responsibility for recruiting (or at least for selecting) his staff, for deciding on their pay, their training, their promotion, their career development, and in the last resort he may have to be given responsibility for firing them.

The whole question of administrative devolution will thus have crucial implications for the reform of central government and for the concept of a single centralised Civil Service. It seems likely to involve a reversal of the centralising trend towards a unified, monolithic Civil Service that has developed over the last fifty years. It may well mean that in the course of time the present distinction between the Civil Service and the rest of the public service will largely break down. It will certainly help to transform our idea of what the Civil Service is. In this case as in others unification will be followed by decentralisation.

Let us now follow the logic of the argument one stage further. The process of analysing the functions of government and devolving clear responsibility for subordinate activities within a framework of policy decisions made at a superior level– in other words the process of introducing accountable management– will shortly begin to converge with the hitherto quite separate process of re-defining the relationship between the central government and the private sector. In the 1960s, as we saw in Chapter 4, Conservative and Labour Governments had both been developing the Companies Acts and institutions like the Monopolies Commission, the Prices and Incomes Board, and so forth, in such a way as to evolve a new framework of public accountability within which private enterprise would be required to operate. It is true that this was happening in a rather blind, piecemeal, zig-zag way, but it was happening none the less and the process is clearly continuing to gather momentum. It is leading us towards a concept of accountable management which will impose on companies the opportunity and the

153

obligation to pursue their own competitive interests to the limit of their energies and abilities, within a framework of targets, objectives and constraints clearly laid down in the interest of employees, shareholders and customers, and in pursuance of wider public interests. This concept of accountable management for private enterprise vis-à-vis the public interest closely parallels the concept of parliamentary accountability for the nationalised industries which has been developed by the Select Committee on Nationalised Industries, and the concepts of accountable management now being developed by the Civil Service itself. It reflects in operational terms the fact that the traditional hard and fast line between the public and private sectors is breaking down.

For practical purposes, from the point of view of central government policies, this will tend to mean that the difference between public servants and private citizens will fade still further. The task of planning and managing the employment and manpower needs of the public services will thus progressively shade into the task of handling employment and manpower questions for the country at large. The combined task will fall to the proposed new Ministry of Employment and Manpower.

SUMMARY

Thus, to summarise our findings in this chapter, the creation of the Civil Service Department in 1968 can be seen as another step in the zigzag course of evolution towards a Prime Minister's Office. Increasing dissatisfaction with existing methods of central government planning and management must lead eventually to the rationalisation within a unified Prime Minister's Office of the present fragmented arrangements for supporting the Prime Minister in his functions as Chief Executive of the government. This in turn will provide the occasion to merge the government's responsibilities for its own internal employment and manpower tasks with its responsibilities for the employment and manpower problems of the country at large, in a fully fledged Ministry of Employment and Manpower.

The unification of responsibility for the central direction of the government under a single Prime Minister's Office will be followed by a process of administrative devolution. The personnel aspects of this process will be handled by the unified Ministry of Employment and Manpower, and the financial aspects (as described in Chapter 7) by the Treasury. This devolution of government work, and the greater degree of openness and accountability that will go with it, will be matched by increasing openness and accountability in the management of large firms, nationalised industries, and the professions. In total, these developments may be regarded as the institutional and procedural reflection of a growing fusion and complementarity between socialism and private enterprise.

NOTES ON CHAPTER 8

General

As always, *The Organisation of British Central Government, 1914–1964* is a valuable source of reference. John P. Mackintosh's *The British Cabinet* (University Paperback—Methuen, 1968) is now the standard book on the development of the Cabinet system from 1660 to the present day. The Fulton Committee's Report (Cmnd. 3638, HMSO: June 1968) and in particular its supporting volumes of evidence and factual analysis are indispensable for any serious student. It is with hesitation that I again bring to the reader's attention my own evidence to the Fulton Committee (Vol. 5 (2), pages 1021–1084), but I believe it to have been important—not least because it may have helped to influence Conservative Party thinking on these matters between 1966 and 1970.

Note 1. R. H. S. Crossman, Ed., *Walter Bagehot: The English Constitution;* Fontana, 1963, page 54.

Note 2. I have not traced the original source of this story. It was quoted by Sir Norman Brook in a talk on Cabinet Government published as No. 5 in a series of Home Office Administrative Studies. HMSO: 1961.

Note 3. David Cecil: *Melbourne;* Pan Books Ltd., 1969; page 390.

Note 4. *Government Statistical Services;* Estimates Committee, Session 1966–67; HMSO: 1966.

Note 5. Brian Chapman: *British Government Observed;* George Allen & Unwin, 1963.

Note 6. Originally published in 1959 as a contribution to *The Establishment*, edited by Hugh Thomas and subsequently reprinted in *Crisis in the Civil Service*, Ed. Hugh Thomas, published by Anthony Blond, 1968.

Note 7. *The Administrators: The Reform of the Civil Service*, by a Fabian Group: Fabian Tract 353, June 1964.

Note 8. John W. Wheeler-Bennett:*John Anderson: Viscount Waverley;* Macmillan, 1962; page 84.

Note 9. See the Fulton Committee's Report, Appendix A, paragraph 3 and footnote.

Note 10. *Ibid.*, paragraphs 1, 2 and 6.

Note 11. Fulton Committee's Report, paragraph 190.

Note 12. *Ibid.* paragraph 177.

Note 13. *'Developments on Fulton': Civil Service and National Whitley Council;* HMSO, March 1969; paragraph 15.

Note 14. Fulton Committee's Report, paragraphs 145, 150 and 154.

Note 15. *First Report from the Select Committee on Procedure, Session 1968–69;* HMSO, pages 26 and following.

9

Government, Parliament and the Law

A reformed Parliament which will be disembarrassed, by
devolution, of the mass of detail with which their progress
is now largely choked.

WINSTON CHURCHILL, 1905 [1]

THE STRUCTURE OF GOVERNMENT

The main changes needed in central government today can now be
summarised as follows.

As chief executive of the government the Prime Minister needs
properly organised official support. A Prime Minister's Office
should be created out of the various fragmented organisations that
support him today.

The number of central government Departments should not exceed
about twelve, as follows:

1. Prime Minister's Office.
2. Ministry of Defence.
3. Ministry of External Affairs.
4. Ministry of Housing, Health and Welfare.
5. Ministry of Education, Science and the Arts.
6. Ministry of Industrial Infrastructure (i.e. Fuel, Power,
   Transport, Communications).
7. Ministry of Industry, Commerce and Trade.
8. Ministry of Local and Regional Government and Environmental Planning.
9. Ministry of Economic and Financial Affairs.
10. Ministry of Employment and Manpower.
11. Home Office.
12. Lord Chancellor's Office.

The Cabinet should contain not more than 16 members. These
would include 12 ministers in charge of the above Departments and
not more than 4 ministers without portfolio.

The managerial and professional functions of central government should be hived off to executive commands and agencies, led and managed on the principles of accountable management and working to a clearly and publicly defined remit from their supervisory minister.

The regional and local functions of government should similarly be hived off to government authorities at the regional and local levels.

Arrangements must be made to ensure that policy research is carried out and is effectively translated into policy planning, that policy planning is effectively translated into action, and that action is effectively monitored as feed-back for future policy-making. In other words, an effective 'circle of control' must be established, linking the future with the present with the past with the future, for every function of government at every level of government.

The whole system must contain within itself the capability to understand the interactive processes of change, so that it can re-organise itself to meet – and indeed to influence – changing circumstances.

In other words, we should now be aiming to raise our whole approach to the problems of government to a higher level of understanding and control than hitherto. We need to regard it as a continually changing totality of activities characterised by:

functions (defence, industry, etc.)
decision levels (political, managerial)
geographical spans (national, regional, local)
time scales (future, present, past).

And we need to try to structure this 'multi-dimensional' system of control so that it adapts itself to changing circumstances and continues to work reasonably well in respect of all the above characteristics, both as a whole and in all of its various parts.

So far as government *administration* is concerned – that is the work of the Executive at central, regional and local levels – the suggestions made in earlier chapters will take us a long way towards meeting these needs. But Parliament and the Law both have a vital part to play. It is to them that we now turn.

GOVERNMENT, PARLIAMENT AND THE LAW

What is Parliament's proper role within a modern system of self-government? How has it changed since Gladstone's day?

In considering these questions, it is important to remember that we are concerned with *action*. What kind of action do we expect Parliament to take? What kind of things do we expect to happen because of Parliament's activities that would not otherwise have happened? Parliament is also, of course, a talking shop as its name suggests, a national forum for discussion and debate. But it is prerequisite to Parliament's effectiveness as such a forum that it shall be capable of effective action. As Bagehot said, 'Human nature despises long arguments which come to nothing, heavy speeches which precede no motion, abstract disquisitions which leave visible things where they are. But all men heed great results.'² What great results do we want from Parliament today?

Parliament's role is to decide on behalf of the community whether to give or withhold final approval of the government's future proposals, present activities, and past actions.

What shall be done? Parliament's job is to discuss and influence future government policies, and give the seal of parliamentary approval to them before they are adopted.

How shall it be done? Parliament's job is to discuss and influence the means used for translating government policies into action, and to give the seal of parliamentary approval to them before they are adopted.

How has it been done? Parliament's job is to examine the success or failure with which government policies have been administered, and to give (perhaps only implicitly) the seal of parliamentary approval before the books are closed.

Parliament has two kinds of mechanism at its disposal for exercising this system of control. The first stems from its responsibility to scrutinise government administration, which derives historically from the traditional parliamentary duty to control taxation and the Crown's expenditure. The second stems from its function as the national legislature, without whose approval new laws cannot be made.

A hundred years ago Parliament was so organised and its procedures were such that it was reasonably well able to carry out these two functions. In an age when the time-scale of human activities was reasonably

159

short and the compass of government reasonably small, debates on annual estimates of expenditure gave Parliament a real opportunity to consider government policies and the means proposed for carrying them out; while the Public Accounts Committee was able, with the support of the Comptroller and Auditor General and the Exchequer and Audit Department, to review the way the money had been spent. In words used by Lord Melbourne in the 1830s, Parliament was able 'to consider the estimates for the public service, to retrench what is superfluous, to correct what is amiss, and to assist the Crown with those supplies and subsidies which it thinks right and necessary to afford.'[3] Likewise, in an age when legislation was comparatively simple and comparatively small in bulk, and when the work of the House of Lords was a more important and integral part of Parliament's proceedings than it is today, Parliament had a real opportunity to examine the probable effects of future legislation; while the system of appeals to the House of Lords as a Supreme Court of Appeal afforded, at least to some extent, an opportunity to monitor the actual effects of legislation and provided some 'feedback' into the legislative process itself.

Today, however, the traditional parliamentary procedures have become inadequate to Parliament's modern task. They have virtually broken down. They still reflect the situation when government was comparatively small, its main concerns being with the historic functions of the Crown, and when government was in a real sense external to society as a whole. In that situation, the Gladstonian Liberals regarded government as a necessary evil and they thought Parliament's main task was to hedge the government with negative constraints, for example by keeping its expenditure down. At the same time they accepted that because of the Crown's special role and functions it should have certain legal privileges. They took it for granted that these privileges should extend to the activities of government officials as servants of the Crown. The situation today is completely different, owing to the huge growth that has taken place in the functions of government and the changed role of government in society. At the same time, Parliament itself is considerably less effective operationally than it used to be, owing to the progressive disintegration of the unified system formerly provided by the two Houses of Parliament working together.

This situation demands a radical transformation of the working relationship between Parliament and the Executive, and systematic changes in parliamentary organisation and procedures. Most of the recent attempts to reform Parliament have not recognised this. They have failed for the same reason as recent attempts to reform our other institutions of government. They have been conceived piecemeal; they have been directed at symptoms; they have failed to identify the underlying long-term problems and to propound systematic, coherent solutions to them.

PARLIAMENTARY CONTROL OF THE EXECUTIVE

Parliament's control of the Executive stemmed originally from its power to control taxation and its power to control government expenditure. The Crown was unable to raise taxes without parliamentary approval, and the Crown was unable to spend money without parliamentary approval of the objects on which expenditure was proposed. A hundred years ago, as we have seen, Parliament's concern was essentially a negative one. We discussed in Chapter 7 some of the effects that that fact has had on the methods of financial control in Whitehall, and some of the difficulties that have arisen with the need for more positive planning and management of government expenditure programmes. What comparable developments have taken place on the parliamentary side?

With the creation of the Public Accounts Committee in 1861 and the enactment of the Exchequer and Audit Departments Act in 1866, Gladstone was able to say that the 'last portion of the circle' of parliamentary control of expenditure was complete.[4]

The circle went as follows:

1. Appropriation, i.e. prior authorisation of specific expenditure by the House of Commons.
2. Issue of funds by the Comptroller and Auditor General in accordance with these appropriations.
3. Access by the Comptroller and Auditor General and his Department to the accounts, showing the actual out-turn of expenditure.
4. Scrutiny of these accounts by the Public Accounts Committee and a report on them to the House.

Basically, this was a two-stage process, involving:

Discussion and approval of the financial implications of government decisions *before* they were carried out.

Scrutiny of the out-turn *afterwards*.

Parliament's procedures were thus designed to handle two kinds of financial questions, corresponding to these two stages.

The Gladstonian circle of control accorded with the ethos of nineteenth-century Liberalism. Its purpose was to set limits to public expenditure and to ensure that these limits were observed. The economic thinking of the time insisted that public expenditure should be kept to a minimum; the government was a mere consumer of wealth, and as far as possible money should be left to fructify in private hands. The notion that public expenditure could be efficiently or productively managed and that this might be the concern of Parliament did not arise.

The Gladstonian financial reforms of the 1860s did not appear like Athene, fully armed from the head of Zeus. They were the climax of a series of changes going back to Burke's Economical Reforms in the 1780s. Moreover, although Gladstone could speak in 1866 of the circle being completed, the task was by no means finished. As he himself said, the Public Accounts Committee had a great deal of detailed work 'of a dry and repulsive kind'[5] to do. Not until twenty years later, in 1886, could it be said that 'general order and regularity . . . have now been established throughout the service in regard to cash accounts.'[6]

These historical facts are of particular interest to us today. For, like the Victorians just over a hundred years ago, we too are now nearing the end of a long period of transition. The outlines of a new 'circle of control' are emerging, which will once again systematise the step-by-step reforms and innovations of the last seventy years.

Since the turn of the century, as we saw in Chapter 7, the following developments have taken place:

Government expenditure and taxation have both grown vastly.

As government has taken on more and more responsibility for the national well-being in every sphere, control of government expenditure has become a very powerful and positive instrument of economic and social policies. The same is true of taxation, especially as regards the sum of the financial relationships between the individual and the State and between the company and the State.

Control over the total combination of government expenditure, taxation and government borrowing, has become the government's most important instrument for steering the national economy.

It has become necessary to plan government expenditure, taxation and borrowing, some years ahead, and to manage them with greater regard to their objectives.

Looking back over the last seventy years one can see that Parliament has been adapting slowly and piecemeal to these new facts of life, just as Whitehall has been.

As early as 1905* Churchill put forward the view that 'Supply Days, so far as any *systematic and scientific examination* of the expenditure of the country was concerned, were a series of farces from beginning to end'.[7] He also said that there were not just two types of financial question – before and after – but three. He called them 'policy', 'merit', and 'audit'. The first was for the Cabinet and the third for the Public Accounts Committee, 'but between these two, there was a lacuna or middle ground which, for want of a better term, he called the *merit* of expenditure, and upon that no control adequately or effectively operated.' Today, sixty-five years later, we talk of policy, *management*, and audit – or perhaps strategy, tactics and review. But the problem is still the same; how to bring these three types of question within a unified circle of control, and to remedy what Churchill called 'the present slipshod and haphazard system'.

After some years of discussion and argument a House of Commons Select Committee on Estimates was set up in 1912. For various reasons it never established itself firmly before being replaced in 1939 (as in 1914) by the war-time National Expenditure Committee. Since 1945 it has done much effective work; the 1961 Plowden Report on Control of Public Expenditure (see Chapter 7), the 1966 Fulton Report on the Civil Service (see Chapter 8) and recent improvements in government statistics (see Chapter 8) all owed their origin to the Estimates Committee. But the philosophy behind the Committee has never been crystal clear. It has always seemed to be operating in a no-man's-land between the debate on policy before the event and the scrutiny of administration afterwards. To describe this no-man's-land as 'administrative policy', as Lord Butler did, is not particularly helpful!

This uneasiness about the Estimates Committee explains why, as long ago as 1945, Lord Campion (then Clerk to the House of Commons) put forward the case for combining the Public Accounts Committee and the Estimates Committee in a single Public Expenditure Committee. The achievements of the war-time National Expenditure Committee and the

* In those days Hansard Reports were published in oratio obliqua.

pre-war experience of the clerks of the financial committees lent support to this proposal. The arguments were as follows:

The examination and control of expenditure by the Accounts and Estimates Committees were incomplete and unsatisfactory.

The functions and organisation of the war-time National Expenditure Committee ought to be retained.

The functions of the Accounts Committee and those of Estimates or Expenditure Committees overlapped, for these Committees might and did work in the same field. It was 'impossible to confine a subject of expenditure of any importance to a single year. The three years period covered by the Accounts and Estimates is the natural unit for this purpose.'[8]

Methods of liaison between committees had been unsuccessful in the past and no system based on separate committees could avoid cases of duplicated work and consequent friction. A more complete and unified system was necessary.

The then Procedure Committee of the House of Commons supported the proposal for a combined Public Expenditure Committee. But it was argued by the Treasury, by members of the Public Accounts Committee and by the Comptroller and Auditor General that parliamentary functions in respect of government accounts and government estimates of expenditure were quite different–the work of the Public Accounts Committee 'is so essentially the checking of an audit; it is not the question of investigating current expenditure'.[8] These arguments were supported by Herbert Morrison, who gave expression to the 'general distaste of any government for powerful investigating committees and the particular dislike of many ministers for the war-time Expenditure Committee'.[8] The Procedure Committee's recommendations were rejected.

Since 1945 further developments have taken place. In particular, various new House of Commons Select Committees have been set up. The Select Committee on Nationalised Industries (see Chapter 4) was appointed in 1956. Since 1966 a number of Specialist Select Committees (most of them temporary) have been appointed on such subjects as Agriculture, Science and Technology, Race Relations, Education, Overseas Development and Scottish Affairs. Although these new

Committees have done good work individually, their piecemeal proliferation, overlapping with the Estimates Committee and the Public
Accounts Committee, has not strengthened Parliament's power to
influence and scrutinise government policies and administration.
Indeed, it has directly weakened the Estimates Committee and by
fragmenting the Select Committee structure as a whole it has tended to
dilute Parliament's powers of systematic scrutiny. Another important
development has been the publication to Parliament of the forward
projections of expenditure compiled by the Public Expenditure Survey
Committee of the Treasury, which was described in Chapter 7. The
Conservative Government published a White Paper on the subject in
December 1963 and the Labour Government published one in February 1966 and another in February, 1969. These publications constituted
an acknowledgement that an important gap now existed in the circle
of parliamentary control, but their *ad hoc* nature left the gap unfilled.

Towards the end of 1969, however, in a report from the House of
Commons Select Committee on Procedure, it was proposed that these
separate strands might be woven into a coherent new system of parliamentary control of public expenditure and administration—the first
stage in a grand design for reforming the relationship between Parliament and the Executive. This was the report of the Procedure Committee's enquiry into parliamentary scrutiny of public expenditure and
administration. The report was hailed by the Economics Editor of *The
Times*[9] as the 'one economic event in the past year that stands out as a
beacon of hope . . . In the fourteen pages of the Committee's report,
Parliament began for the first time in decades to evince at least a desire
to organise itself so that it could be aware of and influence the decisions
of government that determine the character of the society in which we
live.'

The Committee recognised that 'the expansion of government
activity into many fields, and the extension of the time-scale on which
plans for public spending now have to be made, have not been matched
by corresponding developments in the financial procedures of Parliament. Parliament has lacked the information on which to base its
examination of these matters; and the government have not been
required to seek Parliament's formal authorisation before proceeding
with their plans . . .Your Committee believe that the House should now
develop its procedures further, and formally establish a system of
expenditure scrutiny, containing not two elements but three:

First, discussion of the government's expenditure strategy and policies, as set out in projections of public expenditure several years ahead;

Second, examination of the means (including new methods of management) being adopted to implement strategy and to execute policies, as reflected in annual estimates of expenditure;

Third, retrospective scrutiny of the results achieved and the value for money obtained on the basis of annual accounts and related information from departments on the progress of their activities.

These three tasks are closely related to one another. The arrangements for scrutiny by the House must recognise that fact and provide an effective link between the system for allocating resources and the system for getting value for money.'[10]

The Committee made two main sets of recommendations; the first concerned parliamentary consideration of priorities in public expenditure, in other words the government's expenditure strategy and policies; and the second concerned parliamentary scrutiny of administration, in other words the implementation of policies and the results achieved.

Included in the first set were recommendations that every autumn the government should regularly publish forward projections of expenditure and an assessment of future economic developments up to five years ahead, and that Parliament should hold a two-day debate on these publications. The Committee considered that this debate 'should come to occupy as important a place in parliamentary and public discussion of economic affairs as that now occupied by the annual Budget debate'.[11]

Included in the second set of recommendations[12] was a proposal that the Estimates Committee should become a Select Committee on Expenditure. The new Committee should consist of a General Sub-Committee and eight functional sub-committees on:

Industry, Technology, Manpower, Employment.
Power, Transport and Communications.
Trade and Agriculture.
Education, Science and the Arts.
Housing, Health and Welfare.
Law, Order and Public Safety.
Defence.
External Affairs.

Each of these Sub-Committees would have the following terms of reference:

To consider the activities of Departments of State concerned with (naming the particular functional field of administration) and the Estimates of their expenditure presented to this House; and to examine the efficiency with which they are administered.

The task of each Sub-Committee would be threefold:

It should study the expenditure projections for the department or departments in its field, compare them with those of previous years, and report on any major variations or important changes of policy and on the progress made by the departments towards clarifying their general objectives and priorities.

It should examine in as much detail as possible the implications in terms of public expenditure of the policy objectives chosen by ministers and assess the success of the department in attaining them.

It should enquire, on the lines of the present Estimates Sub-Committees, into departmental administration, including effectiveness of management.

The Wilson government accepted the first set of recommendations with commendable promptitude, though with some reservations about the economic information and other supporting information to be published with the forward projections of expenditure. The first of the annual two-day debates was successfully held in January 1970. Much of the credit for the government's readiness to move forward was rightly given to Mr Jack Diamond, the then Chief Secretary to the Treasury.

The Labour Government did not accept the second set of recommendations before the General Election supervened. But there appeared to be a general consensus that the proposed Select Committee on Expenditure should be set up, and Mr Iain Macleod, as Shadow Chancellor of the Exchequer, welcomed the proposal. By early 1971 a new Expenditure Committee had, in fact, taken the place of the old Estimates Committee.

The view is widely held that the report of the 1968–69 Procedure Committee could prove to be a landmark in the reform of British government and in the development of the British constitution. The report recognised in principle the need for Parliament to play its full part in the three-stage circle of control of government corresponding to strategy, tactics and review (see Figure 2 in Chapter 7), and mad practical proposals to that end. But, although I regard it as a privilege to have been associated with the Committee's enquiry as their 'Specialist Adviser', I think the report should be regarded only as a starting point for a more widely ranging approach to the reform of Parliament and its relations with the Executive.

By 1970 a re-definition of the roles of ministers, civil servants and back-bench members of Parliament, was, in fact, beginning to emerge. Once the new Expenditure Committee had successfully established itself, it seemed likely to bring these roles into focus broadly on the following lines.

1. The floor of the House is the right forum for parliamentary debates on policy. Ministers forming the government of the day should answer there for the decisions, including non-decisions, for which they are responsible.

2. A Select Committee of back-benchers is the right forum for the less partisan task of scrutinising administration. 'Administration' in this context refers to work for which officials are primarily responsible. It includes analysing the consequences of different policy options for the future, as well as carrying out administrative action in pursuance of existing policies. Since officials are responsible, it is for officials and not ministers to answer questions about these matters in Select Committee.

3. The distinction between the parliamentary function to which the floor of the House is appropriate and the parliamentary function to which a Select Committee is appropriate corresponds to the distinction between the executive function for which ministers are responsible and the executive function for which civil servants are responsible. Just as work well done by officials contributes to the quality of ministerial decisions on policy, so work well done by a Select Committee can contribute to the quality of policy debates on the floor of the House.

4. The spread of accountable management in Whitehall and the progressive hiving off of the managerial and professional tasks of government to quasi-autonomous commands (as described in Chapter 8) will demand full use of the enlarged channels of parliamentary accounta-

bility which the new Select Committee on Expenditure will provide. Public expenditure today is several hundred times bigger than it was in 1866, and if genuine accountability to Parliament is to be re established there need to be many more 'accounting officers' than there were in Gladstone's time or than there are today. The new Expenditure Committee should be regarded as the modern version of the 1866 Public Accounts Committee, and the enlarged corps of accounting officers should be accountable to Parliament through it.

5. The great expansion of government activity during the last half century now calls for systematic examination of public expenditure by Parliament right across the board, just as it calls for a re-definition of management responsibilities between ministers and officials. (As we saw in Chapter 8, the Fulton Committee half-understood this but failed to appreciate its central importance to the future of the Civil Service.) These two requirements, parliamentary and executive, match and complement each other. Over the years ahead one of the most important tasks of the new Expenditure Committee will be to stimulate the spread of responsible management in Whitehall.

Once it is recognised that the new Expenditure Committee is the modern counterpart of the Public Accounts Committee established by Gladstone, it becomes clear that the Public Accounts Committee, the Nationalised Industries Committee and the various remaining 'specialist' committees should be incorporated within its structure. After all, their *raison d'être* is to scrutinise the effectiveness of government policy and administration in their respective fields. Moreover, it was already becoming clear in 1970 that, as a result of their enquiry into parliamentary scrutiny of taxation, the Select Committee on Procedure were likely to recommend a new Select Committee to scrutinise government administration in the field of taxation and finance. This would, in effect, require a further functional Sub-Committee of the Expenditure Committee to be added to the eight already suggested by the Procedure Committee.[13]

Thus the Expenditure Committee proposed by the Procedure Committee in their 1968–69 Report should be seen as a structure of Committees on Public Expenditure *and Administration*,* on the lines of the chart at Figure 5. The General Committee at its head should have the special role of steering the total programme of work and of enquiring

* And possibly Legislation also see below.

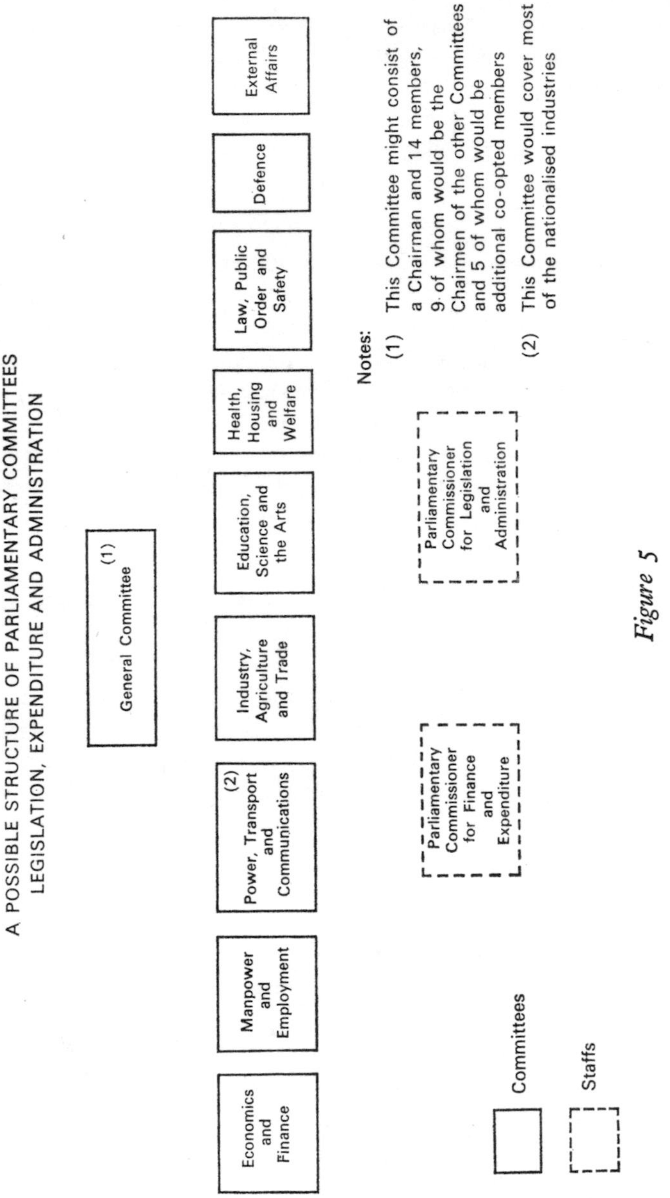

A POSSIBLE STRUCTURE OF PARLIAMENTARY COMMITTEES
LEGISLATION, EXPENDITURE AND ADMINISTRATION

General Committee (1)

| Economics and Finance | Manpower and Employment | Power, Transport and Communications (2) | Industry, Agriculture and Trade | Education, Science and the Arts | Health, Housing and Welfare | Law, Public Order and Safety | Defence | External Affairs |

Parliamentary Commissioner for Finance and Expenditure

Parliamentary Commissioner for Legislation and Administration

Committees

Staffs

Notes:

(1) This Committee might consist of a Chairman and 14 members, 9 of whom would be the Chairman of the other Committees and 5 of whom would be additional co-opted members

(2) This Committee would cover most of the nationalised industries

Figure 5

from time to time into the efficiency with which the proposed Prime Minister's Office is supporting the Prime Minister in his task of conducting the government orchestra as a whole. It will be seen that the chart incorporates a Parliamentary Commissioner for Finance and Expenditure, an up-to-date version of the present Comptroller and Auditor General. He will need to be supported by a Management Analysis and Audit Department, or in other words an up-to-date version of the present Exchequer and Audit Department. This department could take over the public sector functions previously discharged by the Prices and Incomes Board and be reinforced by staff from the Board as well as from the National Economic Development Office, as proposed in Chapter 4.

We can now sum up our discussion on parliamentary control of the Executive as follows.

Governments are committed to place before Parliament annually their firm plans for public spending during the two years immediately ahead and their provisional allocations for the two years after that. The Commons will thus have a regular opportunity to debate the government's medium term priorities and strategies right across the board, on the basis of the most up-to-date information available, when it is not too late to influence decisions. For the first time for many years Parliament may have a chance to participate in shaping future government policy, as Parliament should in any parliamentary democracy worthy of the name.

For this to happen, however, the annual public expenditure debates must be more than just another occasion for party political shadow boxing. The debates must focus on what the expenditure figures mean, not in terms of the familiar clichés and slogans of customary political argument, but in actual terms of schools and roads to be built, health services to be developed, defence capabilities to be streamlined. What choices do the figures imply? What could be achieved by spending so many million pounds more on education or social security or defence? What other programmes would have to be cut, or what taxes would have to be raised, to find the money? What effects would those cuts or higher taxes have? Questions like this are the essential material for any political debate that is to have a practical outcome. The public expenditure White Paper published in December 1969 and the debate on it in January 1970, although a great step forward, did not throw much light on such questions and could not be expected to do so.

To give substance to these debates in future years, is one of the tasks of the new House of Commons Select Committee on Expenditure. But the new Select Committee, once established, will not only give substance to future parliamentary debates on public spending. It will also be part and parcel of a wider series of central government reforms, embracing the work of ministers and civil servants as well as Parliament itself. Looked at this way, some of the doubts that have been expressed about the new Expenditure Committee appear less serious than at first sight. Once it is recognised that a Select Committee is the forum in which officials (not ministers) discharge their accountability to Parliament, ministers need not fear that they will be expected to defend their policies in Select Committee as well as on the floor of the House. Once it is generally recognised that a Select Committee is not the proper forum for political debate, civil servants need not fear that they will become embroiled in political debate between Select Committee members from opposing parties. Back bench protagonists need not fear that the new Committee will ever replace the floor of the House as the main forum for policy debate. Ministers, civil servants and backbenchers alike will all be in a position to keep the new Committee in its proper place, and to see that it does not try (as Congressional Committees in the United States have sometimes seemed to do) to usurp the functions either of the Cabinet or of the House of Commons as a whole.

At the same time, it would be wrong to think that the new arrangements will necessarily make life easier for ministers, civil servants and MPs. Responsibilities will be clarified: ministers' responsibilities for clearly defining policy objectives; civil servants' responsibilities for efficient and humane administration in accordance with their ministers' remit; and MPs' responsibilities for scrutinising the government's actions much more effectively than in the recent past. This may not suit the minister or civil servant who likes fudging things; the minister who is happy enough for the blame for his own mistakes to spill over on to his civil servants; and the civil servant who hides behind his minister's coat tails to escape the consequences of his own laziness or inefficiency. It may not suit those backbench politicians who like to argue on a high plane about great issues while leaving other people to deal with the business of real life. Why, the wind-merchants will ask, should Select Committees be expected to concentrate on so dull and limited a sphere as the whole of government expenditure and administration? 'Hear! hear!' will murmur those ministers and civil servants who believe in keeping parliamentary Select Committees safely out of harm's way!

But in spite of some resistance to the new Expenditure Committee, and to the further developments that will inevitably follow from its creation, it will be very welcome. It will do much to help those ministers who want to pursue effective policies and get things done. It will do much to restore a sense of professionalism and personal responsibility in the Civil Service. And it will do much to reduce the credibility gap between what politicians talk about and what real life is about. It is a big step towards a parliamentary democracy in fact as well as name.

PARLIAMENT AND THE LAW

So much then for Parliament's control over government finance and administration. What of Parliament's legislative role?

Although this is not a field in which I can claim first-hand experience (indeed as a civil servant one was required to have little knowledge and little understanding of the law) it appears that during the last fifty or seventy years Parliament and the Judiciary have lost much of their traditional ability to ensure that the people of this country enjoy an intelligible, equitable and efficient system of law. Officials of the Executive retain an extraordinary degree of immunity in relation to the law. The growth of government has outstripped the capability of Parliament and the Courts to develop any corresponding system of administrative law. This situation has arisen for much the same reasons as administrative confusion in Whitehall: undue secrecy; piecemeal agglomeration of legislative changes over the years according to no comprehensive long-term strategy; and recent approaches to reform that have been directed at symptoms rather than at the underlying causes of the trouble. Even today, many politicians, judges and civil servants appear to be unaware of the need to establish an effective practical system of working relationships between the Legislative, the Judiciary and the Executive.

Parliament has a three-fold duty in respect of legislation, just as it has for controlling government administration. It has a duty to debate the policy for which the government proposes to legislate; to examine the legislative means (i.e. the precise terms of the legislation) proposed for putting the policy into effect; and to review the effects of the legislation in operation. This three-fold duty to scrutinise strategy, tactics and results corresponds to the three-stage circle of parliamentary control—policy, management, and review—over the activities of the Executive described earlier in this chapter. Just as Parliament needs to establish an effective 'link between the system for allocating resources and the system for getting value for money', so Parliament must establish an effective link between the system for deciding the broad substance of new legislation and the system for ensuring that the law is efficiently and equitably administered.

A report published by the Statute Law Society in 1970 on *Statute Law Deficiencies*[14] shows conclusively that the present methods of making the laws and publishing them are inadequate. It quotes the White Paper foreshadowing the Law Commissions Act, 1965, as follows: 'It is today extremely difficult for anyone without special training to discover what the law is on any given topic; and when the law is finally ascertained it is found in many cases to be obsolete and in some cases to be unjust ... English law should be capable of being re-cast in a form which is accessible, intelligible and in accordance with modern needs.' The report continues: 'The problem now is greater than it has ever been. The bulk and the complexity of Statute Law are ever growing and professional users of all descriptions are finding it increasingly difficult to cope with the task of advising their clients as to where exactly they stand in relation to the law.'[15]

One of the reasons for this is the secrecy with which legislation is prepared. As the Statute Law Society say, 'The current practice of the Government is generally to leave proposed legislation in a state of complete secrecy until the introduction of the Bill. This subsequently creates problems for the user and for the member of Parliament as the Bill then takes its normal course under the shadow of the strict Parliamentary time-table. Little time is left between publication and the detailed consideration in Parliament, and subsequently there is a comparative lack of opportunity for outside bodies to digest the proposed legislation and to make their views felt. A greater degree of advance publicity and consultation with appropriate bodies would obviate this situation, although in relation to certain types of legislation (for example fiscal) there may exceptionally be a special need for secrecy.'[16]

Another reason for the present state of the law is that often ministers do not have a clear idea of what they are trying to achieve. 'The drafting process must in the first place have a secure base. If (like the house built on sand) this is lacking, the end product cannot fail to be unsatisfactory. Much of the recent legislation has comprised attempts to remedy in piecemeal fashion bodies of case and statute law which themselves lack any firm structure; the political masters themselves too often do not know exactly what they require of the draftsman.'[17] This piecemeal nature of legislation is the cause of much trouble. 'One of the reasons for the complication and difficulty of the Companies Act is its lack of completeness. No one by reading it could glean any real understanding of company law. Nowhere are the fundamental principles enunciated. Exceptions are laid down to rules which are never stated and which have to be found from a study of the decided cases. The true position emerges, if at all, only when the Act is read against the background of a vast number of decisions, some of which are virtually irreconcilable. All this makes for complication and confusion, not for simplicity and certainty.'[18]

Yet another fault stems from the amount of detail included in the statutes. As the Statute Law Society say, 'United Kingdom law-making is based on the pre-supposition that as little area of discretion as possible should be left to officials and to the courts. It is arguable to what degree a legislature should assert its will. The United Kingdom has tended, particularly in recent times, to confine administrative discretion within narrow limits. Continental legal systems do not generally share the British attitude and in consequence their laws tend to be more general, less detailed and more readily comprehensible. A move towards the Continental attitude to legislation would be welcomed by many in this country. A less detailed statute book does entail a more creative role on the part of the courts although their comparative freedom does not mean allowing their discretion to be absolutely unfettered. The choice is not between complete arbitrariness and absolutely binding rules; the exercise of discretion falls in the middle of these two extremes, and in this exercise principles act as guide posts and not as hitch-posts.'[19] This quotation suggests a parallel between the need to devolve to the Courts responsibility for the detailed interpretation of general legal provisions, and the need to devolve to 'accountable management' the detailed administration of general policies laid down by the ministerial Executive with parliamentary approval. Just as it is now necessary to develop new ways of bringing government officials to account before Parliament for the ways in which they discharge their administrative and management responsibilities, so it may be necessary to develop new ways of making the Courts accountable to Parliament for the way in which they interpret and administer the law.

Again, as the Statute Law Society say, the quality of laws suffers by reason of defects in Parliament's legislative procedures. A Bill is an 'inadequate vehicle for debate of the principles behind it', just as the traditional annual estimates of expenditure are an inadequate vehicle for debating the policies behind them. There is too little time between the publication of a Bill and its detailed discussion in Parliament. Procedural devices such as the guillotine 'often preclude the possibility of full and proper consideration being given to important provisions . . . The Committee stage provides an inadequate vehicle for the debating of committee points . . . No procedure exists in the United Kingdom whereby the proposed legislation is vetted by experts for such purposes as consistency with prior legislation and adequacy of form.'[20]

In short, it appears that the present methods of framing legislation could hardly have been more aptly designed if it had been our intention to produce bad laws. Parliament is asked to pass too many bills in too much of a hurry. Ministers very often have no precise idea of what they want a bill to mean, but are impatient if parliamentary draftsmen ask too insistently for clarification. The Committee stage of legislation in the House of Commons, which should enable Parliament to scrutinise the administrative feasibility of the proposals in a Bill, has declined into just another instalment in the party political mock battle. Bills are sent so late to the House of Lords that their Lordships have too little time to revise them; and in any case the House of Lords has now forfeited most of its credibility as a revising legislature.

Perhaps the most disturbing feature of the Report on Statute Law Deficiencies from which I have quoted was the light it shed on the attitude of members of Parliament towards their legislative duties. In compiling material for this report the Statute Law Society sent a questionnaire to 5,000 'users' of statute law, including barristers, solicitors, accountants and members of Parliament. They sent questionnaires to 966 members of both Houses of Parliament and received 16 replies. The report comments on the questionnaire that 'by far the most noticeable feature was the low rate of response from Parliamentarians (2%). Whether this indicates a lack of interest in the subject matter of the questionnaire or an expression of satisfaction with the status quo is, of course, open to conjecture.'[21] Either way, it appears to show that most members of Parliament do not regard the practical effects of legislation as being of much concern to them. But then what *do* they think their job is ? What do they suppose we pay them for ? One scarcely wonders that a recent survey found that members of Parliament were held lower in public esteem than any other profession, including dustbinmen and clergymen!

176

So much then for the shortcomings of the present legislative procedures. We shall return shortly to possible remedies: the procedures required for debating the strategy of legislation on the floor of the House, as the government's administrative and expenditure strategies are to be debated on the basis of forward projections of expenditure; and the procedures required for scrutinising the detailed legislation implementing the strategy, corresponding to the proposed scrutiny of departmental budgets by a Select Committee on Expenditure.

We now turn to the failure of the law to keep up with the government's growth in size and with its change of character over the last hundred years. This failure takes two closely related forms. First, the law still confers on government today many of the legal privileges traditionally granted to the Crown. Secondly, there is still a presumption on the part of most politicians, government officials and lawyers that the citizen's relationship with government should be on an altogether different footing from his relationships with other parties, and that a different kind of remedy is appropriate in cases of dispute between the citizen and a government body. Both types of anachronism are based on the legal fiction that any government official is a servant of an entity called the Crown.

The privileged legal position of the government takes many forms. It was only as recently as 1947, with the passage of the Crown Proceedings Act, that government agencies and officials were placed in more or less the same position as other organisations in respect of liability for civil action in the courts. Before then, proceedings against the Crown were generally possible only by a procedure known as a petition of right. Thus no proceedings could be brought against the government if an individual were injured by a negligently driven government vehicle or if a government employee suffered from the negligence of the department employing him. Even today there are many instances of government immunity from legal provisions that apply to other organisations and individuals. Civil servants have no contract of employment with the Crown, and a civil servant has no right of action against the Crown for salary due to him in respect of his services. Government departments have been able to claim Crown privilege to avoid disclosing documents in court proceedings, and to claim immunity for damage. Government departments are, in the last resort, judges of whether they should be allowed to erect buildings and other installations, for which other organisations would be refused planning permission. In theory, at least, the Official Secrets Act safeguards the secrecy of every governmental act carried out by every government official, thus putting government departments in a much stronger position to preserve the confidentiality of their activities than any other organisation. Conversely, we find that the Younger Committee on Privacy, set up in 1970 to consider how the individual's right to privacy should be safeguarded, has been precluded by its terms of reference from considering intrusion into privacy by government agencies and departments. As the public sector and the private sector converge, these forms of legal privilege enjoyed by government are increasingly inappropriate and difficult to justify.

Turning now to the question of adjudication between the citizen and the state we find that, as the scale of government activity has grown, the country's judicial system has failed to keep pace with it. Long ago, the courts played an important role in regulating the behaviour of the monarch towards his subjects; the doctrine of *habeas corpus* is a case in point. But as government became more and more closely involved in social and economic administration, it became necessary to set up a whole range of special administrative tribunals to deal with disputes arising between the citizen and the government agency concerned. National Assistance Appeal Tribunals, Lands Tribunals, and a multitude of other tribunals (about 2,000 in all by 1956) came into existence to regulate the discretionary activities of government departments in relation to their clients. They have raised difficult questions about the respective roles of Parliament and the Law.

Marshall and Moodie[22] summarise the situation as follows: 'In this country the mechanisms for the control of power have traditionally been two-fold: first the sanctions of the civil and criminal law applied by the law courts, and secondly the control, exercised, as Burke said, on behalf of the people by the High Court of Parliament. The distinction between the two methods of control is, at least in principle, fairly clear. The function of parliamentary debate is to air grievances against the policy and proposals of Her Majesty's Government, and if possible to get Her Majesty's Ministers to change their minds. It is an argumentative process, rather than a judicial one. The function of the courts on the other hand, is predominantly that of providing remedies for individuals against unlawful damage inflicted on them by other individuals and the process is surrounded by strict rules of procedure and evidence. The extension of State activity and the growth of different kinds of 'damage' to individual interests have destroyed the simplicity of this distinction. A good many recent constitutional disagreements boil down to the question whether a particular type of damage or dispute falls into the area where control ought to be exercised (if at all) by parliamentary means, into that where it ought to be exercised by judicial means, or into some disputed middle ground uneasily and increasingly overcrowded by disputes between private individuals and bodies which are agents (in some sense) of Government and Administration. It must be conceded further that a fair generalisation about the history in this country of individual efforts to attack the exercise of administrative powers in the courts would be that it is a record of comparative failure.'

The basic questions are really as follows: how far should Parliament delegate to the courts responsibility for adjudicating in disputes between citizens and the government? and through what channel of accountability should the judiciary be accountable to Parliament for administering the laws governing relations between the individual and the State?

These questions correspond to comparable questions in the administrative sphere: how far should Parliament encourage Ministers to delegate responsibility to officials for the managerial decisions involved in implementing government policies? and through what channels of accountability should officials be responsible to Parliament for their administration of government policies? In the long run, equity and efficiency respectively require as much devolution as possible. The main argument traditionally put forward by left-wing parliamentarians against devolving administrative justice to the courts has been that judges, like civil servants, have tended to be conservative and therefore to be biased in favour of the private against the public interest. In so far as this may be true, should it not be possible to rectify it by making judges, like officials, properly accountable to Parliament—presumably through the Lord Chancellor, supported by some suitably non-partisan parliamentary agency of the Select Committee type?

There have been three main developments in the spheres of legislation and administrative law in recent years. Law Commissions were set up for England and Scotland in 1965. The Council on Tribunals was set up in 1958, following the report of the Franks Committee appointed after the Crichel Down incident. Finally, the Parliamentary Commissioner for Administration (Ombudsman) was appointed in 1966.

The duty of the Law Commission is 'to prepare and submit to the

179

Lord Chancellor from time to time programmes for the examination of different branches of the law with a view to reform, and to make recommendations as to the agency by which those examinations are to be carried out. In undertaking such examinations the Commission, if it thinks reform is necessary, is to formulate proposals by means of draft Bills. If requested by the Lord Chancellor, it is to prepare comprehensive programmes for the consolidation and revision of the statutory law, and to prepare draft Bills to give effect to these programmes. It is to provide advice and information to Government Departments and other bodies concerned, at the instance of the Government, with proposals for law reform. In the performance of its functions, the Commission is to obtain information as to the legal systems of other countries. The programmes of the Commission, if approved by the Lord Chancellor, are to be laid before Parliament. Likewise, the Commission's proposals for reform, formulated according to an approved programme, are to be laid before Parliament whether or not the Lord Chancellor approves them. Finally, the Commission is to make an annual report to the Lord Chancellor, and he is obliged to lay that report before Parliament with such comments, if any, as he thinks fit to make.'[23]

The establishment of the Law Commission was largely attributable to Lord Gardiner, the Lord Chancellor under the Labour Government from 1964 to 1970. In 1963 he had written in 'Law Reform Now' that 'the complexity of English Law has, by now, reached a degree where the system is not only unknown to the community at large, but unknowable, save to the extent of a few departments, even to the professionals'.[24] Unfortunately, the work of the Law Commission has so far been almost completely hamstrung, not through any fault of its own but by the legislative processes of Parliament itself. As we have seen, these might almost have been designed deliberately to produce the maximum quantity of bad law. The 1964 to 1970 Labour Governments did, as it happens, produce an unusually large quantity of confused and obscure legislation, which has quite swamped the efforts of the newly created Law Commission to improve the quality of the existing law. In legislation as in every other facet of government, it is no use introducing new, modernising organisations into a system which continues to bowl along more merrily than ever in the bad old ways. To achieve effective results it is necessary to understand and tackle the situation as a whole.

The Franks Committee,[25] which led to the creation of the Council on

Tribunals, concluded that when decisions are taken on methods of adjudicating disputes between individuals and the administration, preference should be given, if not to the courts, to an administrative tribunal rather than to a Minister, and that every opportunity should be taken of expressing policy in the form of regulations capable of being administered in a judicial way. Existing tribunals, the Committee thought, 'should properly be regarded as machinery provided by Parliament for adjudication rather than as part of the machinery of administration. Although the relevant statutes do not in all cases expressly enact that tribunals are to consist entirely of persons outside the Government service, the use of the term 'tribunal' in legislation undoubtedly bears this connotation, and the intention of Parliament to provide for the independence of tribunals is clear and unmistakable.' Moreover, the Committee concluded, a general appeal on points of law should be possible from all tribunals; legal representation should be possible in all cases; hearings should be public; reasons should always be given; chairmen of tribunals should be appointed by the Lord Chancellor; and independent councils should be set up to supervise their operations.

The creation of the Council on Tribunals in 1958 confirmed, though only to a limited extent, this swing towards the role of judicial intervention in disputes between the citizen and the government. The Council, appointed by the Lord Chancellor and the Secretary of State for Scotland jointly, is responsible for keeping under review the constitution and working of about 2,000 tribunals. The Council reports annually to the Lord Chancellor and the Secretary of State, who lay the annual report before Parliament with such comments of their own as they wish to make. Members of Parliament, as one might expect, have shown comparatively little interest in the Council's work.

It can be argued – and indeed it has been argued strongly, for example by Professor Mitchell[26] of Edinburgh University – that these administrative tribunals should be fully incorporated in the judicial system of the country, and that the channels of appeal from their findings should culminate in an Administrative Division of the High Court and ultimately in the House of Lords itself. This structure would absorb the Council on Tribunals.

The appointment of the Parliamentary Commissioner or Ombudsman in 1966 represented a shift in the other direction. It was based on the view that Parliament rather than the courts is the right place for ventilating the citizens' grievances and seeking redress for them, and that the Parliamentary Commissioner was needed to help members of Parliament to discharge this task. But there are strong arguments for holding that the business of Parliament is to redress grievances of a general order, not to provide a remedy for the individual citizen in each particular case. After all, Parliament could hardly be expected to provide a remedy for every individual citizen in his disputes with the State. Any arrangement which purports to do this is likely not only to be ineffective in itself, but also to distract public attention from the need for a more effective alternative. It will probably also distract Parliament's attention from its real job of scrutinising the government's overall policies and administrative systems. Certainly, there is little sign some years after the Parliamentary Commissioner's appointment that he is likely to be an important addition to the mechanisms of British government, unless the original concept of his role is fairly radically changed.

THE LEGISLATURE, THE EXECUTIVE AND THE JUDICIARY

In this chapter I have been trying to suggest that reform of the executive arm of government must be paralleled by reforms both of the Legislature and of the Judiciary. It will, in fact, be impossible to reform the Executive without making matching reforms in Parliament and the Courts; each necessarily interacts with the others in our total system of government. Parliament needs to encourage ministers to delegate administrative and financial responsibility to officials and needs to develop its own Select Committee structure to provide a systematic method of bringing officials to account for their discharge of this responsibility; equally Parliament needs to delegate to lawyers and the courts responsibility for the detailed preparation and administration of the laws and needs to develop comparable channels for their accountability.

It is impossible to be dogmatic about the precise organisational changes required in Parliament and the Judiciary for these purposes, but I believe they will prove to be on the following lines:

1. The House of Commons Standing Committees dealing with legislation should be incorporated within the structure of Select Committees on Expenditure and Administration described earlier in this chapter. That would then become a system of Select Committees on Legislation, Expenditure and Administration, as shown in Figure 5.

This would itself remove a fair amount of overlapping membership and duplication of effort that now takes place in existing House of Commons Select and Standing Committees.

2. These Select Committees should include members drawn from the House of Lords as well as the House of Commons. That would further ease the problem of finding competent members to man them.

3. The whole structure of Select Committees would be serviced by the Clerks of Parliament, supported on the one hand by a Parliamentary Commissioner for Finance and Expenditure and his staff (a modernised version of the present Comptroller and Auditor General and the Exchequer and Audit Department) and on the other by a Parliamentary Commissioner for Legislation and Administration (a strengthened version of the present Parliamentary Commissioner for Administration). The staff of the former would include, most importantly, management accountants and economists of the kind recently employed by the Prices and Incomes Board and the staff of the latter would include lawyers and sociologists.

4. These Select Committees would be responsible:

for scrutinising the efficiency of government administration (as recommended by the Procedure Committee in 1968–69),

for scrutinising the administrative feasibility of proposed legislation, and

for examining the adequacy of existing legislation through the reports of such bodies as the Law Commission and the Council on Tribunals.

5. Meanwhile, consideration should be given to transforming the existing structure of administrative tribunals into a structure of administrative courts, responsible through an Administrative Division of the High Court to the House of Lords. Other suggestions, for example for commercial and employment courts, or about the Lord Chancellor's role as custodian of the citizen's interest, or for a Bill of Rights, must also be considered.

OPENNESS AND GEOGRAPHICAL DEVOLUTION

Arrangements on these lines would enable Parliament to delegate to Select Committees much of the detailed business which cannot be handled effectively on the floor of the House and which, if handled there, leaves no time for adequate discussion of wider, more important issues. In this they would correspond to the principle of 'hiving off' in Whitehall. They should do much to remedy Parliament's present inability to discharge its duty to the nation. By providing back-bench MPs with a real opportunity to participate, they should also help to restore Parliament to a sense of competence, personal integrity and self-respect. But in themselves these arrangements will not be enough. Two further changes in Parliament's procedures will be necessary, corresponding to the need for more open administration and to the need for regional and local devolution.

If Parliament is to be a really effective forum for political debate and discussion at the national level and a really effective channel of communication between the people and their representatives in Parliament, its work must be carried out more openly than at present. Parliamentary debates should be made public by whatever communications are available to a modern society; they should be broadcast, by radio if not by television. The main argument put forward against this is that the proceedings of Parliament are boring, unintelligible, esoteric or just plain trivial. For example, in discussing the case for not televising Parliament Allan Segal[27] writes, 'All agree that Parliamentary sittings would have to be telerecorded and edited if infinite hours of boredom resulting from procedural wrangles are to be avoided.' Surely this is very odd. Ought not our legislators to be debating and probing the passionately important issues facing our self-governing society? If they are doing their job properly, how could their proceedings be so boring and trivial that we should want to switch them off? And if they are not doing their job properly, ought we not to know about it, and perhaps switch them right off altogether? Again, so far as Select Committees are concerned, it should become the rule that they sit in public, save in exceptional circumstances when there are special reasons for confidentiality. There can be no doubt that press comment on the progress of a Select Committee's enquiry can contribute significantly to its momentum. This was very noticeable in the enquiry into the future of the United Kingdom Computer Industry carried out by Sub-Committee D of the Select Committee on Science and Technology in 1969–70.

The question of devolution from the national legislature to regional and local legislatures must also be examined more constructively than in the past. The starting point must be an analysis, on the lines suggested in Chapter 6, of the functions of government that are best carried out at the national level, at the regional level, and at the local level. John Mackintosh has summarised the probable outcome.[28] 'The problem of government outside Whitehall has now been examined from both ends, from that of local government reform designed to produce a more democratic and effective series of local councils, and from the opposite end, the need to devolve central government powers, and the most promising solution to emerge takes the form of elected regional councils. These could both be the top tier of a new system of local government and be large enough to undertake regional planning, transport, the preservation of the countryside, and similar essentially local functions at present left to nominated bodies or the central government. Such regional elected councils, perhaps with a few extra powers, could permit all the regional variations of policy and the local control which are a feature of the Stormont system in Northern Ireland, while at the same time meeting the legitimate aspirations of the Welsh and the Scots for a degree of self-government and for jurisdiction over those aspects of policy peculiar to their own countries in a manner which would avoid both the retrograde step of total separation and the unnecessary complications of a formal federal system.'

It is not my purpose here to try to suggest at all precisely the form these regionally elected councils should take, or precisely how the functions of government should be divided between national, regional and local levels. As we have seen in Chapter 6, what is needed is a comprehensive analysis, embracing every function of government, with the aim of reaching a clear view on what decisions we think should be taken nationally, what decisions regionally, and what decisions locally.

THE NEW SYNTHESIS

At the beginning of this chapter I wrote that we need to think of our system of government as a 'multi-dimensional' or multi-faceted system, a totality of activities characterised by functions, decision levels, geographical spans, and time scales. To these four dimensions we now have to add the two more which have been considered in this chapter–the legislative and the judicial. In short, let us take Sir Robert Morant's advice and look at the structure of government as a whole. Let us create a new pattern of government in which Parliament, ministers, civil servants, national corporations, regional government, local government and the judiciary all have their own clearly defined parts to play. Let us reconstruct the public service, as it has evolved since the nineteenth century, to meet the needs of our complex, self-governing society today. By a process of social creativity let us bring a new structure of government into life from the confused jungle of our existing institutions, as Michelangelo released the living form from the inert material of the stone.

In fact, surely we can already see the new structure of government beginning to emerge.

Parliament is beginning to regard the people as partners in the national enterprise rather than as subjects of the Crown. Parliament is gradually beginning to take relatively more interest in the framing and execution of national policies, and relatively less in individual cases.

Ministers are beginning to take more interest in framing broad national policies and translating them into specific policies and operating targets for managerial and executive agencies of government. They are beginning to spend relatively less time on matters of detailed management and administration.

Thus ministers are increasingly beginning to devolve managerial tasks to separate executive agencies outside their ministry – i.e. national boards, corporations and the like.

Ministers will also have to decentralise the detailed decisions concerning particular regions or localities to regional or local authorities. There are some signs that this trend has begun, for example in town planning.

The devolution functionally and geographically of much of the work now centralised in Whitehall will permit drastic reductions in the size of Whitehall departments, which will revert to their proper role of providing a secretariat service to ministers.

It will also permit a significant reduction in the number of departments and in the size of the Cabinet.

The existing structure of administrative tribunals will develop into a rationalised system of judicial administrative courts, flanking the executive at central, regional and local levels and culminating in an Administrative Division of the High Court and ultimately the House of Lords. Similar systems of commercial and employment courts may be needed, as suggested in Chapter 4.

The reform of parliamentary business will consist of: functional devolution to a rationalised Select Committee structure; and geographical devolution to regional and local legislatures. It seems likely also to involve closer integration of the functions of the Commons and the Lords, and the emergence of new organisational structures and procedures which embrace the financial, legislative and judicial functions of Parliament. To borrow the words used by Bagehot about the Cabinet, Parliament will thus emerge as the hyphen which joins, the buckle which fastens, not just the legislative part of the State to the executive part, but the legislative, executive *and* judicial parts of the State together.

That, in outline, is the shape of the new system of government that appears to be emerging in self-governing Britain. The steps required to bring it into being will be discussed in Chapter 11.

NOTES ON CHAPTER 9

General

Ronald Butt's *The Power of Parliament* (Constable, 1967) and Bernard Crick's *The Reform of Parliament* (Weidenfeld and Nicolson, 1964) take two rather different approaches to the problems of parliamentary reform, and provide a valuable background to the subject. I have also found very helpful *Some Problems of the Constitution*, by Geoffrey Marshall and Graeme C. Moodie (Hutchinson University Library, 1967). *The Control of Public Expenditure* by B. Chubb (Oxford University Press, 1955) is an indispensable source of information on parliamentary procedures for controlling public expenditure.

Note 1. Winston Churchill, speaking in the House of Commons; *Hansard* for 26th July 1905, columns 443 and 444.

Note 2. Walter Bagehot: *The English Constitution*; Fontana Library, 1963; page 72.

Note 3. Quoted by Sir L. Woodward in *The Age of Reform: 1815–1870*; page 99.

Note 4. H.C. Debates 1.3.1866, col. 1373. (This short Second Reading Debate–cols. 1368 to 1375–is well worth reading. It is very apt– *mutatis mutandis*–to today's problems.

Note 5. H.C. Debates, 18.4.1861, col. 774.

Note 6. Quoted in Epitome, H.C. 154 of 1937–38, page 190.

Note 7. H.C. Debates, 26.7.1905, cols. 443–444.

Note 8. B. Chubb: *The Control of Public Expenditure*; Oxford University Press, 1955, pages 229 ff.

Note 9. *The Times*, Thursday, 6th November 1969, page 24.

Note 10. *First Report from the Select Committee on Procedure, Session 1968–69*; paragraph 12.

Note 11. *Ibid.*, paragraph 13.

Note 12. *Ibid.*, paragraphs 32 and following.

Note 13. The evidence given to the Select Committee was published as the *Second Special Report from the Select Committee on Procedure: Session 1969–70* in May 1970.

Note 14. *Statute Law Deficiencies: Report of the Committee appointed by the Society to examine the failings of the present Statute Law System*; Sweet and Maxwell on behalf of the Statute Law Society, 1970.

Note 15. *Ibid.*, paragraphs 29 and 30.

Note 16. *Ibid.*, paragraph 36.

Note 17. *Ibid.*, paragraph 46.

Note 18. *Ibid.*, paragraph 63.

Note 19. *Ibid.*, paragraph 69.

Note 20. *Ibid.*, paragraphs 54 and 55.

Note 21. *Ibid.*, Appendix A.

Note 22. Geoffrey Marshall and Graeme C. Moodie: *Some Problems of the Constitution*; page 93.

Note 23. Mr Justice Scarman in *Law Reform*, pages 10 and 11; quoted in *Statute Law Deficiencies*, paragraph 7.

Note 24. *Law Reform Now*: ed. Gerald Gardiner, Q.C., and Andrew Martin; Gollancz, 1964; page 1.

Note 25. See Marshall and Moodie; *op. cit.*, page 113.

Note 26. Professor J. D. B. Mitchell: 'The Constitutional Implications of Judicial Control of the Administration in the United Kingdom': *Cambridge Law Journal*, April 1967.

Note 27. Allan Segal: 'The Case For Not Televising Parliament': Appendix G of Bernard Crick, *op. cit.*

Note 28. J. P. Mackintosh: *The Devolution of Power*; Chatto & Windus and Charles Knight & Co., 1968.

10

The Methodology of Government

The State originated so that people could live, but its
raison d'être now is that people can live the good life.
ARISTOTLE, *Politics*, Book I.2

Reflection on principles, whether those of natural science
or of any other department of thought or action, is commonly called philosophy.

R. G. COLLINGWOOD: *The Idea of Nature*

Previous chapters have brought us to the point where the outline of a
reformed system of government appears to be emerging–a new synthesis incorporating the executive, legislative and judicial elements of
government at national, regional and local levels. The underlying theme
has been that government provides a society with the institutional
mechanism (or circuitry) for taking decisions, and that by understanding how it works it is possible to improve this mechanism. In this
chapter we consider how, under a reformed system of government, it
will be necessary to develop the 'state of the art' of government to tackle
the problems that the future will bring.

The institutional structure and the state of the art are, of course,
closely related. Institutional reform and conceptual evolution must go
hand in hand. Our developing perception of the problems that govern
ment has to handle must be matched by the development of institutions
and procedures for handling them. In turn, the new 'circuitry' introduced by institutional and procedural changes will throw up new decisions to be taken, and by thus posing the problems in a new light will
change our perception of them. Uninitiated commentators sometimes
ask: 'Why all this fuss about institutional changes? Surely what we
need is new policies.' They do not realise that the structure of the
institutions determines to a large extent the manner in which the problems are perceived and thus shapes the policies that are adopted to deal
with them. The converse is also true.

The problem that arises in respect of the concepts and skills and
techniques connected with government work is similar to the institu-

tional problem. New specialisms and professions have proliferated almost as fast as new organs of government. Economists, econometricians, statisticians, systems analysts, operational research scientists, personnel managers, manpower planners, corporate planners, behavioural scientists, sociologists–these are just a few of the professionals whose contributions we now have to pull into a coherent whole, whose specialisms we have to relate to one another in answering the three questions:

what is to be done?

how is it to be done?

how well has it been done?

All these professions and specialisms and all the new techniques like programme budgeting and management by objectives have grown up piecemeal, because they were needed, just as new departments and agencies of government have grown up. How do we reconcile their differing standpoints and combine them to translate the values of society into defined objectives and effective action? How do we gear them to the task of helping us all to live the good life? How do we ensure that they *converge*, in the sense of that word used by Pierre Teilhard de Chardin, as 'the tendency of mankind, during its evolution, to superpose centripetal on centrifugal trends, so as to prevent centrifugal differentiation from leading to fragmentation, and eventually to incorporate the results of differentiation in an organised and unified pattern'?[1]

These are among the questions we consider in this chapter. The answer to them will lead us some way towards a new philosophy of government in tune with actual contemporary needs, in a society whose affairs have become highly complex and in which public decisions have to take account of a far longer time scale than was previously necessary– a society which has become self-governing, and whose citizens rightly pitch their aspirations a great deal higher than their fathers did. It will be a philosophy (or methodology) of government based on the evident need for effective mechanisms of democratic choice.

PRINCIPLES

Some of the principles that underlie any useful consideration of this kind of methodology of government have already appeared in previous chapters in one form or another. It is now time to state three of them explicitly. The first may be called the 'operability' principle. It is closely related to the second which, following Professor Ayer,[2] I shall call the 'verifiability' principle. The third is the 'compatibility' principle. It is simplest to define these negatively.

The operability principle means that it is pointless to conduct the business of government or to discuss it, in terms which, when a conclusion is reached, are incapable of being translated into action. To quote Bagehot's dictum again, 'Human nature despises long arguments which come to nothing—heavy speeches which preclude no motion—abstract disquisitions which leave visible things where they were.'[3]

Similarly, the verifiability principle means that it is pointless to discuss the problems of government in terms which cannot be translated into a reference to real people or real things in the real world.

Much of what at present passes for the currency of political debate and economic discussion is in fact inoperable and unverifiable. Most of us recognise that much politicians' talk is hot air; fewer of us, perhaps, are aware that many of the concepts used by economists, such as the *capacity of the economy* for example, are meaningless since they do not (and never could) represent aggregates of information about real things in the real world.

The compatibility principle means, in effect, that we cannot handle our affairs sensibly with a system of government resembling a tower of Babel. Different departments must be able to make it clear to each other what or which particular things their discourse is about and fit together each other's reports and stories into a single picture of the world.[4] This problem was brought out very clearly in the Estimates Committee's 1966 report on the Government Statistical Services.[5] The following is one example quoted in the Committee's Report:

Most departments keep registers of their sources of statistical information. The departments concerned with economic policy employ four categories of reporting unit: the establishment, the legal entity for tax purposes, the business unit and the enterprise. Both the Ministry of Labour and the Board of Trade maintain registers of establishments (the Ministry of Labour having more than one), which they employ when designing surveys. However, despite regular informal consultation these two sets of registers are not fully compatible, and consequently analyses of variables spanning both departments can be extremely hazardous. Your Committee are also surprised to learn that the Inland Revenue rely on their local Inspectors of Taxes to allocate firms within the Standard Industrial Classification on the basis of 'such knowledge of the activities of the business as he happens to have available'. It is clear that discrepancies between this classification and those made by the Board of Trade and the Ministry of Labour are likely to arise only in cases where the company consists of a number of establishments classified under different headings of the Standard Industrial Classification. But in the absence of a register common to all departments and covering all categories of reporting unit, inconsistencies in coverage and therefore of interpretation are bound to emerge . . . Your Committee regard the establishment of a common register as work which should be accorded the highest priority. They regard it as inexcusable that despite the emphasis laid on productivity by successive governments since the war there is still no regular detailed and accurate source of statistics relating output, earnings and employment other than the Census of Production.[5]

(Productivity, by the way, is a good example of the kind of inoperable, unverifiable concept that recent governments have tried unsuccessfully to conjure with.)

THE SYSTEM CONCEPT

How then are the principles of operability, verifiability and compatibility to be applied? This question brings us back to the cybernetic approach to government mentioned in Chapter 1. The answer lies largely in the development of automatic methods of handling data and in the application of the logically and numerically rigorous techniques of systems analysis and operational research that go with it. The key to understanding this is the concept of *a system*. This concept also provides the common link between all the specialisms and professions mentioned earlier.

The system concept is a very simple one. It is that an organisation is a system ('a set or assemblage of things, connected, associated or interdependent, so as to form a complex unity'—*OED*) for achieving certain objectives; that to a greater or lesser extent these objectives can and must be defined and the extent of their achievement assessed; and that the working of the system and its structure, can be changed so as to improve its performance.

A system may be self-controlling. In other words it may contain a mechanism (or sub-system) for assessing its own performance and for altering its mode of operation accordingly. The mechanical governor is a simple feed-back device of this kind. A system may also be self-adapting or self-organising. It may contain a mechanism for assessing the success or failure with which it is achieving its objectives and for altering its structure accordingly. Social systems–economic, political, administrative, and business systems, for example–are self-organising systems, though their self-organising mechanisms are sometimes crude and unconscious (and sometimes ineffective). As their objectives change, or as their performance declines, a process takes place within them that leads to changes in their mode of operation and their structure. As this process becomes more deliberate and conscious, we can begin to talk of a system planning its own future development. That, of course, is just what this book is all about.

Processing information and making decisions are vital elements in planning and controlling the operations of a system. So is its internal logical hierarchy, its organisational structure. The following example[6] illustrates these points. It may seem trivial, but it does illustrate precisely the kind of systems analysis that is required if government policies, that is to say high-level government decisions, are to observe the principles of operability, verifiability and compatibility.

Imagine a network of pipes through which fluids flow. It has three inflow pipes, into one of which a Red fluid, another a Yellow fluid and the last a Blue fluid, are pumped. It has two outlet pipes, one serving recipient A and the other recipient B. The system looks like Figure 6.

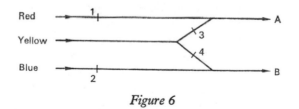

Figure 6

The points marked 1, 2, 3, 4 are valves, which can be fully open, fully closed or at any intermediate, partly open, partly closed, position.

The system works as follows:

(*a*) (i) If A asks for Red, valve 1 must be opened and valve 3 must be closed.

   (ii) If A asks for Yellow, valve 3 must be opened and valve 1 must be closed.

   (iii) If A asks for Orange, valves 1 and 3 must both be opened to the extent that will give the required shade, i.e. the required mixture of Red and Yellow.

(*b*) (i) If B asks for Blue, valve 2 must be opened and valve 4 must be closed.

   (ii) If B asks for Yellow, valve 4 must be opened and valve 2 must be closed.

   (iii) If B asks for Green, valves 2 and 4 must both be opened to the extent that will give the required shade, i.e. the required mixture of Blue and Yellow.

(*c*) A cannot ask for Blue, and B cannot ask for Red.

It will be clear that information must flow between A and valves 1 and 3 and between B and valves 2 and 4, since A's requests determine the correct position of valves 1 and 3 and B's requests determine the correct position of valves 2 and 4. Calculation will also be necessary somewhere on the line of communication between the recipients and the valves, in order to determine the precise position of the valves required to produce a particular shade of Orange or Green at A or B.

Now consider A's requests and B's requests together. There are some things that both cannot have at the same time. Both cannot have a full flow of Yellow at once, assuming that the piping has the same capacity throughout. If A is having a very yellow Orange, B cannot have a very yellow Green. When conflicting demands of this kind come in, a decision is needed: which shall be satisfied and which shall not? Should each be partly satisfied? If so, in what proportions? Even in as simple a situation as this, there are quite a few options to choose from. Somewhere in the system there must be a point to which the relevant information will be sent, which will process the information and establish what options are open, which will decide between them, and which, having made the decision, will send instructions to carry it out. Thus we need to redraw the diagram with the dotted lines representing channels of information (see Figure 7). An information-handling and decision-making network is beginning to take shape.

Sometimes it may be possible to define comprehensively all the possible circumstances which can present themselves to a decision-making system of this kind, and to lay down in advance what decision shall be taken in each. In other words it is possible to 'program' the control mechanism so that it takes the appropriate decisions automatically. This is what is being done when a computer is programmed. It may also be possible to monitor automatically the demands made on the system,

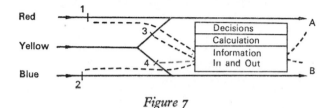

Figure 7

and to operate the controls automatically. In other words it may be possible to automate the whole system. As we shall see later, it will in fact become possible during the next ten or twenty years to automate most routine transactions, including financial transactions, in this kind of way.

If A and B continue to ask for Yellow simultaneously (i.e. continue to make demands on the system which it cannot meet), it may become necessary to alter the system. It might be possible to double the capacity of the Yellow inflow pipe to the point where it divides. Alternatively, it might be possible to discontinue either the Red or the Blue inflow and replace it with a second Yellow inflow. Thus the system needs not just a controlling function to take decisions on how it should operate in the short term, but also a planning function to take decisions about its future shape.

The planning function needs some but not all of the information needed for the controlling function. It needs to know about the demands being made on the system over a period of time, the extent to which they are being met, and the way the system is currently capable of operating. But the planning function also needs other information: about the penalties and benefits which would attach to making various changes in the structure of the system, i.e. information, based on study and experiment, about how the system would operate if it were different. Thus, in the box in Figure 7, Research as well as Calculation is required.

All systems are, however, sub-systems of a larger system. In our example, there will be another system for bringing the Red, Yellow and Blue fluids to the inflow points of the system we have been discussing.

195

The two systems together are thus sub-systems of a system which comprises them both. Now it would clearly be pointless to double the capacity of the Yellow inflow pipe in our system if the adjoining system was incapable of supplying it with a double quantity of Yellow. Thus, to generalise, decisions about structural changes in a sub-system are interdependent with other parts of the system to which it belongs. Such decisions – planning decisions – must, therefore, be taken at a level which is responsible for all the sub-systems which will be affected, i.e. at a higher level than that responsible for controlling the day to day operations of each of the sub-systems. A hierarchical decision-making system on the lines of Figure 8 begins to emerge. In the context of

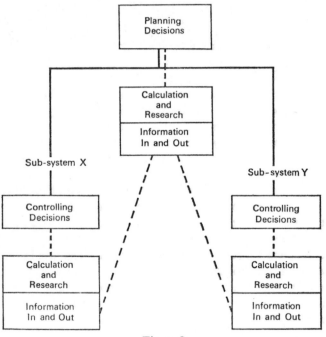

Figure 8

government this might refer to the Prime Minister's Office supported by the Ministry of Defence on the one hand and the Foreign and Commonwealth Office on the other, dealing with some matter of high level external policy on which both military and diplomatic action were required.

It is important to note at this point that the difference between planning and controlling is a purely relative one, corresponding to the difference between policy-making and administration. My superior takes planning decisions about the system whose operations I control, and in controlling my system I take planning decisions about the sub-systems my subordinates control. In other words, we are talking about a hierarchy of decisions. My decisions provide the framework–set the ground rules–for my subordinates' decisions. My superior makes policy for me to administer; in administering it I make policy for my subordinates to administer; and so on down the line. Which explains why everyone in a large organisation believes that policy and administration interact precisely at *his* level!

It is equally important to note that the information upon which the decisions in Figure 8 are based must be compatible between the different decision-makers. Assume that sub-system Y is the set of pipes and valves shown in Figures 6 and 7, carrying red, yellow and blue fluids to recipients A and B, and that sub-system X is the mechanism supplying the red, yellow and blue fluids to sub-system Y. If sub-system X did not recognise the words 'red', 'yellow' and 'blue' but held all its information about its operations under the headings 'scarlet', 'primrose' and 'azure' instead, it would be impossible to plan changes in the total system consisting of sub-systems X and Y, or to evaluate its operations as a whole. (This is the same point as that made by the Estimates Committee about the common register of businesses.) A pre-requisite to coherent decision-making is compatibility of information.

DATA-PROCESSING TECHNOLOGY

This brings us to the technology of government, in other words the technology of data-processing and data-transmission. The computing and communications equipment and facilities now being developed for handling transactions automatically, and automatically capturing, transmitting, storing and manipulating data, are such that quite soon we shall have data networks linking computers with computers; this will enable us to store and process data at the most convenient and economical place, and transmit any we need elsewhere as and when we need it. Thus we shall be able to choose whether we want to centralise the information function shown decentralised in Figure 8, so that it becomes as shown in Figure 9; or whether we would prefer to keep it decentralised. Either way, however, we shall need to make sure that the information flowing from and supporting different parts of the organisation is mutually compatible, in other words that it constitutes an integrated information system, so that it can be 'fitted together into a single picture of the world'.

Data networks are now being developed separately by various government departments, public corporations and large companies for their

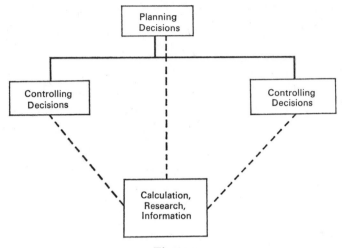

Figure 9

own internal use. This is already happening. In the course of time these separate networks will become linked together and will eventually develop into a single national data network through which the computers and computer terminals of different organisations can communicate with one another, much as people communicate with one another through the telephone system today. (In the course of time a similar development will take place internationally, raising even more complex problems of compatibility.)

In principle, these technical advances should eventually make it possible to monitor the course of social and economic activities much as it is now possible to monitor the flows of traffic in towns or the processes taking place in a chemical plant. In principle, it may eventually make it possible to take action automatically – at least to some extent – to regulate economic affairs, for example, in much the same way as it is now possible to regulate traffic flows or a chemical plant automatically.

This will, however, depend on our developing a degree of understanding about how economic systems work, and also on our developing new institutions and procedures, to the point where we can 'program' our responses to events in advance. This in turn will involve the combined development of the techniques of operational research, statistics and accountancy, together with those of managerial and monetary economics, to the point where we are confident of being able to manipulate economic trends in the direction we desire.

Money can, in fact, be handled automatically just like data. In a sense, the debiting of one person's bank account and the crediting of another's is no more than an accountancy calculation. Bank accounts are now stored on computer file, and there is no doubt that during the next ten or fifteen years we shall see the development of electronic funds transfer. In other words, many of the payments we make today by means of cash or paper instruments like cheques will be made automatically by transferring payments data between the computers of different organisations, including those of the banking and giro systems. The flows of money shown at Figure 1 (p. 107) will progressively become flows of electronic data between the computers of different organisations. As this change occurs these flows of payments data will turn into a much more responsive system than they are today for monitoring and controlling the economy. Money will become a more effective mechanism than it is today for reflecting the values of society in the choices that people actually make and in the ways in which we actually allocate spending power.

The Information Revolution, or Cybernetic Revolution, as it might more accurately be called, is a subject for a whole book on its own—or indeed for many books. But the essence of the matter for our purposes is simple.

Government is about taking decisions and processing information on highly complex issues; that basically is what government is for.

Automatic data-processing (including data-transmission) provides the modern technology for processing information and elucidating the options for decision on highly complex issues; that basically is what automatic data-processing is for.

In other words, automatic data-processing is the technology of modern government. Only by developing its use to the full will it be possible to perform the highly complex, ambitious, inter-related social and economic functions that a modern society demands of its government.

For this reason one of the most important responsibilities of the new parliamentary Select Committees proposed in Chapter 9 will be to stimulate government departments to use this modern technology of government and to develop the application of automatic data-processing and data-transmission in their own fields.[7] Equally important will be the development of safeguards to prevent the abuse of these d a systems, whether by individuals, companies or government departments themselves. This is one aspect of the enquiry into privacy now being conducted by the Younger Committee,[8] though oddly enough the activities of government departments are outside the Committee's terms of reference. The whole question will be a matter for keen parliamentary scrutiny for many years to come.

THE 'SCIENCE' OF GOVERNMENT

To develop the use of data-processing technology in support of their department's activities will be the task of the management services units and statistical units in each department. When we turn from the technology of government to the science of government, we come to the task of the research units.

We can best illustrate the issues that arise here by considering the contribution to long-term strategic planning that policy studies and research may be expected to make. The most important factors bearing on long-term planning are shown in Figure 10. The diagram there is applicable to every department of government–in respect of health or education or transport or defence or whatever its fields of responsibility may be–and also to the government as a whole. In other words, each department including the Prime Minister's Office needs a capability to understand and plan for an evolving situation of the kind shown.

The inner circle in the diagram refers to the government–

(1) employing certain numbers and types of people and other resources,
(2) organised in certain ways,
(3) using certain methods, techniques, systems and procedures,
(4) in order to carry out a certain range of tasks.

All these components of the situation interact on each other. The tasks that have to be done affect the numbers and types of people needed to

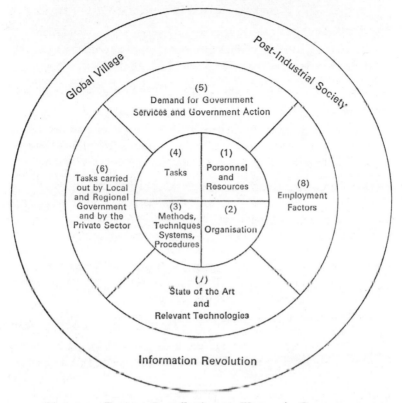

Figure 10. Factors Contributing to Change in Government

do them, and the number and types of people available affect the tasks that can be done. The tasks to be done affect the procedures to be adopted. The techniques used affect the organisation. And so on.

These components of the situation inside government are, of course, also subject to changes generated externally. The tasks of government change in accordance with—

(5) changing demands for government services and government action.

They are also affected by changes in—

(6) the tasks which local and regional authorities, and also the private sector, are capable of carrying out to general satisfaction.

201

The organisation of government and its methods of work are directly affected by–

(7) the state of the art in various disciplines (such as economics) and the state of various technologies (such as computing).

And, of course, the numbers and types of people employed in government depend on–

(8) various employment factors, such as the supply of qualified people coming out of the schools and universities, their career aspirations, and the alternative employment opportunities open to them.

The combination at any one time of these eight factors makes up the total situation prevailing at that time. Changes in each factor are always taking place, so the whole interactive situation is on the move, sometimes evolving faster, sometimes slower, in a never-ending process of change. This process, in turn, is taking place within the context of broad social, economic and technical developments, on a world-wide scale, as shown by the terms 'global village', 'post-industrial society', and 'information revolution' in the outer circle of the diagram.

In the past the process of government evolution generated by these factors and by the combinations between them has taken place higgledy-piggledy, as we have seen. It has not been consciously shaped by any strategic understanding of the long-term trends working on it, or of the interactions between them. For the future we have to shape it more consciously. It will be the task of the departmental research units to provide us with the necessary understanding to do so.

For these research units to be successful they must have certain features. They must work closely with their department's statistical unit and management services unit; they must be linked to the research units in other departments; they must have a considerable degree of professional independence; they must be multi-disciplinary. Let us consider these points in turn.

The reason why a department's research capability must be brigaded closely together with its statistical capability and its management services capability is that the three are necessary in combination to provide an effective planning capability. In other words, relevant information must be acquired; aspects of the situation must be studied; and the necessary changes in management and organisation must be implemented. A combined planning capability of this kind is outlined in the chart of the proposed Prime Minister's Office at Figure 3 on page 150, which shows the Central Statistical Office, a Central Policy Studies Unit, and a Central Management Services Unit, in close proximity to one another.

As we have seen in Chapter 8, the Fulton Committee recognised that 'many of the problems handled by "planning units" will have implications extending beyond the boundaries of a single department. These units may therefore need a measure of central direction if the emerging problems of the country are to be tackled systematically and comprehensively and on the basis of common major hypotheses. The status and location of this central direction, whether by the Cabinet Office, the Treasury, or other machinery, is a question of machinery of government and therefore beyond our terms of reference.'[9]

The arrangement should be on the following lines. Each department—including the Prime Minister's Office—will have its own statistical unit, policy studies or research unit, and management services unit, forming a planning capability within its own field—the field of the Prime Minister's Office being the government as a whole. These units should be detached—hived off—from the ministerial department itself. They should be professional units working to a remit laid down by their minister, but they should not be under his day-to-day control or the day-to-day control of his officials. In the case of the policy studies unit and the management services unit this remit would consist mainly of terms of reference for a series of study projects and 'consultancy assignments'. Whenever necessary these projects and assignments would be carried out by joint teams staffed by the units of more than one department, the terms of reference being laid down jointly by the ministers concerned. As the government builds up a data network shared between different departments, research units working together will find that they already have access to an increasingly common information base.

It should be the rule, rather than the exception, for the reports of the study projects to be published. They will thus form part of the material not just for ministerial decisions but also for parliamentary and public debate about the issues of policy that arise. This is in harmony with the proposals put forward in previous chapters for fuller disclosure and more effective scrutiny of the activities of government departments and of their plans and projections for the future.

A move in this direction would also make it possible to dispense with much of the effort now expended on cumbersome 'one-off' enquiries by Royal Commissions and departmental committees. Because the deliberations of these bodies are not subjected to the stimulus of continuing public discussion, their conclusions are often out of date when they appear; and, even if they are not out of date, they often fail to carry conviction because they have been reached without the genuine involvement and active participation of the interested parties. The recent Redcliffe-Maud Royal Commission on Local Government is a case where something like this appears to have happened. The fact is that these traditional forms of enquiry are out-dated in a society in which public opinion evolves quite rapidly under the impact of modern media of communication. They must be replaced by new forms of enquiry that are both more professional and more responsive to public opinion. This will involve making the results of professional research studies available for parliamentary and public debate.

Given the complexity of the problems and the proliferation of scientific and professional activity, especially in the fields of management and social science, how are we to bring an integrated approach to bear on these problems of research? The answer is that we need a multi-disciplinary approach.

The research unit attached to every major department of state, including the Prime Minister's Office, must be a multi-disciplinary research team. It should be strongly based, not only (or indeed mainly) in the conventional orthodoxy of the department's subject matter, such as defence or transport or education, but in the underlying logical and numerical disciplines of systems analysis, operational research and statistics, and in the behavioural and social sciences.

In particular, the research unit attached to the Prime Minister's Office must be capable of developing a comprehensive analysis of the functions and attributes of the various kinds of political, social and managerial organisations that make up the fabric of government. Most important among these attributes are an organisation's legal, financial and administrative characteristics. These correspond to the three main control mechanisms brought to bear by society on its own activities through the instruments of government–namely legislation, finance and administration. As we have seen in previous chapters, each of these control mechanisms is now labouring under the accretions of a century of piecemeal growth. Much of the responsibility for clearing the jungle and developing a new conceptual and institutional framework will rest with the research unit attached to the Prime Minister's Office. The intellectual horse-power needed for the task will be greater than that which has been evident hitherto in most research in the field of public administration. A more powerfully analytic, even philosophical, cast of mind will be required.

TOWARDS A PHILOSOPHY OF GOVERNMENT

There is, in fact, a close parallel between the organisation of knowledge and the organisation of action, and between the evolution of scientific theories and the evolution of political and administrative institutions.

In a political or administrative organisation, decisions of wide generality provide the framework for decisions of lesser generality and, ultimately, for individual actions. In systems of organised knowledge, theories of wide generality provide the framework for theories of lesser generality and, ultimately, for individual observations. In both types of system a two-way process is at work. General decisions shape individual actions; and the individual actions which become necessary to meet the needs of current circumstances help to re-shape general decisions. In other words, policy-making and administration interact. Similarly, scientific theories shape the interpretation of particular observations; and particular observations help to re-shape general theories. Theorising and experimentation interact.

The process of change in structures of organised action and structures of organised knowledge stems from the need to resolve the contradictions which arise within them. In science, the creative thinker like Copernicus or Newton or Einstein is urged, by this need, to construct simpler, more elegant, more powerful theories which will embrace a wider range of observations and eliminate the inconsistencies between them. What is true of the thinker is also true of the creative statesman and administrator. He is urged to construct a simpler, more coherent, more effective system of organised action, out of a situation where the existing system has grown cumbersome and confused with the passage of time and the increasing demands placed on it, where the conflicts and contradictions within it prevent it working properly, and where the resulting lack of clarity leaves us powerless to understand and solve the problems that come crowding in upon us.

The qualities required for creative administration of this kind are not those of the specialist or those imparted by a formal education in the received ideas of a specialism (however 'relevant' it may seem), but those of men whose vision is whole and whose thinking is geared to action. The 1960s were the decade of the economist. He failed for two reasons: his vision was partial; and his thinking was not geared to action. There are signs that the 1970s may be the decade of the sociologist. He is likely to be unsuccessful too, for the same reasons as the economist, and he in his turn is likely also to be discredited. Perhaps we shall realise then that what we are looking for is not just the next specialist whose nostrums have become fashionable, but the philosopher of organised action.

In fact, we are due for a revival in political philosophy. It is no accident that Locke and Mill, the two outstanding political philosophers in this country in the last three hundred years, lived through those periods in which the most radical changes in government were taking place. As we set about reforming our whole system of government again today, re-shaping the mechanisms of our society for deciding what is to be done to achieve the good life, and bringing our national institutions into line with the advent of self-government and the Cybernetic Revolution, we too will surely make our own contribution to political philosophy. For, once again, we shall regard political philosophy as a serious matter, with practical implications. We shall come to feel, as our Victorian forbears did, that philosophy should be more than word-games and that political studies should be more than a variety of market research.

NOTES ON CHAPTER 10

General

Apart from sources mentioned in previous chapters, the series of Occasional Papers published by HMSO for the Centre for Administrative Studies (formerly sponsored by the Treasury and now by the Civil Service Department) is well worth a reference. Paper No. 1, on *The Design of Information-Processing Systems for Government*, deals in greater detail with some of the ideas in this chapter.

Note 1. Pierre Teilhard de Chardin: *The Phenomenon of Man* (Collins, 1959); Sir Julian Huxley's Introduction, page 14.

Note 2. A. J. Ayer: *Language, Truth and Logic* (Gollancz, 1947), *passim*.

Note 3. *The English Constitution*, Fontana Edition, page 72.

Note 4. Much of this sentence is paraphrased from P. F. Strawson: *Individuals: An Essay in Descriptive Metaphysics* (Methuen, University Paperbacks, 1959), page 38.

Note 5. *Estimates Committee Report on 'Government Statistical Services'* (HMSO: 1966), paragraphs 22 and 24.

Note 6. This example is taken from my memorandum of evidence to the Fulton Committee (Cmnd. 3638; HMSO: 1968; Vol. 5(2), page 1054).

Note 7. For further elaboration of this point, see the *Report on the U.K. Computer Industry* (Volume II, Appendix 79) by the House of Commons Select Committee on Science and Technology, Session 1969–70. HMSO, 13th May 1970.

Note 8. The terms of reference of this Committee, under Mr Kenneth Younger's chairmanship, are 'to consider whether legislation is needed to give further protection to the individual citizen and to commercial and industrial interests, against intrusions into privacy by private persons and organisations or by companies; and to make recommendations'. The appointment of the Committee was announced in Parliament on 23rd January 1970 (*Hansard*, cols. 861–960).

Note 9. Cmnd. 3638 (HMSO: 1968), paragraph 177.

11

Wider Perspectives

Observe how system into system runs,
What other planets circle other suns . . .
All are but parts of one stupendous whole.
POPE: *Essay on Man*

The account given in earlier chapters of recent developments in British government, and the suggestions made about the right way forward into the future, have necessarily been little more than an outline. Little or nothing has been said about vital areas of government such as Law and Order, or External Affairs. Very little has been said about the Trade Unions and the burning question of how to evolve an effective framework of public accountability for them—just as for civil servants, business managers, academics, doctors and scientists. There are other important issues that have not been discussed at all. But I hope that enough has been said to show beyond doubt that 'the old order changeth, yielding place to new'; that an era in the history of British government is drawing to a close, and that the outlines of a new one are beginning to emerge.

In order to clarify the changes that will continue to be needed, and to engage public interest and public support, I believe that we should proceed along the lines recommended by a group of members of Parliament, public administrators, academics and publicists who met under the auspices of PEP (Political and Economic Planning) in 1969.[1] They said:

> The problem concerns the three parts of the State: executive, legislative and judicial. Each of these needs reform, and the reform of each has implications for the others. This interdependence is at the heart of the proposal which we now put forward for three linked inquiries:
> 1. on the structure of executive government at national, regional and local levels,
> 2. on Parliament and the constitution,
> 3. on the liberty of the citizen.

This proposal is not intended to imply that the problem can be divided into rigid compartments. Evidence should be exchanged between the inquiries and there should be joint meetings. Their final reports should complement one another and should together provide the material for an informed public discussion, rather than an oracular pronouncement of ills and remedies.

The inquiries should proceed in such a way that politicians at all levels are fully involved; that the public discussion is wide-ranging; and that the wider perspective is kept constantly in mind. It is this need to bring all aspects of the problem together and to involve different types of expert opinion which has led us to propose these inquiries.

Hence, for the structure of executive government we suggest a modernised form of inquiry instead of the traditional Royal Commission. It should publish six-monthly interim reports and invite comment on them; it should have enough funds to employ advisory panels, consultants and research workers; its members, who should include a full-time chairman, should receive remuneration for their efforts; it should not be obliged to take lengthy oral evidence from interest groups, although they would be welcome to submit memoranda; and there should be a close time-limit on the whole operation.

This inquiry would be concerned primarily with the executive. The other two inquiries, concerned mainly with the legislative and judicial functions of the State, would be undertaken by an all-party Speaker's Conference, comprising members of both Houses of Parliament to consider constitutional aspects, and by a Lord Chancellor's Committee, to consider judicial aspects and particularly civil liberties.[3]

The continuing publication of a regular exchange of views between these three enquiry bodies would enable much sensible discussion to take place about the practical changes that should be introduced—changes of the kind suggested in earlier chapters of this book. It would also help to stimulate public awareness of the effect on government of the deeper social, economic, political and international changes that are always taking place. Some such arrangement might become a permanent feature of our self-organising society.

When our institutions of government took more or less their present form, the keynote of the times was independence–in particular, independence from the Crown. The impetus for the Gladstonian reforms of the late nineteenth century stemmed from the philosophy of *laisser-faire*. God or Nature had arranged things so that, if everyone were left free to go his own way, the best interest of the community would automatically be served. As Pope had said over a century earlier,

'Thus God and Nature fixed the general frame,
And bade self-love and social be the same.'

Professor Basil Willey put the matter concisely, as follows. 'The idea of a state of Nature, especially after Locke, came to be used as a means whereby the new ruling classes could vindicate, against the surviving restraints of the old feudal and ecclesiastical order, their cherished rights of individual freedom and of property . . . Natural Law, sanctioning liberty and progress, was to be the basis of the modern liberal-bourgeois State.'[3] On that basis was founded the political and administrative structure of government that was finally established in Britain in the 1860s.

Today, however, we recognise that it cannot simply be left to God or Nature to ensure that, if everyone pursues his own interest, the best interest of the community will be served. A society that has become self-governing, in which the concepts of systems theory and cybernetics are becoming understood, must *organise itself* so as to achieve a match between the self-interest of individuals and the interest of society as a whole. The message of this book is that the time has come to understand the workings of our institutions of government, to identify their shortcomings, to clarify their purposes, and to re-shape them into an effective control mechanism for a self-organising society. The keynote is no longer independence but interdependence. The mechanistic concept of society as a collection of separate individuals, which grew out of the Reformation and reached its full flower in the political philosophy of Gladstonian Liberalism, is now giving way to an organic concept of society composed of interdependent members, in many ways more akin to the social philosophy of the Middle Ages.

This brings us to the ideology and institutions of politics.

In ideological terms it is surely becoming more and more questionable whether there can be any conflict of principle between socialism and free enterprise if both are feasibly defined. In a society that governs and organises itself, the government must command the topmost decision-making heights; it must be society's representatives who take the national decisions that are of central importance to us all. At the same time, if society is to function at all efficiently, organisations and individuals down the line at lower levels in the community's decision-making hierarchy must have as much freedom as possible to develop and deploy their enterprise as they think best within the framework that society has laid down. Socialism and free enterprise are thus complementary aspects of self-government. The conflict between them, on which our present structure of political debate is based, is indeed a 'bogus dilemma'.[4]

Our existing political parties, like most of our other institutions, are in fact part of our Victorian heritage. So far as their alignment is concerned, the issues between them reflect the economic conflict between working people and owners of property, and the ideological conflict between collectivism and individualism, that actually existed in Victorian times. Some people say this does not greatly matter; are we not always fifty years behindhand in our politics? In a self-governing society we cannot afford to take that view.

We shall be wiser to recognise that a healthy two-sided political debate is an important element in the larger system of British parliamentary democracy. It enables us to choose at intervals between two opposing groups of leaders and two opposing sets of policies. Between general elections it provides us with a built-in safeguard against undue personal aggrandisement or political extremism by the government of the day. Most importantly, the continuing debate between two opposing points of view provides the motive force for government action. It is the engine that drives the machine of government. Thus the basis on which this debate is conducted can determine the whole slant of government, and when the debate loses practical meaning (becomes 'inoperable') the machine loses its drive and runs down.

In other words, we should regard the structure of political conflict like other institutional structures. It becomes out of date from time to time. It no longer matches the issues of the times. It has to be reshaped.

Thus the Whig versus Tory conflict, representing the old divisions between the aristocracy on the one hand and the monarchy and the squirearchy on the other, gave way—after twenty years of political confusion starting in 1846—to the Liberal versus Conservative conflict, more in tune with the division between town and country that arose from the industrial revolution. Similarly, after a period of confusion between 1916 and 1930, the Liberal versus Conservative structure of political conflict gave way to Labour versus Conservative, reflecting the division between organised working people and the owners of capital. We need to understand the causes and mechanisms of these structural changes in politics, which always seem to occur several decades after the economic and social changes that they reflect. We need to understand them for exactly the same reason as we need to understand the processes of institutional change in government–so that we can be ready for them and promote them as necessary.

One cannot help suspecting that we are due for another of these shifts in the structure of political conflict. The existing structure, incorporating the conflict of interest between working people and property owners and the ideological struggle between state ownership and private ownership, gives largely irrelevant–if not positively harmful–results today. It may be that a new basis for a more meaningful political debate will emerge sooner or later on the following lines:

consumers   versus producers
individuals   versus organisations
decentralisers versus centralisers
agnostics   versus authoritarians.

Although other divisions–egalitarians versus elitists, doves versus hawks, radicals versus orthodox–may cut across this alignment, it is not impossible to imagine the 'liberals' in the Conservative and Labour parties joining forces on a platform whose main planks are in the left-hand column above, against the 'conservatives' from both parties who would champion the interests shown in the right-hand column. Precisely how this would come about–whether, for example, by the leader of a progressive Conservative government explicitly adopting a form of *democratic socialism* based on the interests shown in the left-hand column, rather as Peel in 1846 decided to repeal the Corn Laws–is not particularly relevant, except to the career politicians and political gossip columnists who would be directly involved. The point is that some re-alignment of this kind seems inevitable sooner or later, and that it will provide a new driving force for government action when it happens.

However, it is not only the existing *alignment* of political parties that is a product of the Victorian age. The mass political parties are themselves a Victorian creation. They arose to fill a vacuum in social leadership and communication when the rural aristocracy and squirearchy were no longer able to discharge this function in consequence of the industrial revolution and the urbanisation that followed it. Now that political leaders can reach everyone in the country directly through television, radio and the national newspapers, at least some of the *raison d'être* of the nationwide political party has evaporated.

It would be possible to regard the existing type of mass political party indulgently, as Betjemanesque Victoriana. But do these parties not represent a positive institutional hindrance to good government? Do they not ossify the categories of political thinking? Do they not restrict the choice of the electorate? Do they provide a good recruiting ground for Parliament? Does the career ladder of today's professional politician provide good training for statesmen? Is the patronage required to maintain the mass bureaucratised party not a serious cause of inefficiency in the public service? New conditions need new forms of politics. Politicians are in the same boat as the rest of us; they cannot insulate themselves from change.

So we should probably be ready not just for a re-alignment between the existing political parties but also for a decline in the strength of monolithic national parties of any kind. This is likely to be accompanied by greater emphasis on the personalities and policies of individual political leaders, and by a revival of the importance of Parliament and the back-bencher. For those who are committed to the existing order of things in politics the transition to a new order may mean a period of confusion, insecurity, bitterness and betrayal, rather like the periods following 1846 and 1916. Those of us who are not actively committed to the existing forms of party politics will need to understand dispassionately what is happening and do what we can to get it over quickly and smoothly.

There is one further point of great importance. In Chapter 5 we referred briefly to the consequences of growing internationalism. But apart from that one brief reference we have concentrated on the internal structure of British government, rather as if the country was a self-contained unit. The reason for doing so was because this seemed to be the most convenient and manageable way of bringing out the nature of the questions that arise in considering the reform of government.

However, there can be no doubt that international trade and travel, international companies, international financial markets, international government, and indeed every other international activity, will continue to grow. In the course of time, as we move towards one world, we shall see a situation emerging in which our national government becomes—at least in a logical sense—hierarchically subordinate to an international tier of government, in the same way that our local government is hierarchically subordinate to the national government today. Westminster and Whitehall will take their place in a range of parliamentary and government institutions at international, national, regional and local levels. The importance of Westminster as an independent sovereign Parliament will decline, and increasingly it will take on the two-fold function of focussing British national views and interests in the context of international decision-making and of considering how international decisions shall be implemented in the British context.

As this process of evolution takes place we are likely to see a greater proportion of our national energies in the political and administrative fields turning outwards; increasingly our most active politicians and administrators will pursue their careers and seek their achievements in the international arena. As the institutions for a self-governing world evolve, many of the same methodological problems will arise as have arisen in British government in recent decades. Our experience and our success in solving our own problems should enable us to contribute usefully to the further development of international government.

We now stand, just as Newton did in his sphere, on the shoulders of the giants of the past—the great men who have developed the institutions of British government to their present point—and we recognise that we have come to the end of an era in its history. As we peer into the new era that lies ahead our efforts to develop new mechanisms of government may be seen as part of the larger human enterprise.

Teilhard de Chardin, for example, regarded the consciousness of man as the 'specific effect of organised complexity'.[5] He believed that 'we should consider inter-thinking humanity as a new type of organism, whose destiny is to realise new possibilities for evolving life on this planet. Accordingly we should endeavour to equip it with the mechanisms necessary for the proper fulfilment of its task—the psycho-social equivalents of sense organs, effector organs, and a co-ordinating central nervous system with dominant brain; and our aim should be the gradual personalisation of the human unit of evolution—its conversion, on the new level of co-operative inter-thinking, into the equivalent of a person.'[6] One does not have to go all the way with Teilhard—and some people emphatically do not[7]—to see in that broad statement of belief some reflection of the practical proposals and developments discussed in earlier chapters of this book, with the aim of developing more effective mechanisms of decision-making at various levels in society, and supporting these decision mechanisms with responsive information systems.

In conclusion, we may sum up as follows.

The last time Britain faced a comparable situation to the one we face today was in the nineteenth century. The institutions and methods of parliamentary government and local administration inherited from the previous century could no longer cope with the problems of a society which had become largely urban and industrialised. The machinery of the State had become powerless to deal with the massive expansion of private enterprise as a result of the industrial revolution. The universities and the professions were demanding more independence from the Crown and the Church. The people were demanding more self-government. The task of our Victorian predecessors, successfully carried out during the Age of Reform between about 1830 and 1880, was thus to reconstruct Parliament, the Civil Service, and local government; to establish a firm legal basis for the limited liability company and the trade unions; to reform the universities and the professions; and, last but not least, to replace the old political debate between Whigs and Tories, reflecting the burnt out conflicts of a predominantly rural society, with the more meaningful debate between Liberals and Conservatives, reflecting the real, contemporary conflicts between town and country, between the industrialists and the land-owners.

Our task today is comparable to that which faced the Victorians, but subtly different. In the Age of Reform on which we are now embarking, we too have to re-shape Parliament, the Civil Service, local government, industry, the trade unions, the universities, the professions, and the structure of political debate, to meet the changed needs of our society. But this time the problem arises from the massive expansion of the government's activities—of public enterprise, not private enterprise; from the achievement of democratic government, not from the demand for it; from the need to reconcile the interests of industry, trade unions, the universities and the professions with the demands, no longer of the Crown, but of the self-governing people.

By tackling these problems of our own, we may at the same time rediscover our role in the world. For Britain's distinctive contribution to

P   215

history has always been in the sphere of politics, government and the professions – in short in the handling of public affairs – as well as in science and industry. We are rightly proud of how, over the centuries, we have developed new political and administrative institutions to meet the changing needs of the times. In the era now ending, the attainment of self-government has been our main goal; we have sought it at home by successive extensions of the franchise, in Europe by our support for self-determination in the nineteenth and early twentieth centuries, and in our Empire overseas by constitutional advance and peaceful decolonisation.

In the era now beginning the task is related, but different. It is to develop the skills of self-government. By learning how to govern ourselves well, and by evolving new mechanisms of self-government, we shall liberate our own national energies as the Victorians did. We shall also, once again, have something worth offering to the peoples of Europe and the world.

NOTES ON CHAPTER 11

Note 1. The group's findings were published under the title *Renewal of British Government* (PEP Broadsheet 513, July 1969). The moving spirit behind the group's discussions was Max Nicholson. His book *The System: The Misgovernment of Modern Britain* (Hodder & Stoughton, 1967) had made a powerful onslaught on the existing system of government and had elicited proposals for reform from various quarters.

Note 2. Renewal of British Government, page 659. (This sounds formidable, but in fact the broadsheet begins on page 655!)

Note 3. Basil Willey: *The Eighteenth Century Background* (Penguin Books in association with Chatto and Windus, 1962), page 24.

Note 4. See Samuel Brittan's *Left or Right: The Bogus Dilemma* (Secker & Warburg, 1968). We are concerned with the structural and institutional implications of some of the conceptual distinctions discussed by Mr Brittan.

Note 5. Pierre Teilhard de Chardin: *The Phenomenon of Man*, with an Introduction by Sir Julian Huxley (Collins, 1959); page 301.

Note 6. Sir Julian Huxley's Introduction to *The Phenomenon of Man*; page 20.

Note 7. For example Sir Peter Medawar in his review of *The Phenomenon of Man*, originally published in *Mind* and subsequently made available in *The Art of the Soluble* (Pelican Books, 1969).

Index

217

INDEX